Year 4C

A Guide to Teaching for Mastery

Series Editor: Tony Staneff

Contents

Introduction page 4
What is *Power Maths*? page 5
Introduction to the author team page 6
Your *Power Maths* resources page 7
The *Power Maths* teaching model page 10
The *Power Maths* lesson sequence page 12
Using the *Power Maths* Teacher Guide page 15
Power Maths Year 4, yearly overview page 16
Power Maths Year 4, Textbook 4C (Term 3) overview page 16
Mindset: an introduction page 20
The *Power Maths* characters page 21
Mathematical language page 22
The role of talk and discussion page 23
Assessment strategies page 24
Power Maths unit assessment grid page 26
Keeping the class together page 27
Depth and breadth page 28
Same-day intervention page 29
The role of practice page 30
Structures and representations page 31
Practical aspects of *Power Maths* page 32
List of practical resources page 34
Variation helps visualisation page 36
Getting started with *Power Maths* page 37

Unit 11 – Decimals (2) page 38
Lesson 1 – Making a whole page 40
Lesson 2 – Writing decimals page 44
Lesson 3 – Comparing decimals page 48
Lesson 4 – Ordering decimals page 52
Lesson 5 – Rounding decimals page 56
Lesson 6 – Halves and quarters page 60
Lesson 7 – Problem solving – decimals page 64
End of unit check page 68

Unit 12 – Money page 70
Lesson 1 – Pounds and pence page 72
Lesson 2 – Pounds, tenths and hundredths page 76
Lesson 3 – Ordering amounts of money page 80
Lesson 4 – Rounding money page 84
Lesson 5 – Using rounding to estimate money page 88
Lesson 6 – Problem solving – pounds and pence page 92

Lesson 7 – Problem solving – multiplication and division page 96
Lesson 8 – Solving two-step problems page 100
Lesson 9 – Problem solving – money page 104
End of unit check page 108

Unit 13 – Time **page 110**
Lesson 1 – Units of time (1) page 112
Lesson 2 – Units of time (2) page 116
Lesson 3 – Converting times (1) page 120
Lesson 4 – Converting times (2) page 124
Lesson 5 – Problem solving – units of time page 128
End of unit check page 132

Unit 14 – Statistics **page 134**
Lesson 1 – Charts and tables (1) page 136
Lesson 2 – Charts and tables (2) page 140
Lesson 3 – Line graphs (1) page 144
Lesson 4 – Line graphs (2) page 148
Lesson 5 – Problem solving – graphs page 152
End of unit check page 156

Unit 15 – Geometry – angles and 2D shapes **page 158**
Lesson 1 – Identifying angles page 160
Lesson 2 – Comparing and ordering angles page 164
Lesson 3 – Identifying regular and irregular shapes page 168
Lesson 4 – Classifying triangles page 172
Lesson 5 – Classifying and comparing quadrilaterals page 176
Lesson 6 – Deducing facts about shapes page 180
Lesson 7 – Lines of symmetry inside a shape page 184
Lesson 8 – Lines of symmetry outside a shape page 188
Lesson 9 – Completing a symmetric figure page 192
Lesson 10 – Completing a symmetric shape page 196
End of unit check page 200

Unit 16 – Geometry – position and direction **page 202**
Lesson 1 – Describing position (1) page 204
Lesson 2 – Describing position (2) page 208
Lesson 3 – Drawing on a grid page 212
Lesson 4 – Reasoning on a grid page 216
Lesson 5 – Moving on a grid page 220
Lesson 6 – Describing a movement on a grid page 224
End of unit check page 228

Introduction

Foreword by the series editor and author, Tony Staneff

For far too long in the UK, maths has been feared by learners – and by many teachers, too. As a result, most learners consistently underachieve. More crucially, negative beliefs about ability, aptitude and the nature of maths are entrenched in children's thinking from an early age.

Yet, as someone who has loved maths all my life, I've always believed that every child has the capacity to succeed in maths. I've also had the great pleasure of leading teams and departments who share that belief and passion. Teaching for mastery, as practised in China and other South-East Asian jurisdictions since the 1980s, has confirmed my conviction that maths really is for everyone and not just those who have a special talent. In recent years, my team and I at Trinity Academy, Halifax, have had the privilege of researching with and working alongside some of the finest mastery practitioners from the UK and beyond, whose impact on learners' confidence, achievement and attitude is an inspiration.

The mastery approach recognises the value of developing the power to think rather than just do. It also recognises the value of making a coherent journey in which whole-class groups tackle concepts in very small steps, one by one. You cannot build securely on loose foundations – and it is just the same with maths: by creating a solid foundation of deep understanding, our children's skills and confidence will be strong and secure. What's more, the mindset of learner and teacher alike is fundamental: everyone can do maths … EVERYONE CAN!

I am proud to have been part of the extensive team responsible for turning the best of the world's practice, research, insights, and shared experiences into *Power Maths*, a unique teaching and learning resource developed especially for UK classrooms. *Power Maths* embodies our vision to help and support primary maths teachers to transform every child's mathematical and personal development. 'Everyone can!' has become our mantra and our passion, and we hope it will be yours, too.

Now, explore and enjoy all the resources you need to teach for mastery, and please get back to us with your *Power Maths* experiences and stories!

What is *Power Maths*?

Created especially for UK primary schools, and aligned with the new National Curriculum, *Power Maths* is a whole-class, textbook-based mastery resource that empowers every child to understand and succeed. *Power Maths* rejects the notion that some people simply 'can't do' maths. Instead, it develops growth mindsets and encourages hard work, practice and a willingness to see mistakes as learning tools.

Best practice consistently shows that mastery of small, cumulative steps builds a solid foundation of deep mathematical understanding. *Power Maths* combines interactive teaching tools, high-quality textbooks and continuing professional development (CPD) to help you equip children with a deep and long lasting understanding. Based on extensive evidence, and developed in partnership with practising teachers, *Power Maths* ensures that it meets the needs of children in the UK.

Power Maths and Mastery

Power Maths makes mastery practical and achievable by providing the structures, pathways, content, tools and support you need to make it happen in your classroom.

To develop mastery in maths children need to be enabled to acquire a deep understanding of maths concepts, structures and procedures, step by step. Complex mathematical concepts are built on simpler conceptual components and when children understand every step in the learning sequence, maths becomes transparent and makes logical sense. Interactive lessons establish deep understanding in small steps, as well as effortless fluency in key facts such as tables and number bonds. The whole class works on the same content and no child is left behind.

Power Maths

- Builds every concept in small, progressive steps.
- Is built with interactive, whole-class teaching in mind.
- Provides the tools you need to develop growth mindsets.
- Helps you check understanding and ensure that every child is keeping up.
- Establishes core elements such as intelligent practice and reflection.

The *Power Maths* approach

Everyone can!

Founded on the conviction that every child can achieve, *Power Maths* enables children to build number fluency, confidence and understanding, step by step.

Child-centred learning

Children master concepts one step at a time in lessons that embrace a Concrete-Pictorial-Abstract (C-P-A) approach, avoid overload, build on prior learning and help them see patterns and connections. Same-day intervention ensures sustained progress.

Continuing professional development

Embedded teacher support and development offer every teacher the opportunity to continually improve their subject knowledge and manage whole-class teaching for mastery.

Whole-class teaching

An interactive, whole-class teaching model encourages thinking and precise mathematical language and allows children to deepen their understanding as far as they can.

Introduction to the author team

Power Maths arises from the work of maths mastery experts who are committed to proving that, given the right mastery mindset and approach, **everyone can do maths**. Based on robust research and best practice from around the world, *Power Maths* was developed in partnership with a group of UK teachers to make sure that it not only meets our children's wide-ranging needs but also aligns with the National Curriculum in England.

Tony Staneff, Series Editor and author

Vice Principal at Trinity Academy, Halifax, Tony also leads a team of mastery experts who help schools across the UK to develop teaching for mastery via nationally recognised CPD courses, problem-solving and reasoning resources, schemes of work, assessment materials and other tools.

✚ A team of experienced authors, including:

- ⚡ **Josh Lury** – a specialist maths teacher, author and maths consultant with a passion for innovative and effective maths education

- ⚡ **Trinity Academy, Halifax** (Michael Gosling CEO, Tony Staneff, Emily Fox, Kate Henshall, Rebecca Holland, Stephanie Kirk, Stephen Monaghan and Rachel Webster)

- ⚡ **David Board**, **Belle Cottingham**, **Jonathan East**, **Tim Handley**, **Derek Huby**, **Neil Jarrett**, **Stephen Monaghan**, **Beth Smith**, **Tim Weal**, **Paul Wrangles** – skilled maths teachers and mastery experts

- ⚡ **Cherri Moseley** – a maths author, former teacher and professional development provider

✚ Professors Liu Jian and Zhang Dan, Series Consultants and authors, and their team of mastery expert authors:

- ⚡ **Wei Huinv, Huang Lihua, Zhu Dejiang, Zhu Yuhong, Hou Huiying, Yin Lili, Zhang Jing, Zhou Da and Liu Qimeng**

Used by over 20 million children, Professor Liu Jian's textbook programme is one of the most popular in China. He and his author team are highly experienced in intelligent practice and in embedding key maths concepts using a C-P-A approach.

✚ A group of 15 teachers and maths co-ordinators

We have consulted our teacher group throughout the development of *Power Maths* to ensure we are meeting their real needs in the classroom.

Your *Power Maths* resources

To help you teach for mastery, *Power Maths* comprises a variety of high-quality resources.

Pupil Textbooks

Discover, Share, and Think together sections promote discussion and introduce mathematical ideas logically, so that children understand more easily.

Using a Concrete-Pictorial-Abstract approach, clear mathematical models help children to make connections and grasp concepts.

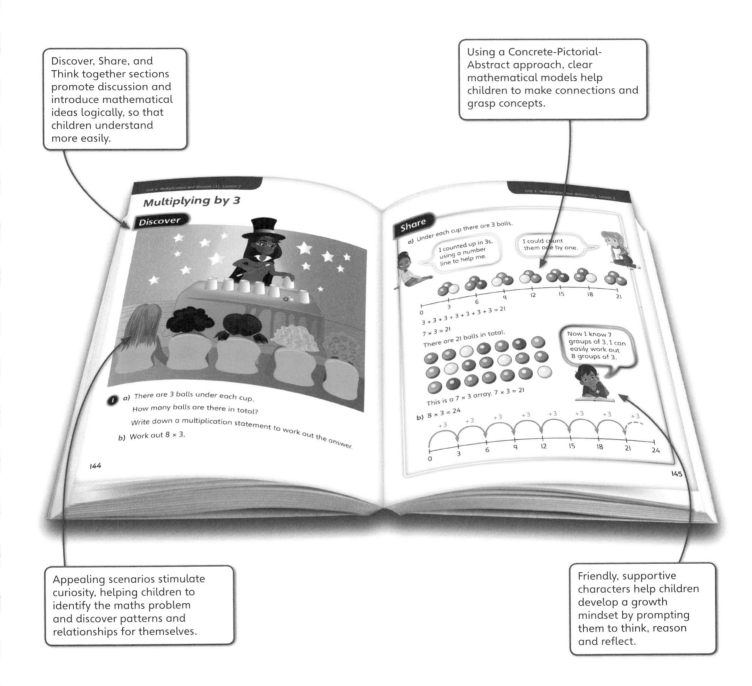

Appealing scenarios stimulate curiosity, helping children to identify the maths problem and discover patterns and relationships for themselves.

Friendly, supportive characters help children develop a growth mindset by prompting them to think, reason and reflect.

The coherent *Power Maths* lesson structure carries through into the vibrant, high-quality textbooks. Setting out the core learning objectives for each class, the lesson structure follows a carefully mapped journey through the curriculum and supports children on their journey to deeper understanding.

Pupil Practice Books

The Practice Books offer just the right amount of intelligent practice for children to complete independently in the final section of each lesson.

The practice questions are for everyone – each question varies one small element to move children on in their thinking. Look at the different parts in question **1**!

Calculations are connected so that children think about the underlying concept. In question **3**, children have to write out the calculation to find the answer. Concepts are presented differently again in question **4** to challenge children.

Practice questions are finely tuned to move children forward in their thinking and to reveal misconceptions.

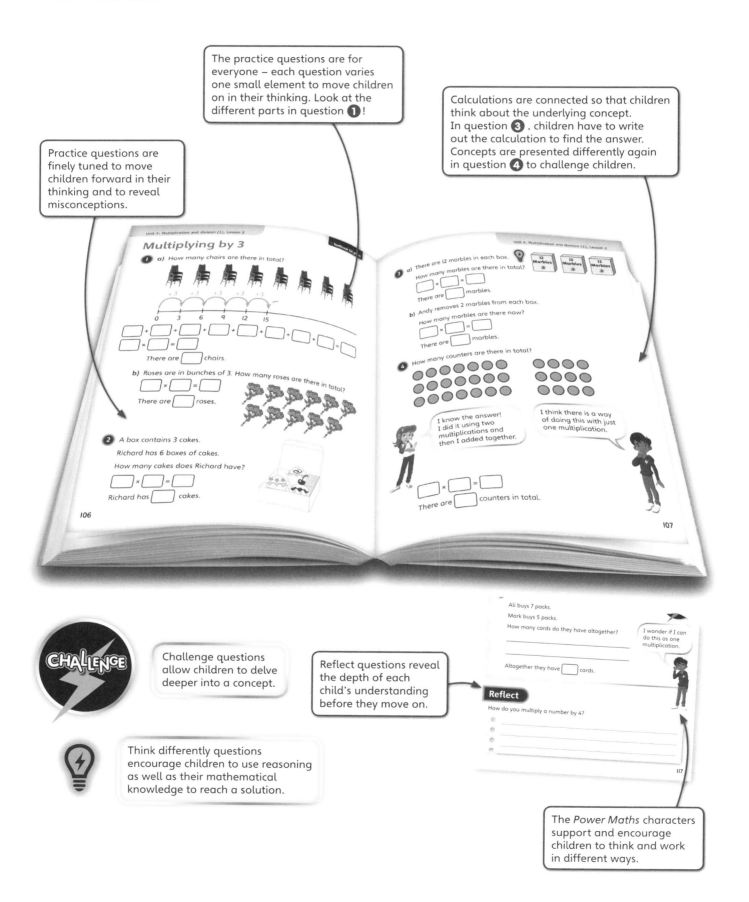

Challenge questions allow children to delve deeper into a concept.

Reflect questions reveal the depth of each child's understanding before they move on.

Think differently questions encourage children to use reasoning as well as their mathematical knowledge to reach a solution.

The *Power Maths* characters support and encourage children to think and work in different ways.

Online subscriptions

The online subscription will give you access to additional resources.

eTextbooks

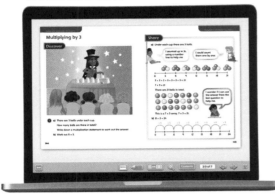

Digital versions of *Power Maths* Textbooks allow class groups to share and discuss questions, solutions and strategies. They allow you to project key structures and representations at the front of the class, to ensure all children are focusing on the same concept.

Teaching tools

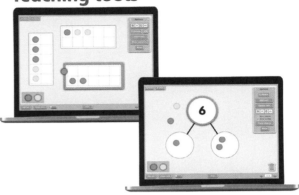

Here you will find interactive versions of key *Power Maths* structures and representations.

Power Ups

Use this series of daily activities to promote and check number fluency.

Online versions of Teacher Guide pages

PDF pages give support at both unit and lesson levels. You will also find help with key strategies and templates for tracking progress.

Unit videos

Watch the professional development videos at the start of each unit to help you teach with confidence. The videos explore common misconceptions in the unit, and include intervention suggestions as well as suggestions on what to look out for when assessing mastery in your children.

End of unit Strengthen and Deepen materials

Each Strengthen activity at the end of every unit addresses a key misconception and can be used to support children who need it. The Deepen activities are designed to be 'Low Threshold High Ceiling' and will challenge those children who can understand more deeply. These resources will help you ensure that every child understands and will help you keep the class moving forward together. These printable activities provide an optional resource bank for use after the assessment stage.

Underpinning all of these resources, *Power Maths* is infused throughout with continual professional development, supporting you at every step.

The *Power Maths* teaching model

At the heart of *Power Maths* is a clearly structured teaching and learning process that helps you make certain that every child masters each maths concept securely and deeply. For each year group, the curriculum is broken down into core concepts, taught in units. A unit divides into smaller learning steps – lessons. Step by step, strong foundations of cumulative knowledge and understanding are built.

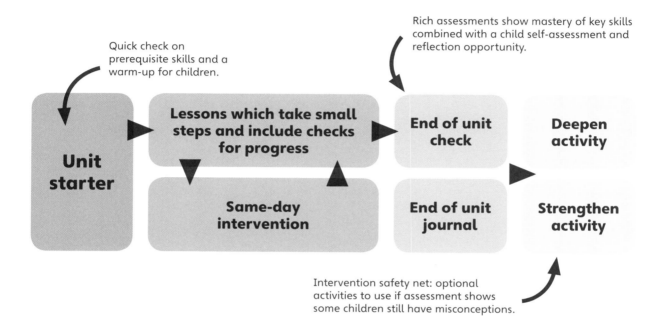

Quick check on prerequisite skills and a warm-up for children.

Rich assessments show mastery of key skills combined with a child self-assessment and reflection opportunity.

Unit starter → **Lessons which take small steps and include checks for progress** → **End of unit check** → **Deepen activity**

Same-day intervention

End of unit journal → **Strengthen activity**

Intervention safety net: optional activities to use if assessment shows some children still have misconceptions.

Unit starter

Each unit begins with a unit starter, which introduces the learning context along with key mathematical vocabulary, structures and representations.

- The Textbooks include a check on readiness and a warm-up task for children to complete.

- Your Teacher Guide gives support right from the start on important structures and representations, mathematical language, common misconceptions and intervention strategies.

- Unit-specific videos develop your subject knowledge and insights so you feel confident and fully equipped to teach each new unit. These are available via the online subscription.

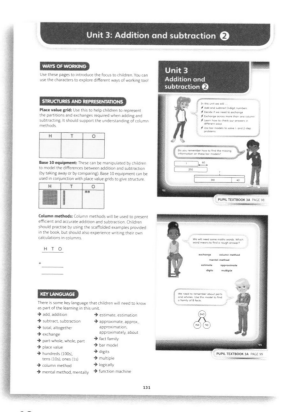

Lesson

Once a unit has been introduced, it is time to start teaching the series of lessons.

- Each lesson is scaffolded with Textbook and Practice Book activities and always begins with a Power Up activity (available via online subscription).

- *Power Maths* identifies lesson by lesson what concepts are to be taught.

- Your Teacher Guide offers lots of support for you to get the most from every child in every lesson. As well as highlighting key points, tricky areas and how to handle them, you will also find question prompts to check on understanding and clarification on why particular activities and questions are used.

Same-day intervention

Same-day interventions are vital in order to keep the class progressing together. Therefore, *Power Maths* provides plenty of support throughout the journey.

- Intervention is focused on keeping up now, not catching up later, so interventions should happen as soon as they are needed.

- Practice questions are designed to bring misconceptions to the surface, allowing you to identify these easily as you circulate during independent practice time.

- Child-friendly assessment questions in the Teacher Guide help you identify easily which children need to strengthen their understanding.

End of unit check and journal

At the end of a unit, summative assessment tasks reveal essential information on each child's understanding. An End of unit check in the Pupil Textbook lets you see which children have mastered the key concepts, which children have not and where their misconceptions lie. The Practice Book includes an End of unit journal in which children can reflect on what they have learnt.
Each unit also offers Strengthen and Deepen activities, available via the online subscription.

The End of unit check presents six to nine multiple-choice questions. These questions are designed to reveal misconceptions and help you target areas that need strengthening.

The Teacher Guide offers support with handling misconceptions.

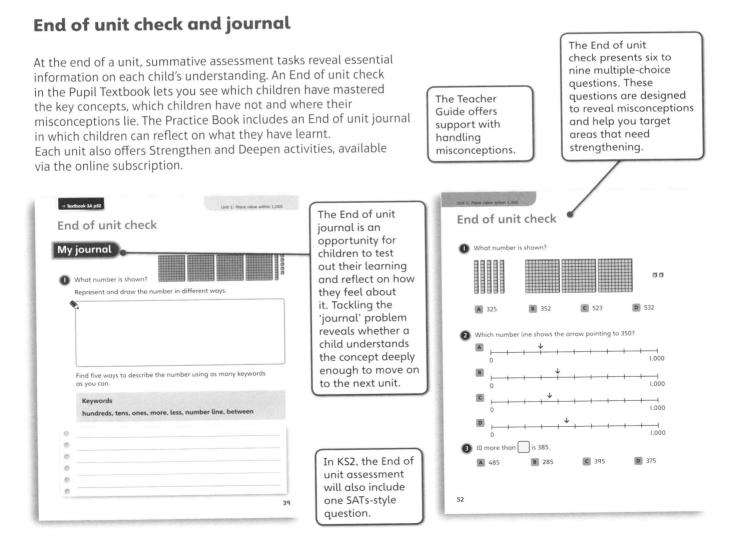

The End of unit journal is an opportunity for children to test out their learning and reflect on how they feel about it. Tackling the 'journal' problem reveals whether a child understands the concept deeply enough to move on to the next unit.

In KS2, the End of unit assessment will also include one SATs-style question.

The *Power Maths* lesson sequence

At the heart of *Power Maths* is a unique lesson sequence designed to empower children to understand core concepts and grow in confidence. Embracing the National Centre for Excellence in the Teaching of Mathematics' (NCETM's) definition of mastery, the sequence guides and shapes every *Power Maths* lesson you teach.

Flexibility is built into the *Power Maths* programme so there is no one-to-one mapping of lessons and concepts meaning you can pace your teaching according to your class. While some children will need to spend longer on a particular concept (through interventions or additional lessons), others will reach deeper levels of understanding. However, it is important that the class moves forward together through the termly schedules.

Power Up ⏱ 5 minutes

Each lesson begins with a Power Up activity (available via the online subscription) which supports fluency in key number facts.

The whole-class approach depends on fluency, so the Power Up is a powerful and essential activity.

TOP TIP
If the class is struggling with the task, revisit it later and check understanding.

Power Ups reinforce key skills such as times-tables, number bonds and working with place value.

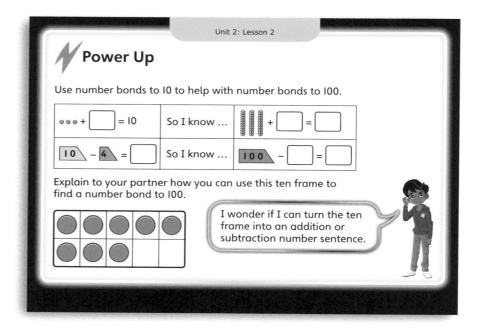

Discover ⏱ 10 minutes

A practical, real-life problem arouses curiosity. Children find the maths through story-telling.

A real-life scenario is provided for the Discover section but feel free to build upon these with your own examples that are more relevant to your class.

TOP TIP
Discover works best when run at tables, in pairs with concrete objects.

Question ❶ a) tackles the key concept and question ❶ b) digs a little deeper. Children have time to explore, play and discuss possible strategies.

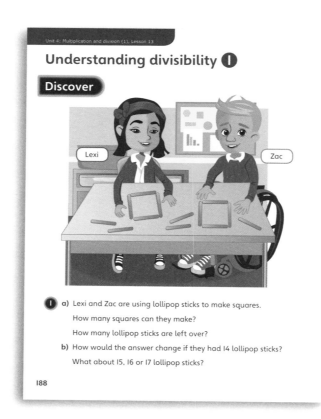

Share ⏱ 10 minutes

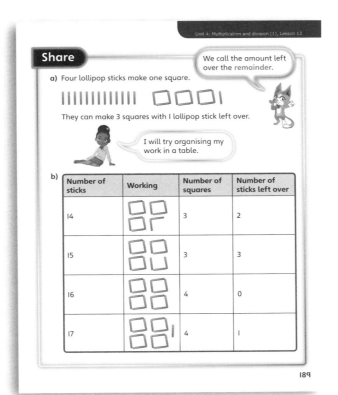

Share

a) Four lollipop sticks make one square.

We call the amount left over the **remainder**.

They can make 3 squares with 1 lollipop stick left over.

I will try organising my work in a table.

b)

Number of sticks	Working	Number of squares	Number of sticks left over
14		3	2
15		3	3
16		4	0
17		4	1

189

Think together

⏱ 10 minutes

Think together

1 Lexi and Zac use more lollipop sticks.

How would you complete the table?

Number of sticks	Working	Number of squares	Number of sticks left over
18		4	
19			
20			

2 a) Describe the pattern that Lexi can see.

I can see a pattern in the number of lollipop sticks left over.

Lexi

b) Is Zac correct?

I don't think you can have more than 3 lollipop sticks left over.

Zac

190

Practice ⏱ 15 minutes

Using their Practice Books, children work independently while you circulate and check on progress.

Questions follow small steps of progression to deepen learning.

TOP TIP
Some children could work separately with a teacher or assistant.

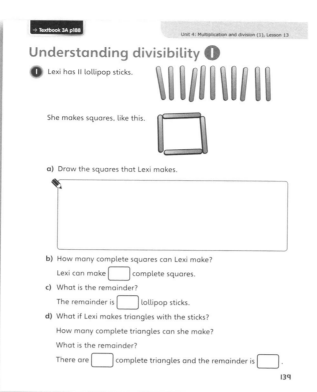

→ Textbook 3A p188

Understanding divisibility ❶

1. Lexi has 11 lollipop sticks.

She makes squares, like this.

a) Draw the squares that Lexi makes.

b) How many complete squares can Lexi make?

Lexi can make ⬚ complete squares.

c) What is the remainder?

The remainder is ⬚ lollipop sticks.

d) What if Lexi makes triangles with the sticks?

How many complete triangles can she make?

What is the remainder?

There are ⬚ complete triangles and the remainder is ⬚ .

139

Are some children struggling? If so, work with them as a group, using mathematical structures and representations to support understanding as necessary.

There are no set routines: for real understanding, children need to think about the problem in different ways.

Reflect ⏱ 5 minutes

'Spot the mistake' questions are great for checking misconceptions.

The Reflect section is your opportunity to check how deeply children understand the target concept.

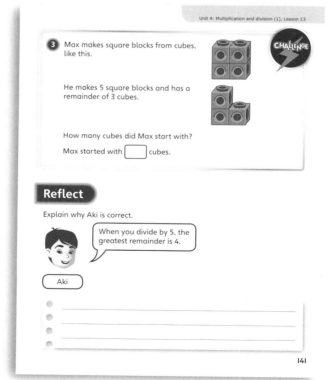

3. Max makes square blocks from cubes, like this. **CHALLENGE**

He makes 5 square blocks and has a remainder of 3 cubes.

How many cubes did Max start with?

Max started with ⬚ cubes.

Reflect

Explain why Aki is correct.

> When you divide by 5, the greatest remainder is 4.

Aki

141

The Practice Books use various approaches to check that children have fully understood each concept.

Looking like they understand is not enough! It is essential that children can show they have grasped the concept.

14

Using the *Power Maths* Teacher Guide

Think of your Teacher Guides as *Power Maths* handbooks that will guide, support and inspire your day-to-day teaching. Clear and concise, and illustrated with helpful examples, your Teacher Guides will help you make the best possible use of every individual lesson. They also provide wrap-around professional development, enhancing your own subject knowledge and helping you to grow in confidence about moving your children forward together.

There is a Teacher Guide per year group for every term with unit and lesson level guidance and support.

Tips and advice on key elements such as C-P-A approaches, misconceptions, language, modelling growth mindsets and same-day intervention.

Annotations for every Pupil Textbook and Practice Book page, providing prompts for key questions to ask to expose understanding and explanations as to why key questions have been chosen.

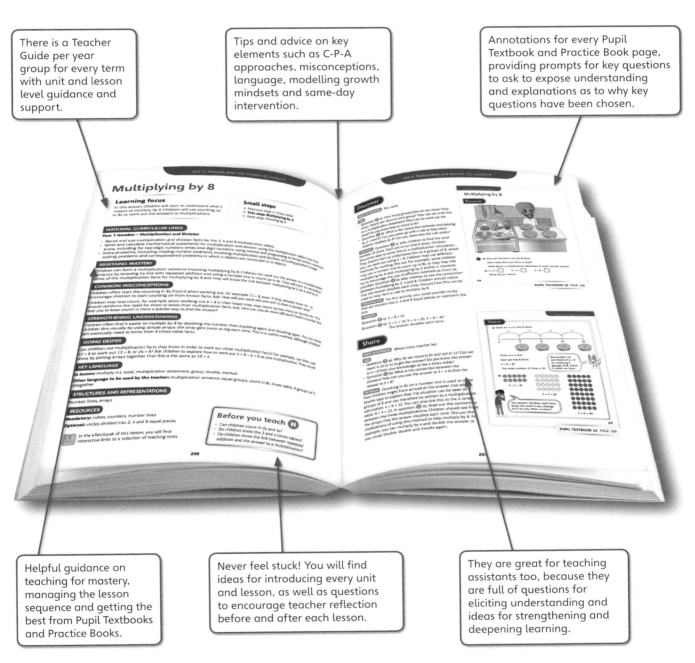

Helpful guidance on teaching for mastery, managing the lesson sequence and getting the best from Pupil Textbooks and Practice Books.

Never feel stuck! You will find ideas for introducing every unit and lesson, as well as questions to encourage teacher reflection before and after each lesson.

They are great for teaching assistants too, because they are full of questions for eliciting understanding and ideas for strengthening and deepening learning.

At the end of each unit, your Teacher Guide helps you identify who has fully grasped the concept, who has not and how to move every child forward. This is covered later in the Assessment strategies section.

Power Maths Year 4, yearly overview

Textbook	Strand	Unit		Number of Lessons
Textbook A / Practice Book A	Number – number and place value	1	Place value – 4-digit numbers (1)	9
	Number – number and place value	2	Place value – 4-digit numbers (2)	9
(Term 1)	Number – addition and subtraction	3	Addition and subtraction	15
	Measurement	4	Measure – perimeter	5
	Number – multiplication and division	5	Multiplication and division (1)	11
Textbook B / Practice Book B	Number – multiplication and division	6	Multiplication and division (2)	15
	Measurement	7	Measure – area	5
(Term 2)	Number – fractions (including decimals)	8	Fractions (1)	7
	Number – fractions (including decimals)	9	Fractions (2)	8
	Number – fractions (including decimals)	10	Decimals (1)	10
Textbook C / Practice Book C	Number – fractions (including decimals)	11	Decimals (2)	7
	Measurement	12	Money	9
(Term 3)	Measurement	13	Time	5
	Statistics	14	Statistics	5
	Geometry – properties of shapes	15	Geometry – angles and 2D shapes	10
	Geometry – position and direction	16	Geometry – position and direction	6

Power Maths Year 4, Textbook 4C (Term 3) Overview

Strand 1	Strand 2	Unit		Lesson number	Lesson title	NC Objective 1	NC Objective 2	NC Objective 3
Number – fractions (including decimals)		Unit 11	Decimals (2)	1	Making a whole	Recognise and write decimal equivalents of any number of tenths or hundredths	Add and subtract fractions with the same denominator	
Number – fractions (including decimals)		Unit 11	Decimals (2)	2	Writing decimals	Find the effect of dividing a one- or two-digit number by 10 and 100, identifying the value of the digits in the answer as ones, tenths and hundredths		
Number – fractions (including decimals)		Unit 11	Decimals (2)	3	Comparing decimals	Compare numbers with the same number of decimal places up to two decimal places		
Number – fractions (including decimals)		Unit 11	Decimals (2)	4	Ordering decimals	Compare numbers with the same number of decimal places up to two decimal places		
Number – fractions (including decimals)		Unit 11	Decimals (2)	5	Rounding decimals	Round decimals with one decimal place to the nearest whole number		
Number – fractions (including decimals)		Unit 11	Decimals (2)	6	Halves and quarters	Recognise and write decimal equivalents to $\frac{1}{4}, \frac{1}{2}, \frac{3}{4}$		

Strand 1	Strand 2	Unit	Lesson title	Lesson number	NC Objective 1	NC Objective 2	NC Objective 3
Number – fractions (including decimals)		Unit 11	Decimals (2)	7	Problem solving – decimals	Solve simple measure and money problems involving fractions and decimals to two decimal places		
Measurement	Number – fractions (including decimals)	Unit 12	Money	1	Pounds and pence	Estimate, compare and calculate different measures, including money in pounds and pence	Solve simple measure and money problems involving fractions and decimals to two decimal places	
Measurement	Number – fractions (including decimals)	Unit 12	Money	2	Pounds, tenths and hundredths	Estimate, compare and calculate different measures, including money in pounds and pence	Solve simple measure and money problems involving fractions and decimals to two decimal places	
Measurement	Number – fractions (including decimals)	Unit 12	Money	3	Ordering amounts of money	Estimate, compare and calculate different measures, including money in pounds and pence	Solve simple measure and money problems involving fractions and decimals to two decimal places	
Measurement	Number – fractions (including decimals)	Unit 12	Money	4	Rounding money	Estimate, compare and calculate different measures, including money in pounds and pence	Solve simple measure and money problems involving fractions and decimals to two decimal places	
Measurement		Unit 12	Money	5	Using rounding to estimate money	Estimate, compare and calculate different measures, including money in pounds and pence		
Measurement		Unit 12	Money	6	Problem solving – pounds and pence	Estimate, compare and calculate different measures, including money in pounds and pence		
Measurement	Number – fractions (including decimals)	Unit 12	Money	7	Problem solving – multiplication and division	Estimate, compare and calculate different measures, including money in pounds and pence	Solve simple measure and money problems involving fractions and decimals to two decimal places	
Measurement	Number – fractions (including decimals)	Unit 12	Money	8	Solving two-step problems	Estimate, compare and calculate different measures, including money in pounds and pence	Solve simple measure and money problems involving fractions and decimals to two decimal places	
Measurement	Number – fractions (including decimals)	Unit 12	Money	9	Problem solving – money	Estimate, compare and calculate different measures, including money in pounds and pence	Solve simple measure and money problems involving fractions and decimals to two decimal places	
Measurement		Unit 13	Time	1	Units of time (1)	Convert between different units of measure [for example, kilometre to metre; hour to minute]		
Measurement		Unit 13	Time	2	Units of time (2)	Convert between different units of measure [for example, kilometre to metre; hour to minute]		
Measurement		Unit 13	Time	3	Converting times (1)	Convert between different units of measure [for example, kilometre to metre; hour to minute]		

Strand 1	Strand 2	Unit		Lesson number	Lesson title	NC Objective 1	NC Objective 2	NC Objective 3
Measurement		Unit 13	Time	4	Converting times (2)	Convert between different units of measure [for example, kilometre to metre; hour to minute]		
Measurement		Unit 13	Time	5	Problem solving – units of time	Convert between different units of measure [for example, kilometre to metre; hour to minute]		
Statistics		Unit 14	Statistics	1	Charts and tables (1)	Interpret and present discrete and continuous data using appropriate graphical methods, including bar charts and time graphs		
Statistics		Unit 14	Statistics	2	Charts and tables (2)	Solve comparison, sum and difference problems using information presented in bar charts, pictograms, tables and other graphs		
Statistics		Unit 14	Statistics	3	Line graphs (1)	Interpret and present discrete and continuous data using appropriate graphical methods, including bar charts and time graphs		
Statistics		Unit 14	Statistics	4	Line graphs (2)	Solve comparison, sum and difference problems using information presented in bar charts, pictograms, tables and other graphs		
Statistics		Unit 14	Statistics	5	Problem solving – graphs	Solve comparison, sum and difference problems using information presented in bar charts, pictograms, tables and other graphs		
Geometry – properties of shapes		Unit 15	Geometry – angles and 2D shapes	1	Identifying angles	Identify acute and obtuse angles and compare and order angles up to two right angles by size		
Geometry – properties of shapes		Unit 15	Geometry – angles and 2D shapes	2	Comparing and ordering angles	Identify acute and obtuse angles and compare and order angles up to two right angles by size		
Geometry – properties of shapes		Unit 15	Geometry – angles and 2D shapes	3	Identifying regular and irregular shapes	Compare and classify geometric shapes, including quadrilaterals and triangles, based on their properties and sizes		
Geometry – properties of shapes		Unit 15	Geometry – angles and 2D shapes	4	Classifying triangles	Compare and classify geometric shapes, including quadrilaterals and triangles, based on their properties and sizes		

Strand 1	Strand 2	Unit		Lesson number	Lesson title	NC Objective 1	NC Objective 2	NC Objective 3
Geometry – properties of shapes		Unit 15	Geometry – angles and 2D shapes	5	Classifying and comparing quadrilaterals	Compare and classify geometric shapes, including quadrilaterals and triangles, based on their properties and sizes		
Geometry – properties of shapes		Unit 15	Geometry – angles and 2D shapes	6	Deducing facts about shapes	Compare and classify geometric shapes, including quadrilaterals and triangles, based on their properties and sizes		
Geometry – properties of shapes		Unit 15	Geometry – angles and 2D shapes	7	Lines of symmetry inside a shape	Identify lines of symmetry in 2D shapes presented in different orientations		
Geometry – properties of shapes		Unit 15	Geometry – angles and 2D shapes	8	Lines of symmetry outside a shape	Identify lines of symmetry in 2D shapes presented in different orientations		
Geometry – properties of shapes		Unit 15	Geometry – angles and 2D shapes	9	Completing a symmetric figure	Complete a simple symmetric figure with respect to a specific line of symmetry		
Geometry – properties of shapes		Unit 15	Geometry – angles and 2D shapes	10	Completing a symmetric shape	Complete a simple symmetric figure with respect to a specific line of symmetry		
Geometry – position and direction		Unit 16	Geometry – position and direction	1	Describing position (1)	Describe positions on a 2D grid as coordinates in the first quadrant		
Geometry – position and direction		Unit 16	Geometry – position and direction	2	Describing position (2)	Describe positions on a 2D grid as coordinates in the first quadrant		
Geometry – position and direction		Unit 16	Geometry – position and direction	3	Drawing on a grid	Plot specified points and draw sides to complete a given polygon		
Geometry – position and direction		Unit 16	Geometry – position and direction	4	Reasoning on a grid	Describe positions on a 2D grid as coordinates in the first quadrant		
Geometry – position and direction		Unit 16	Geometry – position and direction	5	Moving on a grid	Describe movements between positions as translations of a given unit to the left/right and up/down		
Geometry – position and direction		Unit 16	Geometry – position and direction	6	Describing a movement on a grid	Describe movements between positions as translations of a given unit to the left/right and up/down		

Mindset: an introduction

Global research and best practice deliver the same message: learning is greatly affected by what learners perceive they can or cannot do. What is more, it is also shaped by what their parents, carers and teachers perceive they can do. Mindset – the thinking that determines our beliefs and behaviours – therefore has a fundamental impact on teaching and learning.

Everyone can!

Power Maths and mastery methods focus on the distinction between 'fixed' and 'growth' mindsets (Dweck, 2007).[1] Those with a fixed mindset believe that their basic qualities (for example, intelligence, talent and ability to learn) are pre-wired or fixed: 'If you have a talent for maths, you will succeed at it. If not, too bad!' By contrast, those with a growth mindset believe that hard work, effort and commitment drive success and that 'smart' is not something you are or are not, but something you become. In short, everyone can do maths!

Key mindset strategies

A growth mindset needs to be actively nurtured and developed. *Power Maths* offers some key strategies for fostering healthy growth mindsets in your classroom.

It is okay to get it wrong

Mistakes are valuable opportunities to re-think and understand more deeply. Learning is richer when children and teachers alike focus on spotting and sharing mistakes as well as solutions.

Praise hard work

Praise is a great motivator, and by focusing on praising effort and learning rather than success, children will be more willing to try harder, take risks and persist for longer.

Mind your language!

The language we use around learners has a profound effect on their mindsets. Make a habit of using growth phrases, such as, 'Everyone can!', 'Mistakes can help you learn' and 'Just try for a little longer'. The king of them all is one little word, 'yet ... I cannot solve this ... yet!' Encourage parents and carers to use the right language too.

Build in opportunities for success

The step-by-small-step approach enables children to enjoy the experience of success. In addition, avoid ability grouping and encourage every child to answer questions and explain or demonstrate their methods to others.

[1]Dweck, C (2007) *The New Psychology of Success*, Ballantine Books: New York

The *Power Maths* characters

The *Power Maths* characters model the traits of growth mindset learners and encourage resilience by prompting and questioning children as they work. Appearing frequently in the Textbooks and Practice Books, they are your allies in teaching and discussion, helping to model methods, alternatives and misconceptions, and to pose questions. They encourage and support your children, too: they are all hardworking, enthusiastic and unafraid of making and talking about mistakes.

Meet the team!

Flexible Flo is open-minded and sometimes indecisive. She likes to think differently and come up with a variety of methods or ideas.

Determined Dexter is resolute, resilient and systematic. He concentrates hard, always tries his best and he'll never give up – even though he doesn't always choose the most efficient methods!

'Let's try again.'

'Mistakes are cool!'

'Have I found all of the solutions?'

'Let's try it this way ...'

'Can we do it differently?'

'I've got another way of doing this!'

'I'm going to try this!'

'I know how to do that!'

'Want to share my ideas?'

Curious Ash is eager, interested and inquisitive, and he loves solving puzzles and problems. Ash asks lots of questions but sometimes gets distracted.

'What if we tried this ...?'

'I wonder ...'

'Is there a pattern here?'

Miaow!

Sparks the Cat

Brave Astrid is confident, willing to take risks and unafraid of failure. She is never scared to jump straight into a problem or question, and although she often makes simple mistakes she is happy to talk them through with others.

Mathematical language

Traditionally, we in the UK have tended to try simplifying mathematical language to make it easier for young children to understand. By contrast, evidence and experience show that by diluting the correct language, we actually mask concepts and meanings for children. We then wonder why they are confused by new and different terminology later down the line! *Power Maths* is not afraid of 'hard' words and avoids placing any barriers between children and their understanding of mathematical concepts. As a result, we need to be planned, precise and thorough in building every child's understanding of the language of maths. Throughout the Teacher Guides you will find support and guidance on how to deliver this, as well as individual explanations throughout the Pupil Textbooks.

Use the following key strategies to build children's mathematical vocabulary, understanding and confidence.

Precise and consistent

Everyone in the classroom should use the correct mathematical terms in full, every time. For example, refer to 'equal parts', not 'parts'. Used consistently, precise maths language will be a familiar and non-threatening part of children's everyday experience.

Full sentences

Teachers and children alike need to use full sentences to explain or respond. When children use complete sentences, it both reveals their understanding and embeds their knowledge.

Stem sentences

These important sentences help children express mathematical concepts accurately, and are used throughout the *Power Maths* books. Encourage children to repeat them frequently, whether working independently or with others. Examples of stem sentences are:

'4 is a part, 5 is a part, 9 is the whole.'

'There are ... groups. There are ... in each group.'

Key vocabulary

The unit starters highlight essential vocabulary for every lesson. In the Pupil Textbooks, characters flag new terminology and the Teacher Guide lists important mathematical language for every unit and lesson. New terms are never introduced without a clear explanation.

Mathematical signs

Mathematical signs are used early on so that children quickly become familiar with them and their meaning. Often, the *Power Maths* characters will highlight the connection between language and particular signs.

The role of talk and discussion

When children learn to talk purposefully together about maths, barriers of fear and anxiety are broken down and they grow in confidence, skills and understanding. Building a healthy culture of 'maths talk' empowers their learning from day one.

Explanation and discussion are integral to the *Power Maths* structure, so by simply following the books your lessons will stimulate structured talk. The following key 'maths talk' strategies will help you strengthen that culture and ensure that every child is included.

Sentences, not words

Encourage children to use full sentences when reasoning, explaining or discussing maths. This helps both speaker and listeners to clarify their own understanding. It also reveals whether or not the speaker truly understands, enabling you to address misconceptions as they arise.

Working together

Working with others in pairs, groups or as a whole class is a great way to support maths talk and discussion. Use different group structures to add variety and challenge. For example, children could take timed turns for talking, work independently alongside a 'discussion buddy', or perhaps play different *Power Maths* character roles within their group.

Think first – then talk

Provide clear opportunities within each lesson for children to think and reflect, so that their talk is purposeful, relevant and focused.

Give every child a voice

Where the 'hands up' model allows only the more confident child to shine, *Power Maths* involves everyone. Make sure that no child dominates and that even the shyest child is encouraged to contribute – and is praised when they do.

Assessment strategies

Teaching for mastery demands that you are confident about what each child knows and where their misconceptions lie: therefore, practical and effective assessment is vitally important.

Formative assessment within lessons

The Think together section will often reveal any confusions or insecurities: try ironing these out by doing the first Think together question as a class. For children who continue to struggle, you or your teaching assistant should provide support and enable them to move on.

Performance in Practice can be very revealing: check Practice Books and listen out both during and after practice to identify misconceptions.

The Reflect section is designed to check on the all-important depth of understanding. Be sure to review how children performed in this final stage before you teach the next lesson.

End of unit check – Textbook

Each unit concludes with a summative check to help you assess quickly and clearly each child's understanding, fluency, reasoning and problem-solving skills. In KS2 this check also contains a SATs-style question to help children become familiar with answering this type of question.

In KS2 we would suggest the End of unit check is completed independently in children's exercise books, but you can adapt this to suit the needs of your class.

End of unit check – Practice Book

The Practice Book contains further opportunities for assessment, and can be completed by children independently whilst you are carrying out diagnostic assessment with small groups. Your Teacher Guide will advise you on what to do if children struggle to articulate an explanation – or perhaps encourage you to write down something they have explained well. It will also offer insights into children's answers and their implications for the next learning steps. It is split into three main sections, outlined below.

My journal

My journal is designed to allow children to show their depth of understanding of the unit. It can also serve as a way of checking that children have grasped key mathematical vocabulary. Children should have some time to think about how they want to answer the question, and you could ask them to talk to a partner about their ideas. Then children should write their answer in their Practice Book.

Power check

The Power check allows children to self-assess their level of confidence on the topic by colouring in different smiley faces. You may want to introduce the faces as follows:

Power play or Power puzzle

Each unit ends with either a Power play or a Power puzzle. This is an activity, puzzle or game that allows children to use their new knowledge in a fun, informal way. In Key Stage 2 we have also included a deeper level to each game to help challenge those children who have grasped a concept quickly.

How to use diagnostic questions

The diagnostic questions provided in *Power Maths* Textbooks are carefully structured to identify both understanding and misconceptions (if children answer in a particular way, you will know why). The simple procedure below may be helpful:

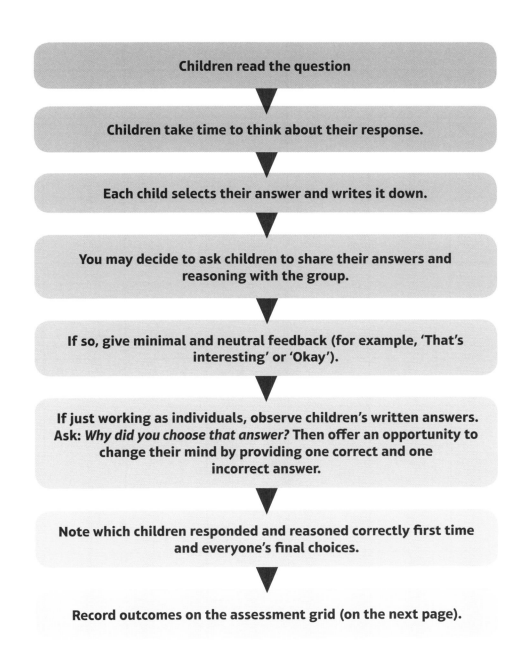

Children read the question

Children take time to think about their response.

Each child selects their answer and writes it down.

You may decide to ask children to share their answers and reasoning with the group.

If so, give minimal and neutral feedback (for example, 'That's interesting' or 'Okay').

If just working as individuals, observe children's written answers. Ask: *Why did you choose that answer?* Then offer an opportunity to change their mind by providing one correct and one incorrect answer.

Note which children responded and reasoned correctly first time and everyone's final choices.

Record outcomes on the assessment grid (on the next page).

Power Maths unit assessment grid

Year ___   Unit ___ _____

Record only as much information as you judge appropriate for your assessment of each child's mastery of the unit and any steps needed for intervention.

Name	Diagnostic questions	SATs-style question	My journal	Power check	Power play/puzzle	Mastery	Intervention/ Strengthen

Keeping the class together

Traditionally, children who learn quickly have been accelerated through the curriculum. As a consequence, their learning may be superficial and will lack the many benefits of enabling children to learn with and from each other.

By contrast, *Power Maths'* mastery approach values real understanding and richer, deeper learning above speed. It sees all children learning the same concept in small, cumulative steps, each finding and mastering challenge at their own level. Remember that when you teach for mastery, EVERYONE can do maths! Those who grasp a concept easily have time to explore and understand that concept at a deeper level. The whole class therefore moves through the curriculum at broadly the same pace via individual learning journeys.

For some teachers, the idea that a whole class can move forward together is revolutionary and challenging. However, the evidence of global good practice clearly shows that this approach drives engagement, confidence, motivation and success for all learners, and not just the high flyers. The strategies below will help you keep your class together on their maths journey.

Mix it up

Do not stick to set groups at each table. Every child should be working on the same concept, and mixing up the groupings widens children's opportunities for exploring, discussing and sharing their understanding with others.

Recycling questions

Reuse the Pupil Textbook and Practice Book questions with concrete materials to allow children to explore concepts and relationships and deepen their understanding. This strategy is especially useful for reinforcing learning in same-day interventions.

Strengthen at every opportunity

The next lesson in a *Power Maths* sequence always revises and builds on the previous step to help embed learning. These activities provide golden opportunities for individual children to strengthen their learning with the support of teaching assistants.

Prepare to be surprised!

Children may grasp a concept quickly or more slowly. The 'fast graspers' won't always be the same individuals, nor does the speed at which a child understands a concept predict their success in maths. Are they struggling or just working more slowly?

Depth and breadth

Just as prescribed in the National Curriculum, the goal of *Power Maths* is never to accelerate through a topic but rather to gain a clear, deep and broad understanding.

"Pupils who grasp concepts rapidly should be challenged through being offered rich and sophisticated problems before any acceleration through new content. Those who are not sufficiently fluent with earlier material should consolidate their understanding, including through additional practice, before moving on."

National Curriculum: Mathematics programmes of study: KS1 & 2, 2013

The lesson sequence offers many opportunities for you to deepen and broaden children's learning, some of which are suggested below.

Discover

As well as using the questions in the Teacher Guide, check that children are really delving into why something is true. It is not enough to simply recite facts, such as '6 + 3 = 9'. They need to be able to see why, explain it, and to demonstrate the solution in several ways.

Share

Make sure that every child is given chances to offer answers and expand their knowledge and not just those with the greatest confidence.

Think together

Encourage children to think about how they found the solution and explain it to their partner. Be sure to make concrete materials available on group tables throughout the lesson to support and reinforce learning.

Practice

Avoid any temptation to select questions according to your assessment of ability: practice questions are presented in a logical sequence and it is important that each child works through every question.

Reflect

Open-ended questions allow children to deepen their understanding as far as they can by discovering new ways of finding answers. For example, *Give me another way of working out how high the wall is … And another way?*

Online materials

For each unit you will find additional strengthening activities to support those children who need it and to deepen the understanding of those who need the additional challenge.

Same-day intervention

Since maths competence depends on mastering concepts one-by-one in a logical progression, it is important that no gaps in understanding are ever left unfilled. Same-day interventions – either within or after a lesson – are a crucial safety net for any child who has not fully made the small step covered that day. In other words, intervention is always about keeping up, not catching up, so that every child has the skills and understanding they need to tackle the next lesson. That means presenting the same problems used in the lesson, with a variety of concrete materials to help children model their solutions.

We offer two intervention strategies below, but you should feel free to choose others if they work better for your class.

Within-lesson intervention

The Think together activity will reveal those who are struggling, so when it is time for Practice, bring these children together to work with you on the first Practice questions. Observe these children carefully, ask questions, encourage them to use concrete models and check that they reach and can demonstrate their understanding.

After-lesson intervention

You might like to use Think together before an assembly, giving you or teaching assistants time to recap and expand with slow graspers during assembly time. Teaching assistants could also work with strugglers at other convenient points in the school day.

The role of practice

Practice plays a pivotal role in the *Power Maths* approach. It takes place in class groups, smaller groups, pairs and independently, so that children always have the opportunities for thinking as well as the models and support they need to practise meaningfully and with understanding.

Intelligent practice

In *Power Maths*, practice never equates to the simple repetition of a process. Instead we embrace the concept of intelligent practice, in which all children become fluent in maths through varied, frequent and thoughtful practice that deepens and embeds conceptual understanding in a logical, planned sequence. To see the difference, take a look at the following examples.

Traditional practice

- Repetition can be rote – no need for a child to think hard about what they are doing.

- Praise may be misplaced.

- Does this prove understanding?

Intelligent practice

- Varied methods – concrete, pictorial and abstract.

- Calculations expressed in different ways, requiring thought and understanding.

- Constructive feedback.

All practice questions are designed to move children on and reveal misconceptions.

Simple, logical steps build onto earlier learning.

C-P-A runs throughout – different ways of modelling and understanding the same concept.

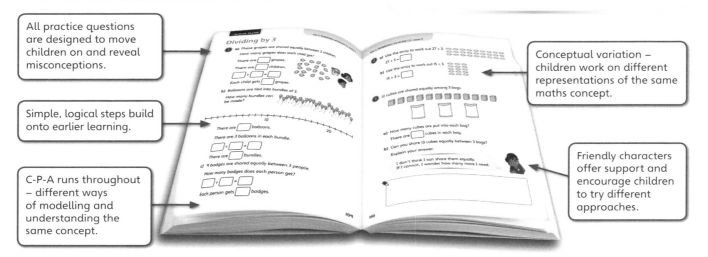

Conceptual variation – children work on different representations of the same maths concept.

Friendly characters offer support and encourage children to try different approaches.

A carefully designed progression

The Practice Books provide just the right amount of intelligent practice for children to complete independently in the final sections of each lesson. It is really important that all children are exposed to the Practice questions, and that children are not directed to complete different sections. That is because each question is different and has been designed to challenge children to think about the maths they are doing. The questions become more challenging so children grasping concepts more quickly will start to slow down as they progress. Meanwhile, you have the chance to circulate and spot any misconceptions before they become barriers to further learning.

Homework and the role of carers

While *Power Maths* does not prescribe any particular homework structure, we acknowledge the potential value of practice at home. For example, practising fluency in key facts, such as number bonds and times-tables, is an ideal homework task, and carers could work through uncompleted Practice Book questions with children at either primary stage.

However, it is important to recognise that many parents and carers may themselves lack confidence in maths, and few, if any, will be familiar with mastery methods. A Parents' and Carers' Evening that helps them understand the basics of mindsets, mastery and mathematical language is a great way to ensure that children benefit from their homework. It could be a fun opportunity for children to teach their families that everyone can do maths!

Structures and representations

Unlike most other subjects, maths comprises a wide array of abstract concepts – and that is why children and adults so often find it difficult. By taking a Concrete-Pictorial-Abstract (C-P-A) approach, *Power Maths* allows children to tackle concepts in a tangible and more comfortable way.

Non-linear stages

Concrete

Replacing the traditional approach of a teacher working through a problem in front of the class, the concrete stage introduces real objects that children can use to 'do' the maths – any familiar object that a child can manipulate and move to help bring the maths to life. It is important to appreciate, however, that children must always understand the link between models and the objects they represent. For example, children need to first understand that three cakes could be represented by three pretend cakes, and then by three counters or bricks. Frequent practice helps consolidate this essential insight. Although they can be used at any time, good concrete models are an essential first step in understanding.

Pictorial

This stage uses pictorial representations of objects to let children 'see' what particular maths problems look like. It helps them make connections between the concrete and pictorial representations and the abstract maths concept. Children can also create or view a pictorial representation together, enabling discussion and comparisons. The *Power Maths* teaching tools are fantastic for this learning stage, and bar modelling is invaluable for problem solving throughout the primary curriculum.

Abstract

Our ultimate goal is for children to understand abstract mathematical concepts, signs and notation and, of course, some children will reach this stage far more quickly than others. To work with abstract concepts, a child needs to be comfortable with the meaning of, and relationships between, concrete, pictorial and abstract models and representations. The C-P-A approach is not linear, and children may need different types of models at different times. However, when a child demonstrates with concrete models and pictorial representations that they have grasped a concept, we can be confident that they are ready to explore or model it with abstract signs such as numbers and notation.

Use at any time and with any age to support understanding.

Practical aspects of *Power Maths*

One of the key underlying elements of *Power Maths* is its practical approach, allowing you to make maths real and relevant to your children, no matter their age.

Manipulatives are essential resources for both key stages and *Power Maths* encourages teachers to use these at every opportunity, and to continue the Concrete-Pictorial-Abstract approach right through to Year 6.

The Textbooks and Teacher Guides include lots of opportunities for teaching in a practical way to show children what maths means in real life.

Discover and Share

The Discover and Share sections of the Textbook give you scope to turn a real-life scenario into a practical and hands-on section of the lesson. Use these sections as inspiration to get active in the classroom. Where appropriate, use the Discover contexts as a springboard for your own examples that have particular resonance for your children – and allow them to get their hands dirty trying out the mathematics for themselves.

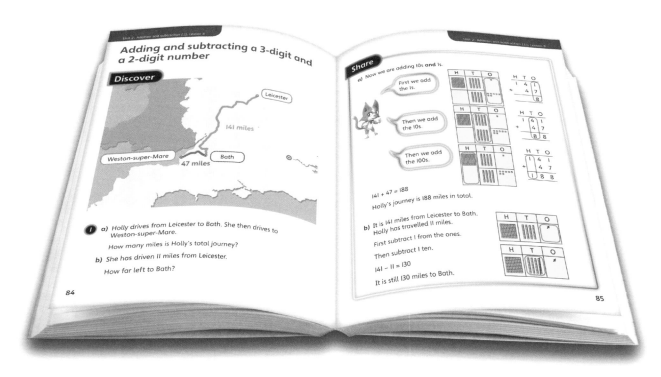

Unit videos

Every unit has a video which incorporates real-life classroom sequences.

These videos show you how the reasoning behind mathematics can be carried out in a practical manner by showing real children using various concrete and pictorial methods to come to the solution. You can see how using these practical models, such as part-whole and bar models, helps them to find and articulate their answer.

Mastery tips

Mastery Experts give anecdotal advice on where they have used hands-on and real-life elements to inspire their children.

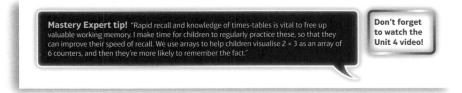

Mastery Expert tip! "Rapid recall and knowledge of times-tables is vital to free up valuable working memory. I make time for children to regularly practice these, so that they can improve their speed of recall. We use arrays to help children visualise 2 × 3 as an array of 6 counters, and then they're more likely to remember the fact."

Don't forget to watch the Unit 4 video!

Concrete-Pictorial-Abstract (C-P-A) approach

Each Share section uses various methods to explain an answer, helping children to access abstract concepts by using concrete tools, such as counters. Remember this isn't a linear process, so even children who appear confident using the more abstract method can deepen their knowledge by exploring the concrete representations. Encourage children to use all three methods to really solidify their understanding of a concept.

Pictorial representation – drawing the problem in a logical way that helps children visualise the maths

Concrete representation – using manipulatives to represent the problem. Encourage children to physically use resources to explore the maths.

Abstract representation – using words and calculations to represent the problem.

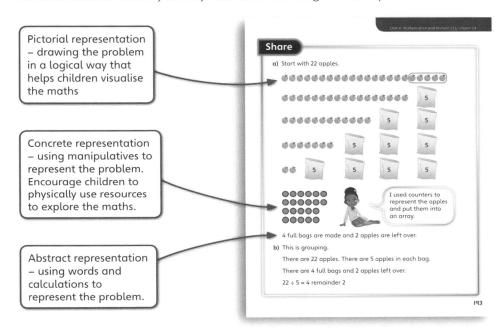

Practical tips

Every lesson suggests how to draw out the practical side of the Discover context.

You'll find these in the Discover section of the Teacher Guide for each lesson.

PRACTICAL TIPS You could use balls, counters or cubes under plastic cups to re-enact the artwork and help children get a feel for this activity.

Resources

Every lesson lists the practical resources you will need or might want to use. There is also a summary of all of the resources used throughout the term on page 34 to help you be prepared.

RESOURCES

Mandatory: cubes, counters, number lines

Optional: balls, plastic cups

List of practical resources

Year 4C Mandatory resources

Resource	Lesson
Blank ten frames	**Unit 11** lesson 1
Hundredths grid	**Unit 11** lessons 1, 6
Lolly sticks	**Unit 15** lesson 10
Metre ruler	**Unit 11** lessons 3, 7
Multilink cubes	**Unit 11** lesson 6
Number cards	**Unit 11** lesson 1
Number lines	**Unit 11** lesson 6
Place value counters	**Unit 11** lessons 1, 2, 3, 4, 6
Rulers	**Unit 14** lessons 1, 2, 3, 4, 5
Squared paper	**Unit 16** lesson 3
Weighing scales	**Unit 11** lessons 4, 7

Year 4C Optional resources

Resource	Lesson
A range of different 2D shapes	**Unit 15** lessons 1, 2, 3, 4, 5, 6, 7, 8, 9, 10
A range of different triangles	**Unit 15** lesson 4
Access to the internet	**Unit 16** lesson 1
Analogue clocks	**Unit 13** lessons 3, 4, 5 **Unit 15** lesson 1
Calendars/year planners	**Unit 13** lesson 5
Cards for pairs game – set of cards, half with a picture of a shape, the other half with the name of a shape	**Unit 15** lesson 6
Chalk	**Unit 16** lesson 4
Chess board	**Unit 16** lesson 6
Clock face	**Unit 15** lesson 1
Crayons	**Unit 12** lesson 1
Computer geometry package	**Unit 16** lessons 2, 3, 4, 5, 6
Digital clocks	**Unit 13** lessons 3, 4, 5
Digital timers/stopwatches	**Unit 13** lesson 1
Examples of 24-hour clock times from everyday life (computer clock, timetables etc.)	**Unit 13** lesson 4
Flash cards	**Unit 13** lesson 5
Geo boards with elastic bands	**Unit 15** lessons 5, 9
Geo strip kit	**Unit 15** lesson 5
Help envelopes	**Unit 14** lesson 5
Large laminated part-whole model	**Unit 11** lesson 1
Measuring jug	**Unit 11** lesson 7
Metre ruler	**Unit 11** lesson 7
Mirrors	**Unit 15** lessons 7, 8, 9, 10
Multilink cubes	**Unit 14** lessons 1, 2
Number cards	**Unit 13** lessons 3, 4, 5
Number lines	**Unit 14** lessons 3, 4, 5
Paper squares	**Unit 15** lessons 1, 6
Pieces of string	**Unit 13** lesson 2
Place value counters	**Unit 11** lesson 5
Place value grid	**Unit 11** lesson 6 **Unit 12** lesson 3
Plastic coins	**Unit 11** lesson 3 **Unit 12** lessons 1, 2, 3, 4, 5, 6, 7, 8, 9
Rulers	**Unit 15** lessons 2, 3 **Unit 16** lesson 3
Set squares	**Unit 15** lesson 2
Simple maps	**Unit 16** lesson 1
Squared paper	**Unit 14** lessons 3, 4, 5 **Unit 16** lesson 3, 4
Sticky labels	**Unit 13** lesson 2
Tape	**Unit 16** lesson 4
Weighing scales and weights	**Unit 11** lesson 7

Variation helps visualisation

Children find it much easier to visualise and grasp concepts if they see them presented in a number of ways, so be prepared to offer and encourage many different representations.

For example, the number six could be represented in various ways:

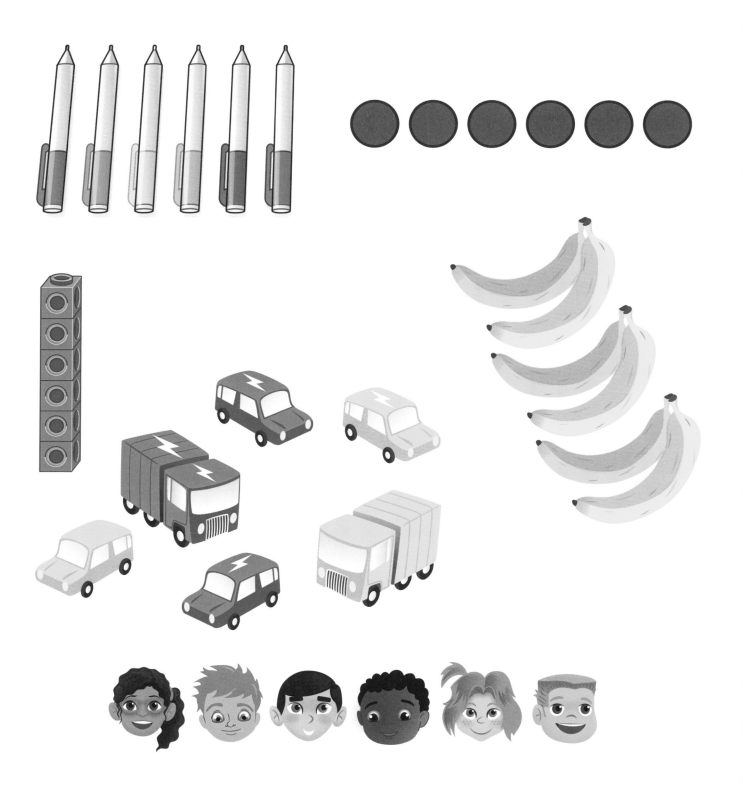

Getting started with *Power Maths*

As you prepare to put *Power Maths* into action, you might find the tips and advice below helpful.

STEP 1: Train up!

A practical, up-front, full-day professional development course will give you and your team a brilliant head-start as you begin your *Power Maths* journey. You will learn more about the ethos, how it works and why.

STEP 2: Check out the progression

Take a look at the yearly and termly overviews. Next take a look at the unit overview for the unit you are about to teach in your Teacher Guide, remembering that you can match your lessons and pacing to your class.

STEP 3: Explore the context

Take a little time to look at the context for this unit: what are the implications for the unit ahead? (Think about key language, common misunderstandings and intervention strategies, for example.) If you have the online subscription, don't forget to watch the corresponding unit video.

STEP 4: Prepare for your first lesson

Familiarise yourself with the objectives, essential questions to ask and the resources you will need. The Teacher Guide offers tips, ideas and guidance on individual lessons to help you anticipate children's misconceptions and challenge those who are ready to think more deeply.

STEP 5: Teach and reflect

Deliver your lesson – and enjoy!

Afterwards, reflect on how it went … Did you cover all five stages?
Does the lesson need more time? How could you improve it?
What percentage of your class do you think mastered the concept?
How can you help those that didn't?

Unit 11
Decimals 2

Mastery Expert tip! "It is essential that children have an understanding of what a decimal looks like visually. I find it best to avoid using base 10 blocks for representing decimals, as this often leads to confusion. A hundredths grid offers a more successful representation."

Don't forget to watch the Unit 11 video!

WHY THIS UNIT IS IMPORTANT

In the previous unit, children were introduced to decimals. This unit builds on the last by exploring decimals in more depth. Children first find number bonds of tenths and hundredths to 1 and show how this links to their bonds to 10 and 100. They start to represent decimals on place value grids and use these grids to help them compare decimals. At this stage, children focus on comparing decimals with the same number of digits. Children begin to use diagrams to understand the decimal equivalents of simple fractions, such as a half and a quarter. Children then progress to rounding decimals to the nearest whole number by considering their position on a number line. Along with the previous unit, these lessons should provide children with a solid introduction to decimals and their link to place value and fractions. This unit is fundamental to further work in Years 5 and 6 on decimals.

WHERE THIS UNIT FITS

→ Unit 10: Decimals (1)
→ **Unit 11: Decimals (2)**
→ Unit 12: Money

This unit builds on children's work in Year 4 on decimals and links closely to all their work on place value and fractions so far.

Before they start this unit, it is expected that children:
· know the decimal equivalent of $\frac{1}{10}$ and $\frac{1}{100}$
· can draw, model and write any number of tenths and hundredths using a hundredths grid, ten frame or bead string
· understand that a tenth arises from dividing 1 by 10 and a hundredth arises from dividing 1 by 100
· understand the use of the decimal point and where it should be placed.

ASSESSING MASTERY

By the end of the unit, children will be able to find the number bond to 1 of a decimal with up to two decimal places. They should be able to round numbers to the nearest whole number and order decimals with the same number of decimal places by comparing digits. Finally, children will know and understand decimal equivalents of simple fractions such as a half and a quarter.

COMMON MISCONCEPTIONS	STRENGTHENING UNDERSTANDING	GOING DEEPER
When finding a number bond to 1, children may add on too much. For example, children may write 0·47 in 0·63 + _ = 1.	Remind children of their bonds to 100 and draw the link to number bonds to 1. In addition, children should be able to use a hundredths grid or bead string to help them visually identify these number bonds.	Using 10 blank place value counters and a place value grid from 10s to hundredths, how many different numbers can children make? What is the greatest number? What is the smallest number?
When comparing decimals, children may compare digits that do not have the same place value. For example, when comparing 23·6 and 9·7 they may compare the 2 (tens) and 9 (ones) as opposed to 2 tens and 0 tens.	Use a number line to help children locate decimals.	Encourage children to explore missing digits in numbers that are in order, such as: 2·_5 < 2·4_ How many different solutions can children find? Now try: 2·_5 < 2·4_ < _·45

WAYS OF WORKING

Use these pages to introduce the unit focus to children as part of a whole-class discussion. You can use the characters to explore different ways of thinking and working, too.

STRUCTURES AND REPRESENTATIONS

Hundredths grid: This is an important representation when children are learning to identify hundredths. Children can use a hundredths grid to work out the missing number.

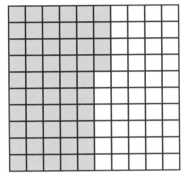

Number line: It is important for children to learn to position a number with one decimal place on a number line. They will learn that, to round a number to the nearest whole number, they need to look at the tenths digit.

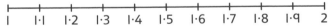

KEY LANGUAGE

There is some key language that children will need to know as part of the learning in this unit.

→ tens (10s), ones (1s), tenths, hundredths, fraction
→ decimal point, decimal place, 0·1, 0·01
→ equivalent, number bond, equivalent fraction
→ whole number, digit
→ rounding, round up, round down, multiply (×), divide (÷)
→ greater than (>), less than (<), equal to (=), smallest, lightest, greatest, heaviest, capacity
→ order, compare, statement, ascending, convert
→ part-whole, place value, bar model

Unit 11
Decimals ❷

In this unit we will …
⚡ Work out what we need to make a whole
⚡ Write a decimal and represent it on a place value grid
⚡ Compare and order decimals
⚡ Round decimals to the nearest whole number
⚡ Learn the decimal equivalents of fractions such as $\frac{1}{2}$, $\frac{1}{4}$ and $\frac{3}{4}$
⚡ Convert different units of measurement

In the last unit, we learnt how to show a decimal.
What decimal is shown here?

6

PUPIL TEXTBOOK 4C PAGE 6

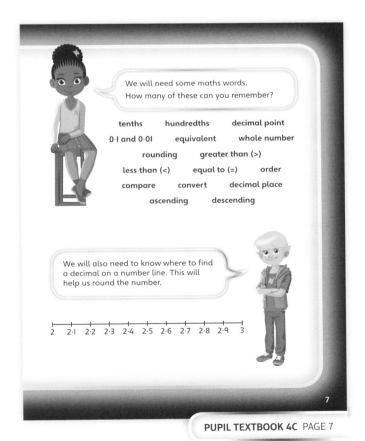

We will need some maths words.
How many of these can you remember?

tenths   hundredths   decimal point
0·1 and 0·01   equivalent   whole number
rounding   greater than (>)
less than (<)   equal to (=)   order
compare   convert   decimal place
ascending   descending

We will also need to know where to find a decimal on a number line. This will help us round the number.

7

PUPIL TEXTBOOK 4C PAGE 7

Making a whole

Learning focus

In this lesson, children will understand that given a number of tenths or hundredths they can make the number bond up to 1.

Small steps

→ Previous step: Dividing by 10 and 100
→ **This step: Making a whole**
→ Next step: Writing decimals

NATIONAL CURRICULUM LINKS

Year 4 Number – Fractions (Including Decimals)
- Recognise and write decimal equivalents of any number of tenths or hundredths.
- Add and subtract fractions with the same denominator.

ASSESSING MASTERY

Children can find the number bond to 1 using a ten frame and hundredths grid and can write them onto a part-whole model.

COMMON MISCONCEPTIONS

Children may not be secure with their number bonds to 10 and 100 and may miscalculate the number that makes the number bond to 1. For example, they may think that, if they had 0·36, they would need 0·74 to make the number bond to 1. Ask:

- *What number do you need to add to make [1/10/100]? How do you know?*

STRENGTHENING UNDERSTANDING

Provide children with a ten frame and hundredths grid. When dealing with tenths and hundredths, encourage children to say them aloud to highlight the value of the digits and to count in tenths or hundredths when making a whole. For example, 0·8 is '8 tenths' or 0·45 is '45 hundredths'.

GOING DEEPER

Ask children to make a whole using three numbers instead of two. Give them one number and ask how many different ways they can make a whole. For example, 0·2 + __ + __ = 1. This could be represented on a part-whole model. Also encourage children to link making a whole to subtraction, such as 1 – 0·72 = __.

KEY LANGUAGE

In lesson: tenths, hundredths, whole, part-whole, statement, number bond

STRUCTURES AND REPRESENTATIONS

hundredths grid, part-whole model, bar model and ten frame

RESOURCES

Mandatory: hundredths grid, blank ten frames, number cards, 1s and tenths (0·1) place value counters

Optional: large laminated part-whole model

 In the eTextbook of this lesson, you will find interactive links to a selection of teaching tools.

Before you teach

- Do children know their number bonds to 10 and 100?
- Can children represent tenths on a ten frame and hundredths on a hundredths grid?
- Can children represent tenths and hundredths on a part-whole model?

Discover

WAYS OF WORKING Pair work

ASK

- Question **1** a): *What is the value of the 7 in 0·7 kg?*
- Question **1** a): *How could you represent 0·7?*
- Question **1** b): *What number is shown here?*
- Question **1** b): *How could you represent 0·46?*

IN FOCUS Encourage children to use resources and model each question in a concrete way. Children may use a hundredths grid or a ten frame to work out the missing number. Some children may need to count up in tenths or hundredths. For example, to get the number bond to 1 for 0·46, some children may individually count 54 squares on a hundredths grid. Encourage children to use a more efficient method, such as identifying that there are 5 columns of ten and then 4 ones.

PRACTICAL TIPS Ensure children have tenths counters and ten frames. Since Jamie has 0·7 kilograms of strawberries, ask them to show the value of the 7 using their counters on the ten frame.

ANSWERS

Question **1** a): Jamie needs to pick another 0·3 kilograms of strawberries.

Question **1** b): Alex needs to pick another 0·54 kilograms of strawberries.

Share

WAYS OF WORKING Whole class teacher led

ASK

- Question a): *What number are you starting with? How can you use a hundredths grid to show this? What do you need to look at to help you make a whole?*
- Question b): *Can you see how this works on a part-whole model?*

IN FOCUS Show children the hundredths grid of 0·7 (7 tenths) and count aloud as a class so that they know it is 0·7. Can children explain why the number bond to 1 is 0·3? Similarly, show children the hundredths grid of 0·46. Explain a more efficient way of identifying this as 0·46 without counting each individual hundredth. For example, show children that there are 4 columns of ten and 6 ones. Can children explain why the number bond to 1 is 0·54 without having to count each hundredth? Encourage children to see the link to the number bonds to 100.

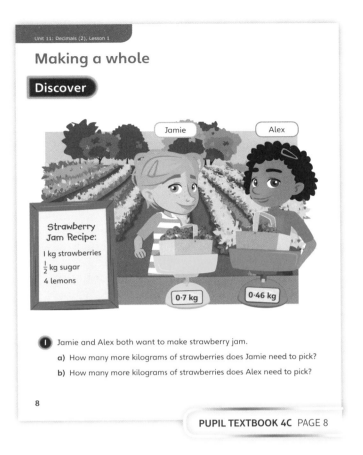

Making a whole

Discover

Strawberry Jam Recipe:
1 kg strawberries
½ kg sugar
4 lemons

1 Jamie and Alex both want to make strawberry jam.

a) How many more kilograms of strawberries does Jamie need to pick?

b) How many more kilograms of strawberries does Alex need to pick?

8

PUPIL TEXTBOOK 4C PAGE 8

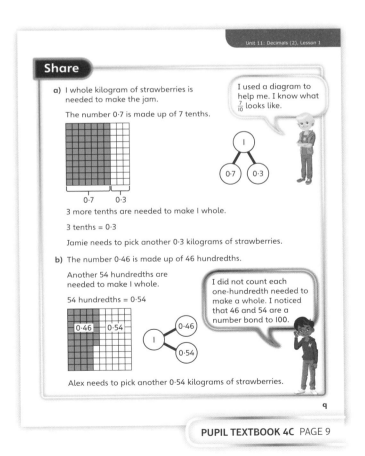

PUPIL TEXTBOOK 4C PAGE 9

Think together

WAYS OF WORKING Whole class teacher led (I do, We do, You do)

ASK

- Question ❷: *What numbers are shown here? Can you represent these on a hundredths grid? What number is needed to make a whole?*
- Question ❸ a): *What amounts of water does Jamilla have? What do they add up to? What number is needed to make the whole 1 litre?*

IN FOCUS Questions ❶ and ❷ look at making a whole from tenths and hundredths, which are represented using ten frames, hundredths grid and part-whole models. Encourage children to make their own representations for each question. Ensure children are aware that they are dealing with tenths and hundredths and not whole numbers when calculating the number bond to 1. Count up in tenths and say the numbers aloud to reinforce this.

STRENGTHEN To support understanding, represent question ❸ using an actual jug and cups, counters or a hundredths grid. Children could also use three different colours to represent the three different cups and help them calculate the number bond to 1.

DEEPEN Ask children to give more than one answer for question ❸ c). Ask children if it is possible to give an answer that has tenths and hundredths in it. Can they give examples?

ASSESSMENT CHECKPOINT Can children successfully represent their answers on a hundredths grid and on part-whole models?

ANSWERS

Question ❶ a): $0{\cdot}6 + 0{\cdot}4 = 1$

Question ❶ b): $0{\cdot}8 + 0{\cdot}2 = 1$

Question ❶ c): $0{\cdot}83 + 0{\cdot}17 = 1$

Question ❷ a): Missing whole is 1

Question ❷ b): Missing part is 0·5

Question ❷ c): Missing part is 0·73

Question ❷ d): Missing part is 0·01

Question ❸ a): Jamilla needs another 0·2 litres.

Question ❸ b): Luis needs another 0·37 litres.

Question ❸ c): Numerous answers are possible, as long as the three numbers add to 1.

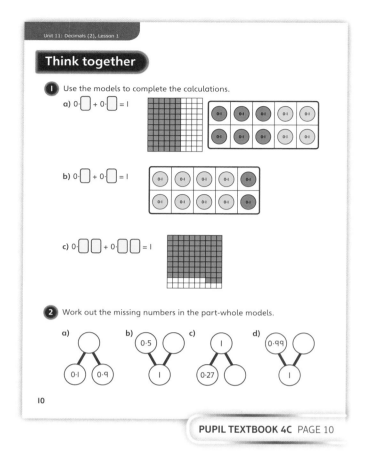

PUPIL TEXTBOOK 4C PAGE 10

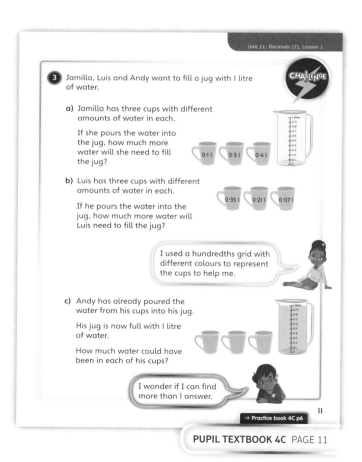

PUPIL TEXTBOOK 4C PAGE 11

Practice

WAYS OF WORKING Independent thinking

IN FOCUS Question **3** consolidates the representations on part-whole models. Children should use 1s and tenths counters to physically replicate the same part-whole models as in the questions. They should then manipulate the counters to make the number bonds to 1.

STRENGTHEN In question **2**, children can use a hundredths grid to replace the bar models. This may help them to more readily see how to make a whole. When diagrams are not given, encourage children to use concrete resources to make their own representations.

DEEPEN Explore question **5** further by asking children if there are any different digits they could use that would still make the number sentences correct. Can they explain why? Question **6** can also be explored further. Ask children to identify different ways to complete the cross diagrams. Challenge children to create their own version of this question and share it with a partner.

ASSESSMENT CHECKPOINT Children should now be confident in using a ten frame, hundredths grid or a part-whole model to make a whole if they are given a number of tenths or hundredths. Ask children to model one of the parts of question **3**, explaining why they would place certain counters in certain sections of the part-whole model. Do they use sound reasoning and demonstrate a deep understanding when explaining their thinking?

ANSWERS Answers for the **Practice** part of the lesson appear in the separate **Practice and Reflect answer guide**.

Reflect

WAYS OF WORKING Independent thinking

IN FOCUS This activity checks children's understanding of how to make a whole from different numbers of tenths. Children should see links with the number bonds to 10 and 100.

ASSESSMENT CHECKPOINT Children can make a selection of number bonds to 1 and confidently explain their decisions using the correct vocabulary and sound reasoning.

ANSWERS Answers for the **Reflect** part of the lesson appear in the separate **Practice and Reflect answer guide**.

After the lesson ⏸

- Are children confident with tenths and hundredths?
- Can children make the number bonds to 1 using a ten frame, hundredths grid or part-whole model?

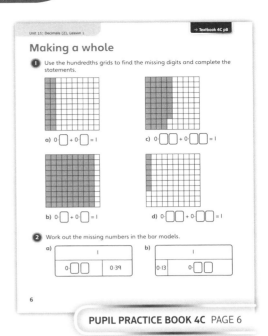

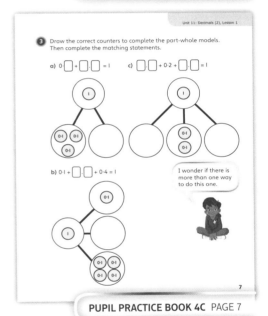

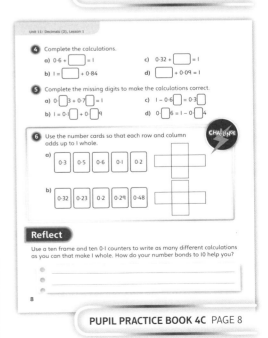

Writing decimals

Learning focus

In this lesson, children will learn that a number with up to two decimal places can be made up of some 10s, 1s, tenths and hundredths.

Small steps

→ Previous step: Making a whole
→ **This step: Writing decimals**
→ Next step: Comparing decimals

NATIONAL CURRICULUM LINKS

Year 4 Number – Fractions (Including Decimals)

Find the effect of dividing a one- or two-digit number by 10 and 100, identifying the value of the digits in the answer as ones, tenths and hundredths.

ASSESSING MASTERY

Children can represent numbers with up to two decimal places using counters and a place value grid and, given a pictorial representation, can write a number with up to two decimal places. Children recognise that a number up to two decimal places can be made up of some 10s, 1s, tenths and hundredths.

COMMON MISCONCEPTIONS

Children may confuse the place value and size of a number. They may, for example, see 2 ones and 7 hundredths as 2·7, missing that the value of the tenth is 0. Ask:
• *How would you write 2 tenths and 7 hundredths? Are there any 0s in this number? What does the 0 represent?*

STRENGTHENING UNDERSTANDING

Children who need support with representing numbers up to two decimal places should recap representing 1-digit numbers. Ask children to show a 1-digit number on a place value grid. Explain that we can now add some tenths and this will give us a number with one decimal place. Next, explain that we can also add some hundredths and this will create a number with two decimal places. Encourage children to write out the numbers, for example 7·23 as 7 ones, 2 tenths and 3 hundredths. They can then represent each part on a place value grid.

GOING DEEPER

Ask children to represent the number 5·63 in different ways. For example, do they represent this as 5 ones, 6 tenths and 3 hundredths or 5 ones and 63 hundredths? Ask children to explain why these are equal.

KEY LANGUAGE

In lesson: hundreds, tens (10s), ones (1s), tenths (0·1), hundredths (0·01), decimal place

STRUCTURES AND REPRESENTATIONS

place value grid, bar model, hundredths grid, part-whole model

RESOURCES

Mandatory: place value counters

 In the eTextbook of this lesson, you will find interactive links to a selection of teaching tools.

Before you teach

• Can children represent 1-, 2- and 3-digit numbers using a place value grid?
• Do children know the place value of each digit in whole numbers?

Discover

Writing decimals

Discover

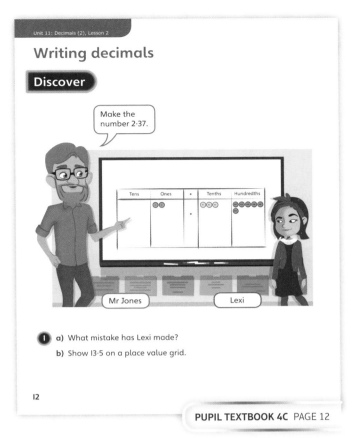

WAYS OF WORKING Pair work

ASK

- Question ① a): *What is the value of the 2? What is the value of the 3? What is the value of the 7?*
- Question ① a): *How can you tell how many 1s, tenths and hundredths Lexi has used?*
- Question ① a): *What number has Lexi made?*
- Question ① b): *How can you partition your number? How can you tell how many 10s and how many 1s there are? What about how many tenths and how many hundredths?*

IN FOCUS Question ① b) provides children with a number and asks them to make a representation of it. Encourage children to partition the number and discuss the place value headings that will be needed in their place value grid. Will they need a hundredths column?

PRACTICAL TIPS Encourage children to use counters and a place value grid or a hundredths grid to represent Lexi's number from question ①. Encourage children to partition the number into 1s, tenths and hundredths until they see that Lexi has made a mistake.

ANSWERS

Question ① a): Lexi has 6 hundredths instead of 7 hundredths.

Question ① b): 13·5 can be represented on a place value grid with 1 ten, 3 ones and 5 tenths.

In the textbook image:

Make the number 2·37.

Mr Jones   Lexi

① a) What mistake has Lexi made?
b) Show 13·5 on a place value grid.

12

PUPIL TEXTBOOK 4C PAGE 12

Share

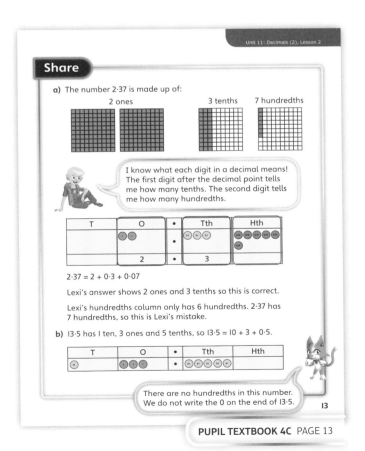

WAYS OF WORKING Whole class teacher led

ASK

- Question a): *What is the number 2·37 made up of? Which parts of the number has Lexi got correct? What is Lexi's mistake?*
- Question b): *What is the number 13·5 made up of? Why do you not have any hundredths?*

IN FOCUS Show children the diagram of 2·37 represented by the hundredths grids. Can children explain why the value of the 3 is 3 tenths and why the value of the 7 is 7 hundredths? Explain that the first number after the decimal point tells us how many tenths there are and the second number after the decimal point tells us how many hundredths there are.

In the textbook image:

Share

a) The number 2·37 is made up of:

2 ones   3 tenths   7 hundredths

I know what each digit in a decimal means! The first digit after the decimal point tells me how many tenths. The second digit tells me how many hundredths.

T	O	•	Tth	Hth
		•		
	2	•	3	

2·37 = 2 + 0·3 + 0·07

Lexi's answer shows 2 ones and 3 tenths so this is correct.

Lexi's hundredths column only has 6 hundredths. 2·37 has 7 hundredths, so this is Lexi's mistake.

b) 13·5 has 1 ten, 3 ones and 5 tenths, so 13·5 = 10 + 3 + 0·5.

T	O	•	Tth	Hth
		•		

There are no hundredths in this number. We do not write the 0 on the end of 13·5.

13

PUPIL TEXTBOOK 4C PAGE 13

Think together

WAYS OF WORKING Whole class teacher led (I do, We do, You do)

ASK

- Question ❶ a): *What is the value of the 5, the 4 and the 9?*
- Question ❶ b): *What is the value of the 0, the 2 and the 6?*
- Question ❷: *What is the value of each column in the place value grids? Can you write the value under each column of your own place value grids?*
- Question ❸: *What is $\frac{1}{10}$ the same as? What is $\frac{1}{100}$ the same as? What number has Ebo shown? How many different numbers can you make using five counters?*

IN FOCUS In question ❸, children write decimals from numbers they have created themselves, using a place value grid and five counters. It highlights the importance of 0 and when we do and do not need to include it. Can children explain why 12·2 and 12·20 have the same value?

STRENGTHEN To support understanding, represent all the numbers on a place value grid and ask children to write the value at the bottom of each place value heading. Separate the 10s, the 1s, the tenths and the hundredths. Clearly associate each digit with the particular place value and say this aloud. For example, 0·7 is 7 tenths. This will help children understand the numbers.

DEEPEN Give children numbers using place value counters (but not a grid). Provide the numbers out of order, not arranged as 10s, 1s, tenths and hundredths, and ask them to write down what number is shown. This will help them understand that the order the parts are presented in does not matter, but the value does.

ASSESSMENT CHECKPOINT Can children represent numbers up to two decimal places on a place value grid? Do children understand that a number up to two decimal places is made up of some 10s, 1s, tenths and hundredths?

ANSWERS

Question ❶ a): 5·49 is equal to 5 ones, 4 tenths and 9 hundredths. 5·49 = 5 + 0·4 + 0·09

Question ❶ b): 0·26 is equal to 0 ones, 2 tenths and 6 hundredths. 0·26 = 0·2 + 0·06

Question ❷ a): 0·03

Question ❷ b): 0·3

Question ❷ c): 0·33

Question ❸: Various answers, such as 20·21, 21·02, 21·2, 22·01, 22·1, 1·22, 10·22, 12·02, 12·2, etc.

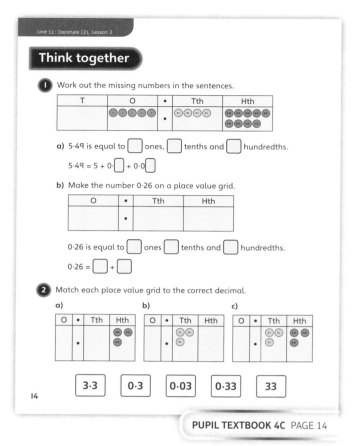

PUPIL TEXTBOOK 4C PAGE 14

PUPIL TEXTBOOK 4C PAGE 15

Practice

WAYS OF WORKING Independent thinking

IN FOCUS Questions **1** to **4** aim to consolidate children's understanding of representations of numbers up to two decimal places. Children can make their own representations and should understand that a number is made up of 10s, 1s, tenths and hundredths and that these can be shown and written in different ways.

STRENGTHEN Children can use place value grids and counters to represent the numbers. When numbers are not given in the order of 10s, 1s, tenths and hundredths, encourage children to reorder them.

DEEPEN Question **6** can be explored further by asking children how many different ways they can write the same number. Ask children if there are other ways they can represent a number such as 13·45. For example, they could represent this as 1 ten, 3 ones and 45 hundredths or as 1 ten, 3 ones, 4 tenths and 5 hundredths. Can they explain why these are equal?

ASSESSMENT CHECKPOINT Children should be confident in representing numbers up to two decimal places using a place value grid. They should also be able to write the number when presented with a representation of it.

ANSWERS Answers for the **Practice** part of the lesson appear in the separate **Practice and Reflect answer guide**.

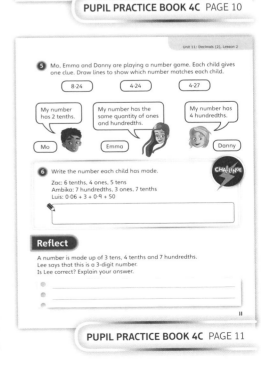

PUPIL PRACTICE BOOK 4C PAGE 9

PUPIL PRACTICE BOOK 4C PAGE 10

Reflect

WAYS OF WORKING Independent thinking

IN FOCUS This question checks for understanding of place value. The number given has three parts, so children may assume it is a 3-digit number. Children need to realise this is not always the case. Children should be able to explain what a 3-digit number is.

ASSESSMENT CHECKPOINT Children explain that the number is 30·47. They need to realise that even though 1s are not mentioned, we do not ignore that part when writing the decimal.

ANSWERS Answers for the **Reflect** part of the lesson appear in the separate **Practice and Reflect answer guide**.

After the lesson

- Can children represent a number up to two decimal places on a place value grid?
- Can children work out what numbers are represented by given representations?

PUPIL PRACTICE BOOK 4C PAGE 11

Comparing decimals

Learning focus

In this lesson, children will compare decimal numbers by looking at the largest place value and then moving to the next largest place value.

Small steps

→ Previous step: Writing decimals
→ **This step: Comparing decimals**
→ Next step: Ordering decimals

NATIONAL CURRICULUM LINKS

Year 4 Number – Fractions (Including Decimals)

Compare numbers with the same number of decimal places up to two decimal places.

ASSESSING MASTERY

Children can compare decimal numbers using a place value grid and place value counters. They compare decimal numbers by looking at which number has the largest place value.

COMMON MISCONCEPTIONS

Children may not look at the largest place value first when comparing decimal numbers. Ask:
• *Which number has the higher value, 2·17 or 2·71? My number is 5·15. Can you think of a number that is larger than this?*

STRENGTHENING UNDERSTANDING

Recap comparing 2- or 3-digit numbers. Ask children to show a selection of these numbers on a place value grid. Explain that we need to look at the largest place value to help us compare the numbers. If the largest place value does not help us, then we must look at the next largest place value. Encourage children to write the numbers underneath the place value grid.

GOING DEEPER

Ask children to compare decimal numbers that are represented in different ways or that do not have the same number of decimal places. For example, ask: *Which is bigger, 5 ones and 2 tenths or 3 tenths and 5 ones? or Which is bigger, 4·5 or 4·25?*

KEY LANGUAGE

In lesson: tens (10s), ones (1s), tenths, hundredths, statement, compare, less than, greater than, decimal, place value

STRUCTURES AND REPRESENTATIONS

place value grid, hundredths grid

RESOURCES

Mandatory: place value counters, metre ruler

Optional: plastic coins

 In the eTextbook of this lesson, you will find interactive links to a selection of teaching tools.

Before you teach

• Can children represent decimal numbers in a place value grid?
• Can children compare 2- and 3-digit numbers?
• Are children confident using the inequality signs < and >?

Discover

ASK

- Question ❶ a): *How can you represent Bella and Zac's numbers on a place value grid? How can you tell how many 1s, how many tenths and how many hundredths each number has? How can you decide which number is larger?*
- Question ❶ b): *What numbers are you comparing in this question? Why does it not help to compare the 1s and tenths? Which place value do you need to look at?*

IN FOCUS For each question, encourage children to make the numbers with counters on a place value grid. Ask them to partition the numbers into 1s, tenths and hundredths. They should start to see that, to compare the numbers, they first need to look at the largest place value, then the next place value, and so on.

PRACTICAL TIPS Recreate a similar activity in the classroom. Measure two items of similar height and give children the measurements in the same format. For example: *Isabelle's chair is 0·43 metres tall. My chair is 0·49 metres tall.* Ask children to model the heights using a place value grid and counters.

ANSWERS

Question ❶ a): 0·67 m < 0·76 m, so Zac is correct.

Question ❶ b): Zac is correct as 0·79 is greater than 0·76.

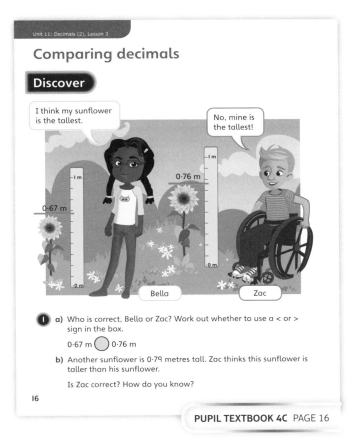

PUPIL TEXTBOOK 4C PAGE 16

Share

WAYS OF WORKING Whole class teacher led

ASK

- Question ❶ a): *How can you represent these numbers on place value grids? When comparing the numbers, why do you need to start by looking at the largest place value? How many 1s do the numbers have? Why does this not help you to compare the numbers? Why do you not need to look at the hundredths to compare the numbers?*
- Question ❶ a): *What do the < and > signs mean?*
- Question ❶ b): *What numbers are you comparing now? Why do you need to look at the hundredths to compare the numbers? Which number is bigger?*

IN FOCUS For question ❶ a), model the numbers on a place value grid. Say how many 1s each number has. Can children explain why this does not help them find the answer? Say how many tenths each number has. Can children explain which number is bigger/smaller now? Can children explain why it is not necessary to look at how many hundredths each number has? Discuss the inequality sign and ensure children are able to use it correctly.

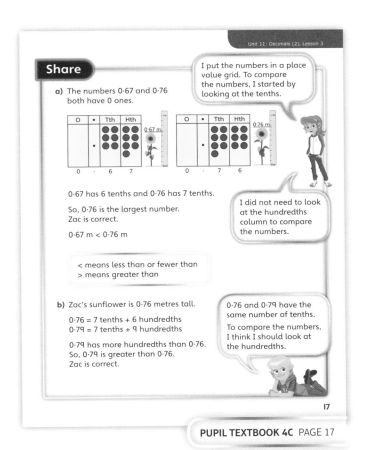

PUPIL TEXTBOOK 4C PAGE 17

Think together

Whole class teacher led (I do, We do, You do)

ASK

- Question **1**: *Which numbers do you need to represent in the place value grid? How many 1s and tenths are there in 2·4 and 2·7? Who has jumped the farthest?*
- Question **2**: *Can you represent £1·43 and £1·41 on a place value grid? Which place value is going to help you compare the numbers this time?*

IN FOCUS Question **3** looks at comparing decimal numbers that are represented in different ways. It also deals with comparing numbers that do not have the same number of decimal places. Encourage children to make the numbers in a place value grid and write each number as a decimal. Children need to understand that to compare the numbers they need to look at the largest place value first.

STRENGTHEN To support understanding, represent the numbers on a place value grid. Separate the 10s from the 1s from the tenths from the hundredths. Clearly associate each digit with the particular place value. Instead of just displaying the counters in the place value grids, make sure you write the numbers under each place value column; this will help children understand the size of the numbers and help them to compare the numbers.

DEEPEN Provide numbers represented by place value counters that are not given in the order of 10s, 1s, tenths and hundredths. This will help deepen their understanding that the order does not matter but that it is important to always compare the largest place value first.

Ask children to compare numbers that have a different number of decimal places, as in question **3**.

ASSESSMENT CHECKPOINT Children should be able to evaluate decimals by comparing the 1s, tenths and hundredths. Are they able to compare decimal numbers using a place value grid and place value counters? Children need to understand that to compare decimal numbers they need to start by looking at the largest place value.

ANSWERS

Question **1**: 2·4 = 2 ones and 4 tenths
2·7 = 2 ones and 7 tenths
7 is greater than 4
2·7 > 2·4
Jen jumped the farthest.

Question **2** a): £1·43 is greater than £1·41, so Max has the most money.

Question **2** b): £1·46 is greater than £1·43, so Richard now has the most money.

Question **3** a): 31·12 is greater than 30·42.
30·3 is greater than 3·24.

Question **3** b): 31·12 is the greatest number overall.

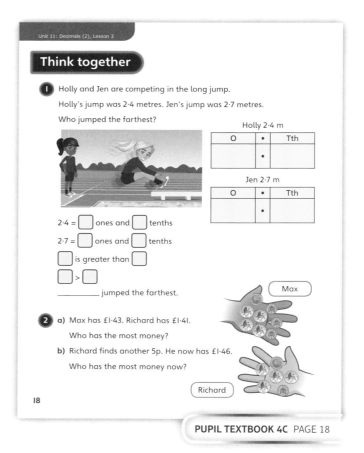

PUPIL TEXTBOOK 4C PAGE 18

PUPIL TEXTBOOK 4C PAGE 19

Practice

→ Textbook 4C p16

WAYS OF WORKING Independent thinking

IN FOCUS
- Question **2** highlights the misconception that more counters mean a bigger number. Encourage children to explain what the numbers are made up of and which place value helps them compare the numbers.
- Questions **4** to **6** are more abstract with no pictorial representations given. Ensure concrete resources are available to children as they may need to make their own representations of the number sentences.

STRENGTHEN In question **1**, children can use a place value grid with the headings clearly labelled. Encourage children to write question **1** d) in order of place value size. This may help them understand which number is larger.

Assist children in writing out the numbers as decimals when they are not presented in this way.

DEEPEN Comparing decimals can be further explored by giving children numbers that have a different number of decimal places.

Give children two numbers and ask them to give examples of numbers that are in between these values. For instance, which numbers are between 3·1 and 3 ones, 1 tenths and 9 hundredths? Are they able to explain how they know?

THINK DIFFERENTLY Question **5** asks children to consider more deeply the place value of digits within decimal numbers. Finding multiple potential answers will cement this learning.

ASSESSMENT CHECKPOINT Children should now be confident comparing decimals that have the same number of decimal places using a place value grid.

ANSWERS Answers for the **Practice** part of the lesson appear in the separate **Practice and Reflect answer guide**.

Reflect

WAYS OF WORKING Independent thinking

IN FOCUS This **Reflect** question checks children's understanding of comparing decimal numbers. It encourages them to explain the process in their own words. Children may need to use a place value grid to help them compare the numbers.

ASSESSMENT CHECKPOINT Children can explain how to compare decimal numbers. They should realise that they need to start by looking at the largest place value, then the next largest place value, and so on.

ANSWERS Answers for the **Reflect** part of the lesson appear in the separate **Practice and Reflect answer guide**.

After the lesson ⏸

- Can children compare decimal numbers that have the same number of decimal places?
- Can children work out what numbers are represented by the diagrams in the questions?
- Do children understand that to compare numbers they need to start by looking at the largest place value?

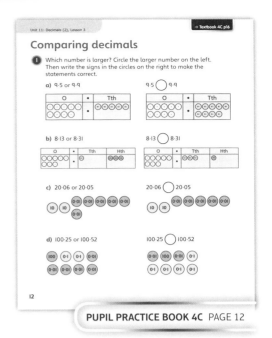

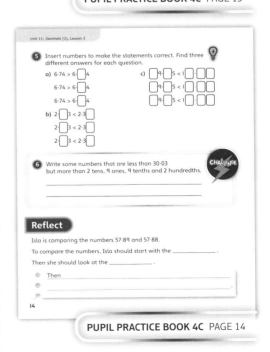

Ordering decimals

Learning focus

In this lesson, children will order numbers with up to two decimal places.

Small steps

→ Previous step: Comparing decimals
→ **This step: Ordering decimals**
→ Next step: Rounding decimals

NATIONAL CURRICULUM LINKS

Year 4 Number – Fractions (Including Decimals)

Compare numbers with the same number of decimal places up to two decimal places.

ASSESSING MASTERY

Children can order decimal numbers using a place value grid and place value counters. They start by looking at the largest place value.

COMMON MISCONCEPTIONS

When comparing decimals, children may not start by looking at the largest place value and then the next largest place value and so on. For example, to order 6·16, 5·09 and 6·12, children must focus on the 1s and then the hundredths. Ask:
• *Will focusing on the tenths help you in comparing these numbers?*
• *Which place value should you look at first when comparing numbers?*

STRENGTHENING UNDERSTANDING

Children who need support ordering decimal numbers should first recap ordering whole numbers. Ask children to show these numbers on a place value grid. Explain that they need to look at the largest place value to help them order the numbers. If this does not help, then they must look at the next largest place value and so on. Encourage children to write out the numbers underneath the place value grid.

GOING DEEPER

Give children some decimal numbers that are in order and ask them to place a number that would fit in the sequence. For example, ask children which numbers would replace the question mark in the sequence 5·67, 5·72, ?, 5·81. Is it possible to give an answer that has only one decimal place? Ask children to represent their answers on a place value grid. Alternatively, ask children to order numbers that do not have the same number of decimal places.

KEY LANGUAGE

In lesson: tens (10s), ones (1s), tenths, hundredths, smallest, largest, greatest, lightest, heaviest, compare, ascending

STRUCTURES AND REPRESENTATIONS

place value grid, number line

RESOURCES

Mandatory: place value counters, weighing scales

 In the eTextbook of this lesson, you will find interactive links to a selection of teaching tools.

Before you teach

• Can children represent decimal numbers in a place value grid?
• Can children order whole numbers?
• Could children identify the number if given a number of 10s, 1s, tenths and hundredths?

Discover

WAYS OF WORKING Pair work

ASK

• Question ① a): *How can you represent the rabbits' masses on a place value grid? How can you tell how many 1s, how many tenths and how many hundredths there are?*

• Question ① a): *How can you decide which of the three numbers is the smallest? Why does it not help to compare the tenths?*

• Question ① b): *Where would the second heaviest rabbit be in the order from lightest to heaviest? What numbers is this position in between? Which place values need to be the same when working out Flopsy's mass? Is there more than one answer?*

IN FOCUS For each question, encourage children to make the numbers on a place value grid and ask children to partition the numbers into 1s, tenths and hundredths. Children should start to see that to order the numbers they need to look at the largest place value, then the next place value and so on.

PRACTICAL TIPS Recreate the scene in the classroom using classroom objects and scales, or ask children to bring in stuffed animals from home.

ANSWERS

Question ① a): Lily is the lightest, Bob is second lightest and Molly is the heaviest.

Question ① b): Flopsy's mass could be 2·12 kg, 2·13 kg or 2·14 kg.

(Note: it is also possible to have an infinite number of answers that go into thousandths and ten thousandths, etc. For example, Flopsy's mass could be 2·121 kg. Here though, we are focusing on two decimal places.)

Share

WAYS OF WORKING Whole class teacher led

ASK

• Question ① a): *How have the numbers been represented on the place value grids? What does each blue counter represent? Why do you need to follow Flo's example and start by looking at the largest place value? How many 1s do the numbers have?*

• Question ① a): *How do you know that Lily is the lightest rabbit without looking at the tenths or hundredths? Why does it not help to compare the tenths? How many hundredths do the numbers have? How do you know which number is the biggest?*

• Question ① b): *Which two rabbits is Flopsy's mass between? Why do you need to look at the hundredths to decide on Flopsy's mass? What could Flopsy's mass be? Is there more than one answer?*

IN FOCUS For question ① a), show children the numbers on a place value grid. Can children explain why this means Lily is the lightest rabbit without having to compare the tenths or hundredths? For 2·15 and 2·11, say aloud how many tenths each number has. Can children explain why comparing the 1s and tenths for these numbers does not help? Say how many hundredths each number has. Can children explain which number is bigger/smaller now?

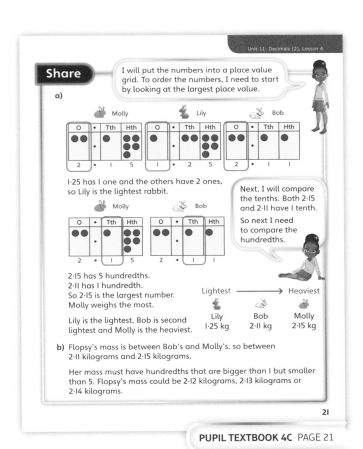

Think together

Whole class teacher led (I do, We do, You do)

ASK

• Question **1** : *How many 1s and tenths does each number have?*
• Question **2** : *How many 10s, 1s, tenths and hundredths does each number have? Which place value is going to help you order the numbers? Do you need to look at all the place values?*
• Question **4** a): *Can you make each number in a place value grid?*
• Question **4** b): *Is there more than one possible way to order the numbers? Discuss with a partner.*

IN FOCUS Question **4** gives children some decimal numbers that are in order and asks them to identify the mistake or fill in the missing digits. Encourage children to make the numbers in a place value grid and write each number as a decimal. For question **4** b), encourage children to give more than one answer.

STRENGTHEN To support understanding, represent the numbers on place value grids and separate the 10s from the 1s from the tenths from the hundredths. Clearly associate each digit with the particular place value. Instead of just displaying the counters in the place value grids, ensure you also put the numbers under each place value column. This will help children understand the size of the numbers and help them order the numbers.

DEEPEN Provide partitioned numbers where one of the place value columns has been left empty. For example, ask children to order 4 tens and 4 tenths; 4 tens, 4 ones and 4 hundredths; 4 ones, 4 tenths and 4 hundredths. Children may have the misconception that 4 tens and 4 tenths is the smallest as it only contains 2 parts, so this exercise will help them understand the importance of place value. Encourage children to make these numbers in a place value grid.

ASSESSMENT CHECKPOINT Can children order decimal numbers using a place value grid and place value counters? Children need to understand that to order decimal numbers they need to start by looking at the largest place value. Children should be able to order decimals by comparing the 1s, tenths and hundredths.

ANSWERS

Question **1** : Smallest 1·2, 1·9, 2·1 Largest

Question **2** : Largest 25·31, 19·07, 15·62 Smallest

Question **3** : Smallest 1·43, 1·53, 2·33 Largest

Question **4** a): 9·82 is in the wrong place

Question **4** b): Various possible answers, for example
　　　　　5·31,　5·33,　5·54,　6·09,　6·12
　　　　　5·32,　5·33,　5·54,　6·09,　6·13

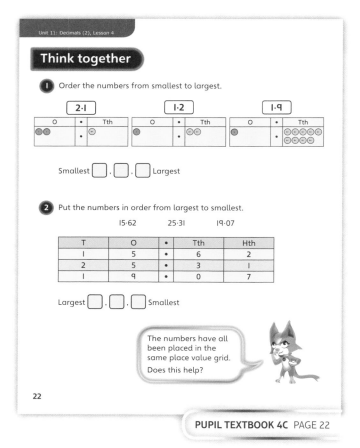

Unit 11: Decimals (2), Lesson 4

Think together

1 Order the numbers from smallest to largest.

| 2·1 | | 1·2 | | 1·9 |

Smallest ☐ . ☐ . ☐ Largest

2 Put the numbers in order from largest to smallest.

15·62　　　25·31　　　19·07

T	O	•	Tth	Hth
1	5	•	6	2
2	5	•	3	1
1	9	•	0	7

Largest ☐ . ☐ . ☐ Smallest

The numbers have all been placed in the same place value grid. Does this help?

22

PUPIL TEXTBOOK 4C PAGE 22

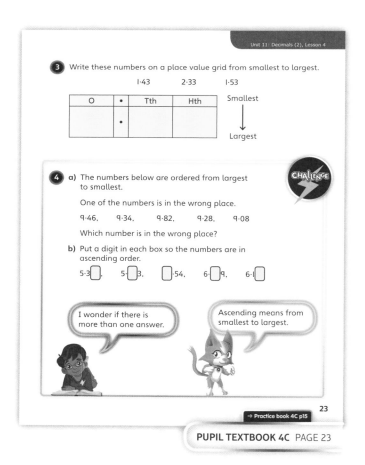

Unit 11: Decimals (2), Lesson 4

3 Write these numbers on a place value grid from smallest to largest.

1·43　　　2·33　　　1·53

O	•	Tth	Hth
	•		

Smallest
↓
Largest

4 a) The numbers below are ordered from largest to smallest.

CHALLENGE

One of the numbers is in the wrong place.

9·46,　　9·34,　　9·82,　　9·28,　　9·08

Which number is in the wrong place?

b) Put a digit in each box so the numbers are in ascending order.

5·3☐,　　5·☐3,　　☐·54,　　6·☐9,　　6·1☐

I wonder if there is more than one answer.

Ascending means from smallest to largest.

23

→ Practice book 4C p15

PUPIL TEXTBOOK 4C PAGE 23

Practice

WAYS OF WORKING Independent thinking

IN FOCUS Question **7** encourages children to problem solve and order decimal numbers. Encourage children to make the numbers on a place value grid and manipulate the counters until the numbers are in ascending order.

STRENGTHEN Encourage children to make each number on a place value grid. To start with, focus on numbers that only involve comparing the tenths, then progress to numbers that involve looking at other place value columns.

DEEPEN Ask children if they can come up with more than one answer for some of the numbers in question **7**. They should discuss and compare their answers with a partner.

THINK DIFFERENTLY Question **6** aims to highlight the mistake that the largest number means the fastest time. Encourage children to think about this carefully. It may help them to relate the context to whole numbers in order to unpick this difficult misconception. For example, ask children if it is faster to complete a race in 30 seconds or 40 seconds. Does this mean the larger number is the faster time? Highlight that the context here shapes the answer.

ASSESSMENT CHECKPOINT By the end of the **Practice** section, children should be confident in using a place value grid to order decimals that have the same number of decimal places. Successful work in answering questions **3** and **4**, including modelling the answers in a place value grid with counters and then writing the numbers, should indicate a sound understanding of the concept.

ANSWERS Answers for the **Practice** part of the lesson appear in the separate **Practice and Reflect answer guide**.

Reflect

WAYS OF WORKING Pair work

IN FOCUS This assesses a child's understanding of ordering decimal numbers and whether they can coherently describe their reasoning to a partner using mathematical language such as place value, greater than and less than.

ASSESSMENT CHECKPOINT Children can explain how to order decimal numbers. They need to realise that they need to start by looking at the largest place value and then the next largest place value and so on.

ANSWERS Answers for the **Reflect** part of the lesson appear in the separate **Practice and Reflect answer guide**.

After the lesson ⏸

- Can children make numbers in a place value grid to help them order decimal numbers?
- Can children order decimal numbers that have the same number of decimal places?
- Do children understand that to order decimal numbers they need to start by looking at the largest place value?

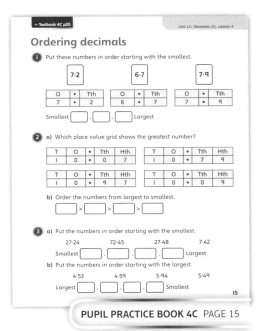

PUPIL PRACTICE BOOK 4C PAGE 15

PUPIL PRACTICE BOOK 4C PAGE 16

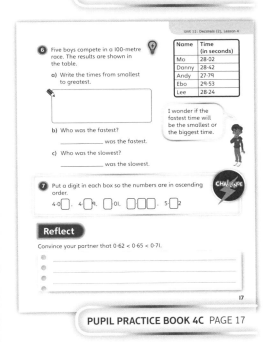

PUPIL PRACTICE BOOK 4C PAGE 17

Rounding decimals

Learning focus

In this lesson, children will round a decimal to the nearest whole number by looking at the tenths digit. They will place decimal numbers on a number line.

Small steps

→ Previous step: Ordering decimals
→ **This step: Rounding decimals**
→ Next step: Halves and quarters

NATIONAL CURRICULUM LINKS

Year 4 Number – Fractions (Including Decimals)

Round decimals with one decimal place to the nearest whole number.

ASSESSING MASTERY

Children can round a number with one decimal place to the nearest whole number using a number line. They understand that to round a number to the nearest whole number they need to look at the tenths digit.

COMMON MISCONCEPTIONS

A common misconception occurs when children do not understand that within a number with one decimal place, the tenths digit determines what the number will round to. For example, they may see 8·2 and think it rounds to 9 because 8 is greater than 5. Children need to understand that the number in the tenths column determines the nearest whole number. Ask:
• *What would you round 8·2 to as the nearest whole number? Why? Which is the important place value here?*

Some children may also incorrectly round a number to the nearest 10. For example, some children may round 17·6 to 20. Ask:
• *What do we mean by a whole number? What is the closest whole number to 17·6?*

STRENGTHENING UNDERSTANDING

Children who need support with rounding to the nearest whole number should recap rounding to the nearest 10. For example, ask children to round 27 to the nearest ten and then explain how they did this (by looking at the 1s digit). Explain that we can round to the nearest whole number by looking at the tenths digit. Encourage children to place the number on a number line so they can clearly see the nearest whole number.

GOING DEEPER

Give children a whole number and ask if they can say what the number might have been before it was rounded to the nearest whole. Challenge them to find two or more answers.

KEY LANGUAGE

In lesson: tens (10s), ones (1s), tenths, number line, round up, round down, decimal place, whole number, digit

STRUCTURES AND REPRESENTATIONS

number line, place value grid, number cards

RESOURCES

Optional: place value counters

 In the eTextbook of this lesson, you will find interactive links to a selection of teaching tools.

Before you teach

• Do children know that if the place value is 5 or more they round up to the next whole number, 10 or 100?
• Can children identify the tenth digit in a decimal number?
• Can children place decimals with one decimal place on a number line?

Discover

Pair work

ASK

- Question ❶ a): *How many grams of sugar are in one serving of cereal?*
- Question ❶ a): *Can you place 6·8 on a number line?*
- Question ❶ b): *Can you place 1 on a number line? Which numbers would round to 1?*
- Question ❶ b): *What does 'one decimal place' mean?*

IN FOCUS In question ❶ a), encourage children to find or write the number on a number line. Some children may need support deciding which whole numbers 6·8 lies between. Encourage children to look at the tenths when rounding to the nearest whole number. They should see that Mo is correct.

PRACTICAL TIPS Recreate this activity by looking at the labels on various empty cereal packets or food wrappers and rounding some of the values to the nearest whole number.

ANSWERS

Question ❶ a): Mo is correct. The amount of sugar is closer to 7 grams.

Question ❶ b): The smallest possible amount of salt is 0·5 grams.

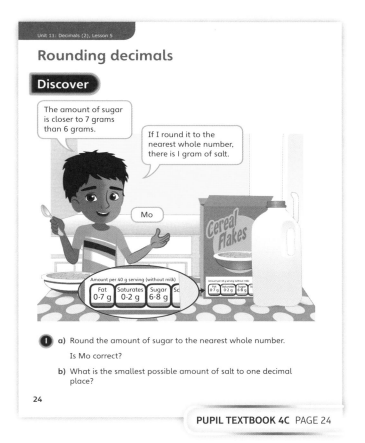

PUPIL TEXTBOOK 4C PAGE 24

Share

Whole class teacher led

ASK

- Question ❶ a): *Which whole number is 6·8 closer to: 6 or 7? Which part of the number helps you decide?*
- Question ❶ b): *Do you need to look at the numbers below or above 1? How do you know?*

IN FOCUS For question ❶ a), show children the number line from 6 to 7 and explain that we need to look at the tenths. If the number of tenths is 5 or more, then we round up to the next one. Remind children that a tenth is the first number after the decimal point.

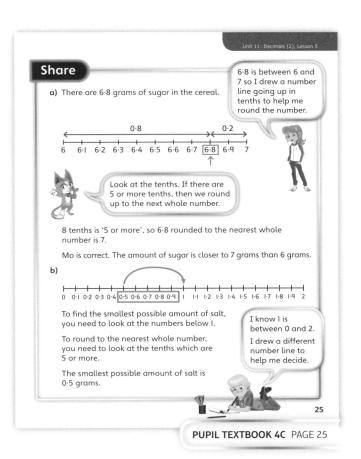

PUPIL TEXTBOOK 4C PAGE 25

Think together

WAYS OF WORKING Whole class teacher led (I do, We do, You do)

ASK

- Question **1** a): *What is the value of the tenths digit in the number 4·2? Is 4·2 closer to 4 or 5?*
- Question **1** b): *Which whole numbers does 12·5 lie between? What do you do when the tenths digit is 5 or more?*
- Question **2**: *Can you place each of the numbers on a number line? Which numbers round to 8?*
- Question **3**: *Which place value do you need to look at when rounding to the nearest whole number/10/100?*

IN FOCUS Question **3** challenges children to round to different values. Remind children that to round to the nearest 10 they need to look at the ones column and to round to the nearest 100 they need to look at the tens column. Encourage children to use a number line to help them.

STRENGTHEN To support understanding, represent each number on a number line and ask children to decide which whole number it is closer to. Encourage children to always identify the tenths digit and decide if it is 5 or more.

DEEPEN Give children a decimal number that rounds to the same number whether it is rounded to the nearest whole number, nearest 10 or nearest 100. For example, 199·7, rounded to the nearest whole number is 200. It is also 200 when rounded to the nearest 10 or the nearest 100. Ask children to explore other numbers that follow this pattern. Extend this to see if children can think of a number that rounds to the same number when rounded to the nearest whole and 10 but a different number when rounded to the nearest 100. For example, 19·6 rounds to 20 when rounded to the nearest whole number or nearest 10, but when rounded to the nearest 100 it is 0. Can they explain why this is? What are the smallest and largest numbers they can think of that this would work for?

ASSESSMENT CHECKPOINT Can children round numbers to the nearest whole number using a number line? Children need to understand that to round a number with one decimal place to the nearest whole number, they need to look at the tenths digit.

ANSWERS

Question **1** a): 4·2 is between 4 and 5.
4·2 rounded to the nearest whole number is 4.

Question **1** b): 12·5 is between 12 and 13.
12·5 rounded to the nearest whole number is 13.

Question **2**: Jamilla is incorrect. 8·5 rounds to 9.

Question **3** a): Max gets 71; Lexi gets 70; Kate gets 100.

Question **3** b): Various possible answers, between 444·5 and 544·4. Working backwards, 500 could have been 450 before Kate rounded to the nearest 100. 450 could have been 445 before Lexi rounded to the nearest 10. 445 could have been 444·5 before Max rounded it to the nearest whole number.

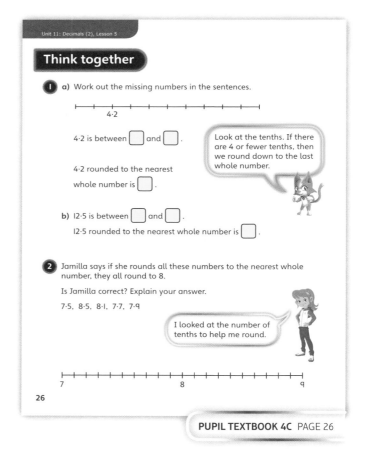

PUPIL TEXTBOOK 4C PAGE 26

PUPIL TEXTBOOK 4C PAGE 27

Practice

→ Textbook 4C p24

WAYS OF WORKING Independent thinking

IN FOCUS Question **6** reinforces the value of the tenths and that they need to be 5 or more to round up to the next whole number and 4 or less to round down to the previous one. Encourage children to explain why their answers round to 80.

STRENGTHEN Children can place the numbers on a number line before writing their answers. When number lines are not given, persuade them to draw one of their own and label it going up in tenths.

DEEPEN Explore question **5** further by asking children to come up with more than one answer. Ask children what the smallest and largest value would be to go in each blank box. Can they explain their answers?

ASSESSMENT CHECKPOINT Children should now be confident in rounding a decimal number to the nearest whole number. They should also be able to write the numbers on a number line. Successful responses to questions **1** a) to **1** c) will demonstrate their confidence in these skills.

ANSWERS Answers for the **Practice** part of the lesson appear in the separate **Practice and Reflect answer guide**.

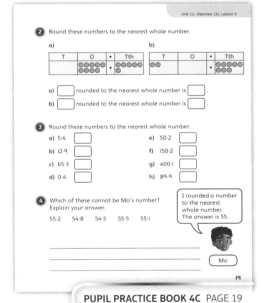

PUPIL PRACTICE BOOK 4C PAGE 18

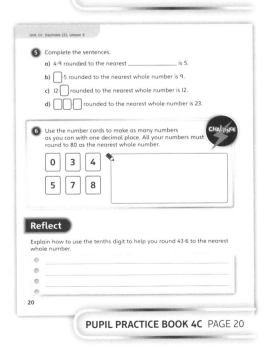

PUPIL PRACTICE BOOK 4C PAGE 19

Reflect

WAYS OF WORKING Independent thinking

IN FOCUS This activity checks children's understanding of rounding to the nearest whole number. Children may need to use a number line to help them formulate their response. They should be confident in their explanation that if the tenths digit is 5 or more, they round up to the next whole number.

ASSESSMENT CHECKPOINT Children should answer that the number 43·6 rounds to 44 as the nearest whole number. As part of their explanation, they should describe how the tenths are used to determine this, as 6 tenths is '5 or more'.

ANSWERS Answers for the **Reflect** part of the lesson appear in the separate **Practice and Reflect answer guide**.

After the lesson ⏸

- Can children represent a number with one decimal place on a number line?
- Can children round a number with one decimal place to the nearest whole number?

PUPIL PRACTICE BOOK 4C PAGE 20

Halves and quarters

Learning focus

In this lesson, children will represent fractions and decimals using a number line and a hundredths grid. They will learn the decimal equivalents for $\frac{1}{2}$, $\frac{1}{4}$ and $\frac{3}{4}$.

Small steps

→ Previous step: Rounding decimals
→ **This step: Halves and quarters**
→ Next step: Problem solving – decimals

NATIONAL CURRICULUM LINKS

Year 4 Number – Fractions (Including Decimals)

Recognise and write decimal equivalents to $\frac{1}{4}$, $\frac{1}{2}$, $\frac{3}{4}$.

ASSESSING MASTERY

Children can write the decimal equivalents for $\frac{1}{2}$, $\frac{1}{4}$ and $\frac{3}{4}$ and can accurately represent them on a number line and hundredths grid.

COMMON MISCONCEPTIONS

Some children will make the mistake of taking the numbers in the fraction and changing them into a decimal. They may, for example, think that $\frac{1}{4} = 1\cdot4$. Children need to understand what the fraction is telling them in order to find its decimal equivalent. Show children representations on a hundredths grid and number line in order to secure this understanding and avoid the misconception. Ask:

- *What does this fraction mean? How many hundredths does this fraction have? How do you know?*

STRENGTHENING UNDERSTANDING

Strengthen understanding of the decimal equivalents of $\frac{1}{4}$ and $\frac{3}{4}$ by showing them on a hundredths grid. First, have children practise colouring in $\frac{1}{4}$ and $\frac{3}{4}$, then talk about the decimal equivalents. It may be necessary to use a place value grid to show, for example, 25 hundredths as a decimal.

GOING DEEPER

Ask children to make decimal equivalents for fractions that are equivalent to $\frac{1}{2}$, $\frac{1}{4}$ and $\frac{3}{4}$. For example, ask children to find the decimal equivalent of $\frac{2}{4}$. Ask questions such as: *What fraction is equivalent to 5 tenths?*

KEY LANGUAGE

In lesson: fraction, decimal, tenths, hundredths, part, equivalent, equivalent fraction

Other language to be used by the teacher: whole, whole number

STRUCTURES AND REPRESENTATIONS

hundredths grid, number line, bar model

RESOURCES

Mandatory: hundredths grid, number line from 0 to 1, multilink cubes, blank place value counters

Optional: place value grid

 In the eTextbook of this lesson, you will find interactive links to a selection of teaching tools.

Before you teach

- Can children represent a fraction on a number line and on a hundredths grid?
- Can children represent hundredths on a hundredths grid?
- Do children know what equivalent means?

Discover

WAYS OF WORKING Pair work

ASK

• Question **1** a): *Ebo says that 0·5 is the same as $\frac{1}{2}$. What does $\frac{1}{2}$ mean?*
• Question **1** a): *How can you represent $\frac{1}{2}$?*
• Question **1** b): *What fraction full is Amelia's jug?*
• Question **1** b): *How can you represent $\frac{3}{4}$?*

IN FOCUS This part of the lesson focuses on the decimal equivalents of $\frac{1}{2}$ and $\frac{3}{4}$. Begin by recapping with children what a fraction means. $\frac{1}{2}$ is 1 out of 2 equal parts and $\frac{3}{4}$ is 3 out of 4 equal parts.

PRACTICAL TIPS For each question, encourage children to make their own representation of the fraction. Children may use a number line or a hundredths grid to represent the fraction.

ANSWERS

Question **1** a): $\frac{1}{2}$ is equivalent to 0·5, so Ebo is correct.

Question **1** b): $\frac{3}{4}$ as a decimal is 0·75.

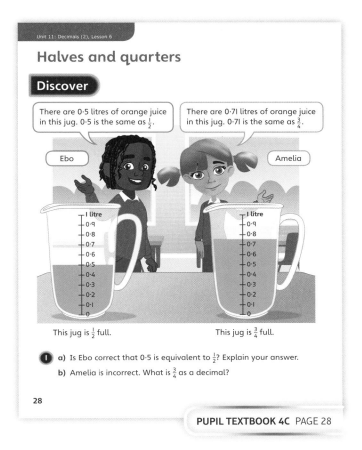

PUPIL TEXTBOOK 4C PAGE 28

Share

WAYS OF WORKING Whole class teacher led

ASK

• Question **1** a): *How full is Ebo's jug? How can you use a number line to show this?*
• Question **1** b): *What does $\frac{3}{4}$ mean? How can you use a hundredths grid to show this? What do you need to look at to help you change the fraction to a decimal?*

IN FOCUS Discuss where $\frac{3}{4}$ is on the number line. Explain that $\frac{3}{4}$ is exactly halfway between 0·7 and 0·8. Can children explain why this is 0·75? This is where some children may give an answer of 7·1. Avoid this misconception by showing children the hundredths grid. Can children see that $\frac{3}{4}$ is shaded? Discuss how many small squares are shaded. Encourage children to say this as 75 hundredths. Can children explain why $\frac{3}{4}$ is equivalent to 0·75? A place value grid may be needed to remind children what 75 hundredths looks like as a decimal.

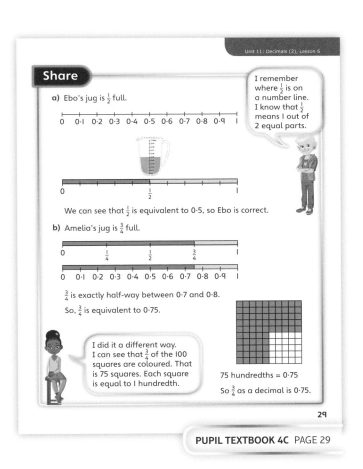

PUPIL TEXTBOOK 4C PAGE 29

Think together

WAYS OF WORKING Whole class teacher led (I do, We do, You do)

ASK

- Question ❶: *Can you see $\frac{1}{4}$ on the hundredths grid? How many hundredths are shaded in? What is 25 hundredths as a decimal?*
- Question ❷: *Can you shade $\frac{1}{2}$ of your hundredths grid? How many hundredths do you need to colour? How many tenths are coloured? What is 5 tenths as a decimal?*
- Question ❸ a): *Can you write each diagram as a fraction or a decimal?*
- Question ❸ b): *Can you use some of the resources and items on your table to demonstrate 0·25?*

IN FOCUS Questions ❶ and ❷ look at using hundredths grid to write the decimal equivalents for $\frac{1}{4}$ and $\frac{1}{2}$. Encourage children to make their own representations for each question. Ensure children are aware that they are dealing with hundredths and not whole numbers when looking at the hundredths grid. Say the numbers aloud to reinforce this.

STRENGTHEN To support understanding, ensure children have access to and use hundredths grids. For question ❸ b), encourage children to write 25 hundredths on a place value grid so they can see why it is 0·25. They should also look at ❸ a) to help them think of different ways of representing the decimal.

DEEPEN For question ❸ b), can children offer an equivalent fraction to 0·25 that is not $\frac{1}{4}$? Encourage children to represent $\frac{1}{2}$ and $\frac{3}{4}$ in as many different ways as they can.

ASSESSMENT CHECKPOINT Questions ❶ and ❷ will provide an indication of whether children can accurately represent their answers on a hundredths grid and then translate their work with the physical resources into a more abstract written format.

ANSWERS

Question ❶: $\frac{1}{4}$ is equivalent to 25 hundredths.

$$\frac{1}{4} = 0·25$$

Question ❷: $\frac{1}{2}$ is equivalent to 50 hundredths.

$\frac{1}{2}$ is equivalent to 5 tenths.

$$\frac{1}{2} = 0·5$$

Question ❸ a): 3·4 is the odd one out as all the other representations show $\frac{3}{4}$ (or 0·75).

Question ❸ b): Various possible representations.

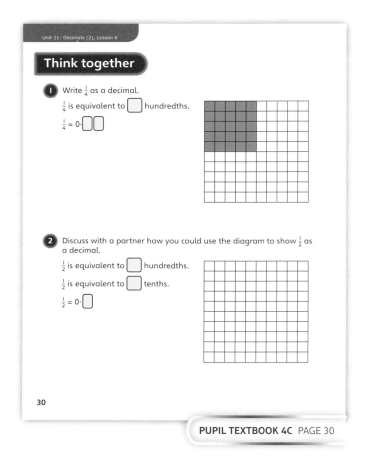

Think together

❶ Write $\frac{1}{4}$ as a decimal.

$\frac{1}{4}$ is equivalent to ☐ hundredths.

$\frac{1}{4} = 0·$ ☐☐

❷ Discuss with a partner how you could use the diagram to show $\frac{1}{2}$ as a decimal.

$\frac{1}{2}$ is equivalent to ☐ hundredths.

$\frac{1}{2}$ is equivalent to ☐ tenths.

$\frac{1}{2} = 0·$ ☐

30

PUPIL TEXTBOOK 4C PAGE 30

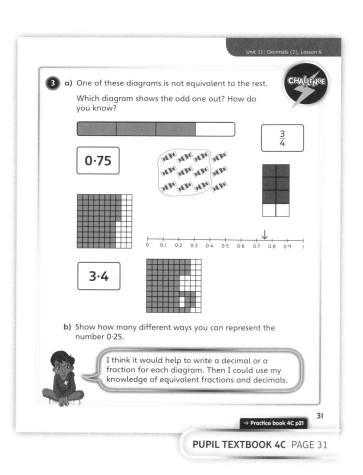

❸ a) One of these diagrams is not equivalent to the rest.

Which diagram shows the odd one out? How do you know?

CHALLENGE

0·75

$\frac{3}{4}$

3·4

b) Show how many different ways you can represent the number 0·25.

I think it would help to write a decimal or a fraction for each diagram. Then I could use my knowledge of equivalent fractions and decimals.

31

→ Practice book 4C p21

PUPIL TEXTBOOK 4C PAGE 31

Practice

WAYS OF WORKING Independent thinking

IN FOCUS Question **5** consolidates the equivalence of 0·5 and $\frac{1}{2}$. Children could work out $\frac{1}{2}$ of 12, but discuss with them whether this is necessary. Ask children what they know about $\frac{1}{2}$ and 0·5. What can they say about the number of apples each child has? This should reinforce the equivalency of $\frac{1}{2}$ and 0·5.

STRENGTHEN For all questions where diagrams are not provided, encourage children to make their own representations. For question **6**, encourage children to use counters to represent the problem. This may help them to see how many counters there are in total. They can also convert 0·25 to a fraction and draw a bar model to represent the problem.

DEEPEN Question **6** can be explored further by asking children to find the total number of counters if 6 white counters represented 0·75 of the total counters. How many grey counters are there?

THINK DIFFERENTLY Question **4** provides an alternative representation. Encourage children to convert the decimals to fractions and think about how they would colour the fractions in.

ASSESSMENT CHECKPOINT By the end of **Practice**, children should be confident in writing the decimal equivalents for $\frac{1}{2}$, $\frac{1}{4}$ and $\frac{3}{4}$ using a hundredths grid and a number line. Their responses to question **3** should indicate their level of understanding and highlight any areas where further practice may be necessary.

ANSWERS Answers for the **Practice** part of the lesson appear in the separate **Practice and Reflect answer guide**.

Reflect

WAYS OF WORKING Independent thinking

IN FOCUS In this part of the lesson, children must demonstrate the equivalency of 0·75 and $\frac{3}{4}$. Suggest that they colour the hundredths grid. Do children understand what they need to do and how many squares need to be coloured?

ASSESSMENT CHECKPOINT Children should use the hundredths grid provided to show that 0·75 is equivalent to $\frac{3}{4}$. Children should recognise that $\frac{3}{4}$ is 75 hundredths and colour the squares accordingly. They should then be able to write this as 0·75.

ANSWERS Answers for the **Reflect** part of the lesson appear in the separate **Practice and Reflect answer guide**.

After the lesson ⏸

- Can children show the decimal equivalents for $\frac{1}{2}$, $\frac{1}{4}$ and $\frac{3}{4}$ on a hundredths grid?
- Can children locate and write the decimal equivalents for $\frac{1}{2}$, $\frac{1}{4}$ and $\frac{3}{4}$ on a number line?

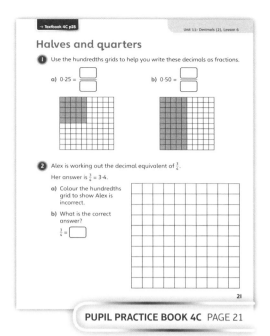

PUPIL PRACTICE BOOK 4C PAGE 21

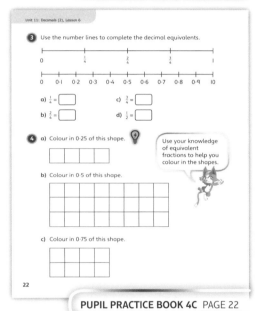

PUPIL PRACTICE BOOK 4C PAGE 22

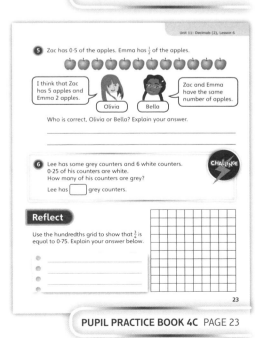

PUPIL PRACTICE BOOK 4C PAGE 23

Problem solving – decimals

Learning focus

In this lesson, children will convert between different units of measurement and solve simple problems.

Small steps

→ Previous step: Halves and quarters
→ **This step: Problem solving – decimals**
→ Next step: Pounds and pence

NATIONAL CURRICULUM LINKS

Year 4 Number – Fractions (Including Decimals)

Solve simple measure and money problems involving fractions and decimals to two decimal places.

ASSESSING MASTERY

Children can convert between different units of measurement, including grams to kilograms, litres to millilitres, and kilometres to metres to centimetres and vice versa.

COMMON MISCONCEPTIONS

Children may use the incorrect number when converting. Use real-life objects where possible, for example show children a metre ruler. Ask:
• *Can you find 100 centimetres? Is 100 centimetres the same as 1 metre?*

Children may not know whether to multiply or divide to convert between measurements. For instance, when converting 5 millilitres to litres, they may try 5 × 1,000. Show children a litre jug to help them understand. Ask:
• *What does 5 millilitres look like? Is 5,000 litres a realistic answer?*

STRENGTHENING UNDERSTANDING

Children who need support converting between measurements should focus on one conversion to begin with. Centimetres and metres is a good starting point as children can use a metre ruler to help them convert. Talk about whether the number will be bigger or smaller before they work anything out. For example, when converting 60 centimetres to metres, do they think the number is going to be bigger or smaller than 60? Ask them to explain how they know.

GOING DEEPER

Ask children to solve problems that involve converting between units. For example, ask children to find the perimeter of a rectangle with a length of 3 kilometres and a width of 440 metres. They could represent this in a diagram.

KEY LANGUAGE

In lesson: kilometres, metres, centimetres, litres, millilitres, kilograms, grams, mass, convert, capacity, cube, cylinder, units, divide (÷), heaviest, lightest

STRUCTURES AND REPRESENTATIONS

bar model

RESOURCES

Optional: metre ruler, weighing scales and weights, measuring jug

 In the eTextbook of this lesson, you will find interactive links to a selection of teaching tools.

Before you teach

• Do children know how to multiply and divide by 10, 100 and 1,000?
• Are children confident measuring in centimetres, millilitres and grams?

Discover

WAYS OF WORKING Pair work

ASK

- Question **1**: *What does it mean if the scale is balanced? Are both of these scales balanced?*
- Question **1** a): *What is the mass of 2 cubes? How could you work out the mass of 1 cube?*
- Question **1** b): *How many cubes are on the left-hand side of the scale? What is the mass of the cubes?*
- Question **1** b): *How many grams are in a kilogram? How can you convert 2 kilograms to grams?*

IN FOCUS For question **1** b), encourage children to use 10 cubes and a counter to represent the second scale. Remind them that each cube weighs 150 grams. Can they say the combined mass in grams of the 10 cubes on the left-hand side of the scale? Can they say the mass in grams of the object on the right-hand side of the scale? Allow children to say the units of each mass so they realise it is necessary to convert between units. Encourage children to use their concrete objects or draw a bar model to show what is happening in this problem and get them to write the masses in grams.

PRACTICAL TIPS Recreate the **Discover** scene using classroom equipment and balance scales, if available.

ANSWERS

Question **1** a): The mass of 1 cube is 150 grams.

Question **1** b): The mass of the cylinder is 500 grams.

Share

WAYS OF WORKING Whole class teacher led

ASK

- Question **1** a): *How do you know the mass of 2 cubes is 300 grams? How can you use a bar model to show this?*
- Question **1** b): *How can you use a bar model to show the mass of the 10 cubes and the cylinder? How can you work out the mass of the cylinder?*

IN FOCUS Show children the diagram of the bar model for question **1** b) with the cubes and cylinders. Can children see why the 10 cubes and cylinder are together in 1 bar and why 2 kg is written at the top of the bar? Explain that to work out the mass of the cylinder we need to be dealing with the same units of measurement. Can children explain why 2 kilograms is 2,000 grams? Can children see why they need to subtract 1,500 from 2,000 to find the mass of the cylinder?

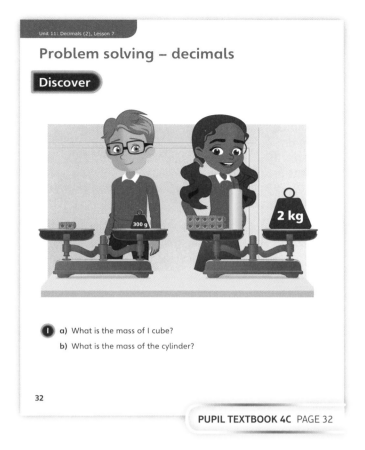

Problem solving – decimals

Discover

1 a) What is the mass of 1 cube?
   b) What is the mass of the cylinder?

32

PUPIL TEXTBOOK 4C PAGE 32

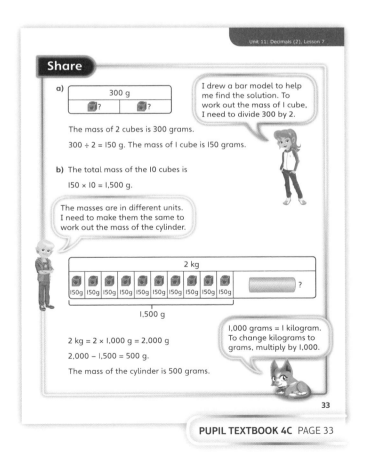

Share

a) [300 g]
   [?] [?]

The mass of 2 cubes is 300 grams.

$300 \div 2 = 150$ g. The mass of 1 cube is 150 grams.

I drew a bar model to help me find the solution. To work out the mass of 1 cube, I need to divide 300 by 2.

b) The total mass of the 10 cubes is

$150 \times 10 = 1,500$ g.

The masses are in different units. I need to make them the same to work out the mass of the cylinder.

[2 kg]
[150g 150g 150g 150g 150g 150g 150g 150g 150g 150g] [ ] ?
[1,500 g]

2 kg $= 2 \times 1,000$ g $= 2,000$ g

$2,000 - 1,500 = 500$ g.

The mass of the cylinder is 500 grams.

1,000 grams = 1 kilogram. To change kilograms to grams, multiply by 1,000.

33

PUPIL TEXTBOOK 4C PAGE 33

Think together

WAYS OF WORKING Whole class teacher led (I do, We do, You do)

ASK

• Question **1** a): *If 1 kilogram is 1,000 grams, what is 7 kilograms?*
• Question **1** d): *Can you partition 7,300 m into 1,000s and 100s? What is 7,000 metres in kilometres?*
• Question **1** f): *In millilitres, what is the combined total of 5,000 ml and 300 ml?*

IN FOCUS Encourage children to think carefully about whether they are going to multiply or divide for each question. Ensure children show the calculation they are doing and always write the units after every number.

STRENGTHEN To support understanding, question **2** could be represented using metre rulers. Give children some questions using smaller numbers, for example, converting 65 centimetres to metres or 2 metres to centimetres. Children can then use the rulers to help them.

DEEPEN Question **1** can be explored further by asking children to write their answers as decimal numbers. For example, instead of 3,600 g = 3 kg and 600 g, ask children to write it as 3·6 kg. Question **3** can also be explored further by asking children to give their answers in kilometres as well as centimetres and metres.

ASSESSMENT CHECKPOINT Can children convert between grams and kilograms, litres and millilitres, kilometres and metres, metres and centimetres?

ANSWERS

Question **1** a): 7 kilograms = 7,000 grams.

Question **1** b): 3,600 g = 3 kg and 600 g.

Question **1** c): 9 kilometres = 9,000 metres.

Question **1** d): 7,300 m = 7 km and 300 m.

Question **1** e): 6,000 millilitres = 6 litres.

Question **1** f): 5 l and 300 ml = 5,300 ml.

Question **2**: Luis needs to swim 20 lengths.
50 m × 20 = 1,000 m or 1 km.

Question **3** a): There are 100 centimetres in 1 metre.

Question **3** b) i): 700 cm = 7 m

Question **3** b) ii): 12 m = 1,200 cm

Question **3** b) iii): 450 cm = 4 m and 50 cm

Question **3** b) iv): 395 cm = 3 m and 95 cm

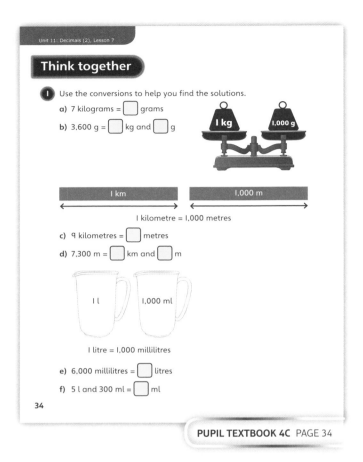

PUPIL TEXTBOOK 4C PAGE 34

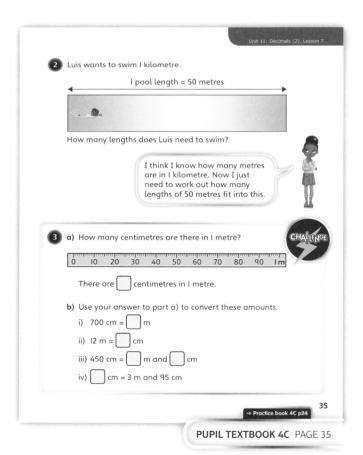

PUPIL TEXTBOOK 4C PAGE 35

Practice

WAYS OF WORKING Independent thinking

IN FOCUS Question **4** consolidates children's understanding of converting between centimetres and metres. Encourage children to convert all the numbers to the same unit, for example, all to metres or all to centimetres. Discuss with children which may be more useful.

STRENGTHEN For question **3**, show children real-life examples. For instance, show children what 8 millilitres of water looks like. Show children a bucket and 1 litre of water. Ask them if it would be logical to have a bucket that held 8 millilitres. This may help them to visualise the size of the measurements.

DEEPEN Question **7** can be explored further by asking children if they can represent the measurements in different ways. For example, 8 kg and 300 g + 1 kg and 700 g = 10 kg could be represented by 100 g + 2.9 kg + 7 kg = 10 kg. How many different ways can children come up with?

THINK DIFFERENTLY Question **5** encourages children to think a little differently in their problem solving, while also converting between units. Children may need reminding of the definition of perimeter. They need to realise that if they know one length, they will also know the other length. Ask them how they will work out the remaining distance of the two widths, and then one width.

ASSESSMENT CHECKPOINT By the end of **Practice**, children should be confident in converting between grams and kilograms, litres and millilitres, kilometres and metres, metres and centimetres. The ability to successfully answer all parts of questions **6** and **7** will indicate whether they need further practice or are mastering this skill.

ANSWERS Answers for the **Practice** part of the lesson appear in the separate **Practice and Reflect answer guide**.

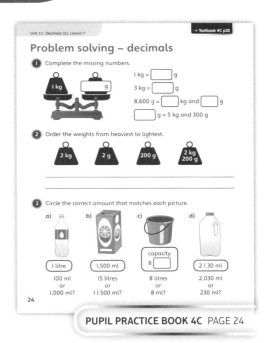

PUPIL PRACTICE BOOK 4C PAGE 24

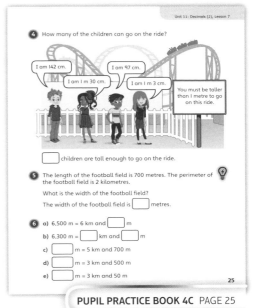

PUPIL PRACTICE BOOK 4C PAGE 25

Reflect

WAYS OF WORKING Independent thinking

IN FOCUS This activity checks children's understanding of converting between measurements. Children should be able to confidently explain without looking back at the conversions in the workbook.

ASSESSMENT CHECKPOINT Children can explain how to convert between grams and kilograms or litres and millilitres or kilometres and metres. They offer a confident answer using accurate conversions and key vocabulary.

ANSWERS Answers for the **Reflect** part of the lesson appear in the separate **Practice and Reflect answer guide**.

After the lesson

- Can children convert between grams and kilograms, litres and millilitres, kilometres and metres, metres and centimetres?

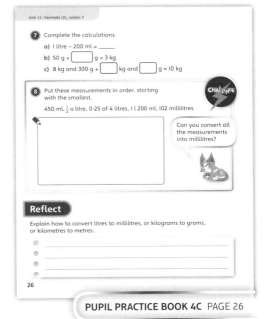

PUPIL PRACTICE BOOK 4C PAGE 26

End of unit check

Don't forget the *Power Maths* unit assessment grid on p26.

WAYS OF WORKING Group work adult led

IN FOCUS These questions are designed to draw out particular misconceptions or misunderstandings. Question **6** is a SATS-style question which focuses on converting grams into kilograms. Children need to link this to the work they have just completed on decimals and their knowledge of how many grams are in a kilogram.

ANSWERS AND COMMENTARY By the end of the unit, children will be able to find the number bond to 1 of a decimal with two decimal places. They will be able to round numbers to the nearest whole number and order decimals with the same number of decimal places by comparing digits. Finally, children will know and understand decimal equivalents of simple fractions such as a half and a quarter.

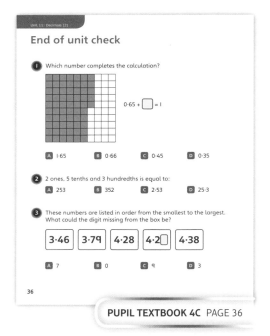

PUPIL TEXTBOOK 4C PAGE 36

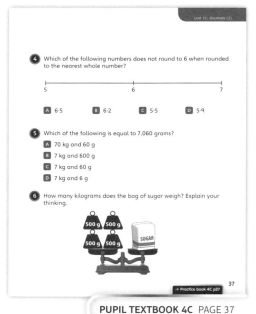

PUPIL TEXTBOOK 4C PAGE 37

Q	A	WRONG ANSWERS AND MISCONCEPTIONS	STRENGTHENING UNDERSTANDING
1	D	A suggests children added together the 1 and 0·65. B suggests they just added 1 to 65.	For question 1, children should count the squares. Encourage children to count in 10s, not 1s, where possible.
2	C	B suggests children have confused tenths with 10s and hundredths with 100s. D suggests children are confused about where to put the decimal point.	For question 2, children might find a place value grid and counters help them better understand the value of the number.
3	C	A, B and D suggest children are unsure about hundredths.	
4	A	C and D suggest children do not understand the '5 or above' rule of rounding up.	For question 4, children should place the numbers on a number line to help them.
5	C	A, B and D suggest children do not understand how to convert between units.	
6	2 kg	2,000 g suggests children are not yet confident converting g to kg.	

My journal

WAYS OF WORKING Independent thinking

ANSWERS AND COMMENTARY Children may make the numbers on a place value grid to help them understand the size of the numbers and what each digit in each number represents. Encourage children to read the numbers aloud. They should take care not to read the two digits after the decimal as a double digit, so they should avoid saying 'zero point twenty-seven' for '0·27' and instead say 'zero point two seven'. Children may also compare just two of the numbers, as opposed to finding similarities and differences about all three.

What is the same? Children may offer answers such as:
• They are all greater than 0.
• They all contain the digits 2 and 7.
• All the numbers have a decimal point in them.
• Two of the numbers have 2 numbers after the decimal (the other just has 1).
• 7·2 and 7·20 are equivalent.

What is different?
• One number does not show any hundredths.
• Two numbers start with a 7, the other one does not.

Power check

WAYS OF WORKING Independent thinking

ASK
• Can you explain how to round a number with one decimal place to the nearest whole number?
• Are you able to put some decimals in order?

Power puzzle

WAYS OF WORKING Pair work or small groups

IN FOCUS This puzzle focuses on children understanding and applying the conversion between litres and millilitres. These can be difficult questions in assessments. Children should look at the information that they are given (one glass holds 200 ml) and then gradually work down the list, finding the other values. As children work through, they should realise they need to use their knowledge of multiplication and division from earlier units to find the answers to the last questions. For instance, they need to be able to multiply by 200 or count in 200s.

ANSWERS AND COMMENTARY

Glass = 0·2 litres. Jug = 1 litre (5 × 200 = 1,000 ml = 1 l).
Bucket = 7 litres (7 × 1 = 7 l). Barrel = 140 litres (20 × 7 = 140 l).
Paddling pool = 1,120 litres (8 × 140 = 1,120 litres).

After the unit ⏸

• Can children find the number bond of a decimal to 1? Can they accurately represent a decimal on a place value grid or other representation?
• Can children round a number to the nearest whole number and compare and order numbers that have the same number of decimal places?
• Can children convert between common units of measurement?

PUPIL PRACTICE BOOK 4C PAGE 27

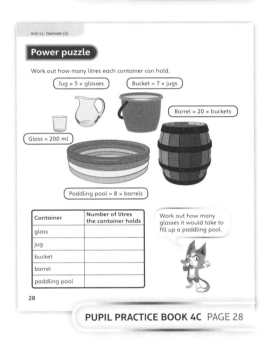

PUPIL PRACTICE BOOK 4C PAGE 28

Strengthen and **Deepen** activities for this unit can be found in the *Power Maths* online subscription.

Unit 12
Money

Don't forget to watch the Unit 12 video!

Mastery Expert tip! "Children have only just formally been introduced to the decimal point in the previous unit so spend time introducing these key concepts. I recreated a lot of shopping scenes in class, with plenty of £·p price tags, and encouraged children to add mentally and find the change!"

WHY THIS UNIT IS IMPORTANT

This unit is the first time children are introduced to the £·p notation. Children will learn that the decimal point separates the pounds from the pence. They will round money to the nearest 10p and £1 to help them estimate total costs and will start to add and subtract simple amounts of money, but without needing to formally add decimals. Children will know already that 100p is equal to £1 and will use this knowledge to help them with their addition. They will go on to multiply and divide amounts of money and solve word problems about money.

WHERE THIS UNIT FITS

→ Unit 11: Decimals (2)
→ **Unit 12: Money**
→ Unit 13: Time

Children have already worked with money and been formally introduced to decimals. Now they will learn how to write about money using £·p. Children should already be confident in knowing that 100p is equal to £1 and should be able to work out how much money is shown in notes and coins.

Before they start this unit, it is expected that children:
- know how to convert between pounds and pence
- can round amounts to the nearest 10 and 100
- can use a variety of methods to count amounts of money.

ASSESSING MASTERY

By the end of the unit, children will be able to record money using the £·p notation. They will understand that the decimal point separates pounds and pence. They will know how to convert between pounds and pence and vice versa. They will be able to write money such as 3p in £s. Children will round amounts to the nearest 10p and £1 to help them estimate totals. They will compare and order amounts of money to work out the cheapest and most expensive items. Finally, children will solve money problems involving four rules of numbers.

COMMON MISCONCEPTIONS	STRENGTHENING UNDERSTANDING	GOING DEEPER
Children incorrectly write amounts of money when they have money less than £1. For example, children write 30p as £0·3 and 3p as £0·30.	Encourage children to think of the difference between amounts such as £3, 30p and 3p. Link their knowledge on number with tenths and hundredths as decimals. Use a place value table to help children find the correct place for each digit.	Explore the minimum number of coins children need to make particular amounts or ask how many ways they can make this amount. For example, find all the ways of making 50p using their times-table knowledge.
Children think that more coins equals a greater amount of money.	Children should make amounts using pennies. For example, to show that 50p is greater than 8 × 5p coins, ask children to select the correct number of pennies for each amount and compare.	Explore what it means to find an under and over estimate. Ask children why, when adding amounts of money, it might be useful to overestimate if they have just £20 to spend.

Introduce the unit using whole class discussion. Use simple amounts of money to give children examples of ordering, rounding and what it means to have change. Ask children which of Flo's words they are familiar with and use terminology in sentences about money.

STRUCTURES AND REPRESENTATIONS

Number lines: These are used to add amounts. Children will benefit from seeing the addition and jumps of money using this model.

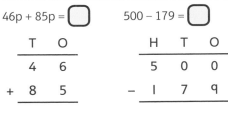

Column addition and subtraction: Adding and subtracting amounts of money using the column method allows children to use familiar methods to work with money.

46p + 85p = ◯   500 − 179 = ◯

```
    T   O
    4   6
+   8   5
  _____
```

```
  H   T   O
  5   0   0
− 1   7   9
  _____
```

KEY LANGUAGE

There is some key language that children will need to know as part of the learning in this unit.

→ notes
→ coins
→ pounds (£)
→ pence (p)
→ add (+)
→ subtract (−)
→ change
→ round to the nearest
→ order
→ greater than (>)
→ less than (<)
→ cheaper
→ more expensive
→ estimate
→ over estimate
→ under estimate
→ total

PUPIL TEXTBOOK 4C PAGE 38

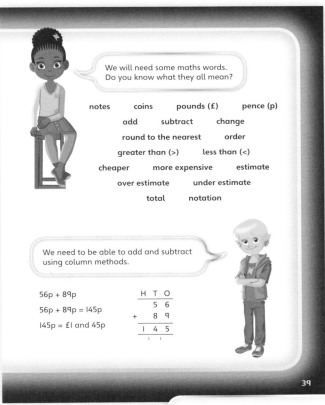

PUPIL TEXTBOOK 4C PAGE 39

Pounds and pence

Learning focus

In this lesson, children will add pence, breaking the pound boundary, and pounds and pence. Children will write totals as pence, pounds and pence, and using a decimal point.

Small steps

→ Previous step: Problem solving – decimals
→ **This step: Pounds and pence**
→ Next step: Pounds, tenths and hundredths

NATIONAL CURRICULUM LINKS

Year 4 Measurement – Money
- Estimate, compare and calculate different measures, including money in pounds and pence.
- Solve simple measure and money problems involving fractions and decimals to two decimal places.

ASSESSING MASTERY

Children will understand that there are 100p in £1 and will explore various ways of making a pound and other totals by adding a range of coins together. Children will be confident writing totals in pence, pounds and pence, and with a decimal point.

COMMON MISCONCEPTIONS

When recording amounts, children may not be clear where and when to use the signs £, p and ·. Ask:
- *What does the £ sign represent? What does the p sign represent? Where should £ be used? Where should p be used?*

STRENGTHENING UNDERSTANDING

Strengthen understanding by providing children with physical coins to move around, pair up and count. A number line or hundredths grid will help children with addition. Hundredths grids are particularly useful to show reaching £1 and breaking the boundary.

GOING DEEPER

Challenge children to find a range of methods or come up with a variety of ways to make a given total.

KEY LANGUAGE

In lesson: pence (p), pounds (£), decimal point

Other language to be used by the teacher: coins, total, altogether, one hundred, multiples

STRUCTURES AND REPRESENTATIONS

part-whole models

RESOURCES

Optional: plastic coins, crayons

 In the eTextbook of this lesson, you will find interactive links to a selection of teaching tools.

Before you teach

- Do children recognise British coins and notes?
- Do children know how much each coin and note is worth?
- Do children know basic equivalence (ten 10p coins make £1, two 5p coins make 10p)?

Discover

WAYS OF WORKING Pair work

ASK

- Question **1** a): *What coins does Bella have? How are you going to find the total? Could you make the coins easier to count?*
- Question **1** b): *What does 'pounds' mean? How will the total look different in pounds and pence?*

IN FOCUS In questions **1** a) and **1** b), children must recognise the value of each coin and add them together correctly. Question **1** b) will highlight whether children know there is 100p in £1 and whether they understand and can use the pound sign and decimal point.

PRACTICAL TIPS Recreate the **Discover** scene of Bella counting her pounds and pence. Give children plastic coins matching the coins Bella has.

ANSWERS

Question **1** a): Bella has 236p.

Question **1** b): £2 and 36p or £2·36
Bella has £2·36.

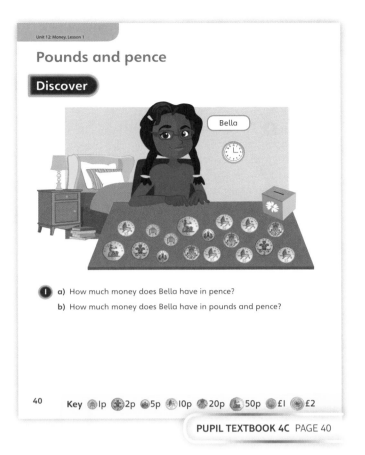

PUPIL TEXTBOOK 4C PAGE 40

Share

WAYS OF WORKING Whole class teacher led

ASK

- Question **1** a): *What coins could you use to make 100p? Are there different ways to make 100p? What coins are left over? How can you count these left-over coins?*
- Question **1** b): *How many pence are there in £1? If 100p is £1, how many pounds will 200p be? How do you write £2? Where does the pound sign go?*
- Question **1** b): *What units do you use for the 36? Why is the 36 in pence and not pounds? What does the decimal point tell you? Do you need the £ sign when using a decimal point? Do you need the p sign when using a decimal point?*

IN FOCUS Ensure children understand that there are 100p in £1, and therefore 200p is equivalent to £2. Explain that the 36p remains pence because it is less than 100p and you can only exchange for one pound at 100p. Using a decimal point ensures children understand that it comes after the whole pounds.

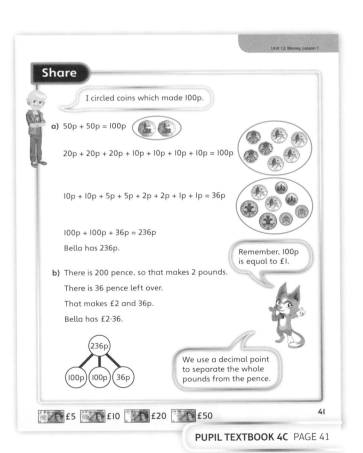

PUPIL TEXTBOOK 4C PAGE 41

Think together

WAYS OF WORKING Whole class teacher led (I do, We do, You do)

ASK

• Question ❶: *Can you make Lexi's coins easier to count by making pounds? How many pounds are there? How many coins are left that do not make one pound? What is the total of these coins in pence?*

• Question ❷: *How many pounds can you make? How many coins are left over? Will the left-over coins be pounds or pence? What is the total of these coins?*

• Question ❸: *What is the total value of Danny's coins? What is the total value of Emma's coins? How can you compare amounts of coins?*

IN FOCUS Question ❸ gives children the opportunity to explore equivalence. Discuss ways to compare the amounts – converting all into pence or all into pounds.

STRENGTHEN Children may find it beneficial having plastic coins available to move around and group into 100s or other amounts. In order to group coins to make 100p, children may find it helpful to use a hundredths grid. Encourage children to use number bonds to 10 or use the larger coins first to help them make 100p.

DEEPEN Challenge children to find alternative ways of making 100p and to explain which way was the most efficient and why.

ASSESSMENT CHECKPOINT Check to see if children can find totals of a range of coins and whether they can write amounts in pence, pounds and pence, and pounds. Do children know when it is appropriate to use the '£', 'p' and '·' signs and why? Do they know that 100p and £1 are equivalent and can they find an efficient way to make 100p given a range of coins?

ANSWERS

Question ❶ a): Lexi has 324 pence.

Question ❶ b): Lexi has 3 pounds and 24 pence.

Question ❶ c): £3·24

Question ❷: There is £4·17 in the purse.

Question ❸: Danny is incorrect. Danny and Emma have the same amount because 10 × 10p = £1. Danny has more coins than Emma, but each of Danny's coins is worth less than Emma's coin.

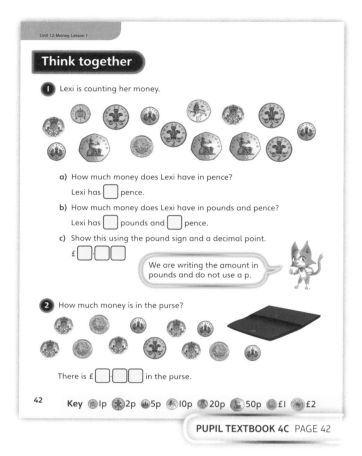

Practice

→ Textbook 4C p40

WAYS OF WORKING Independent thinking

IN FOCUS Question **6** focuses on equivalence. Children must convert amounts from pence to pounds and vice versa. Children are expected to convert both ways so will need to think carefully whether they are dividing or multiplying by 100.

STRENGTHEN Children need to keep a running total when completing question **3**. To help children keep track of the amount, encourage the use of a hundredths grid or number line. Encourage children to make the whole pounds first and regularly add up their notes and coins so far. To complete questions **5** to **7**, children might need to use plastic coins or draw coins, circle amounts to 100p or £1, or used coloured crayons to pair up bonds to 100.

DEEPEN For question **1**, ask children to find different ways of making 100p using the given coins and then to explain which is the most efficient method and why. Deepen understanding of question **3** by asking children to investigate different ways to make the given amounts.

ASSESSMENT CHECKPOINT Assess whether children can add pounds and amounts under 100p together. Children should be secure in their knowledge that 100p makes £1 and should be able to choose suitable coins to make a given amount.

ANSWERS Answers for the **Practice** part of the lesson appear in the separate **Practice and Reflect answer guide**.

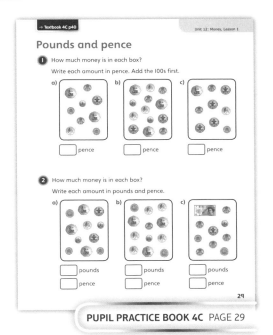

PUPIL PRACTICE BOOK 4C PAGE 29

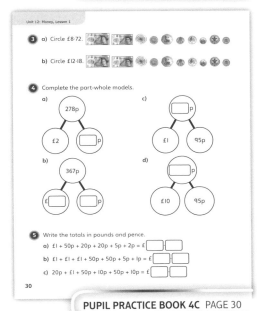

PUPIL PRACTICE BOOK 4C PAGE 30

Reflect

WAYS OF WORKING Independent thinking

IN FOCUS This section gives children a final chance to reflect on the three different ways to record amounts. Children will be able to use the images to work out one way of writing the total, then use their knowledge of multiplying or dividing by 100 to convert. The question also requires children to use their knowledge of the '£', 'p' and '·' signs.

ASSESSMENT CHECKPOINT Children should now be aware of the three different ways of recording amounts and be able to convert from pence to pounds and from pounds to pence. Do children have an efficient method for grouping coins? Can they use appropriate signs correctly?

ANSWERS Answers for the **Reflect** part of the lesson appear in the separate **Practice and Reflect answer guide**.

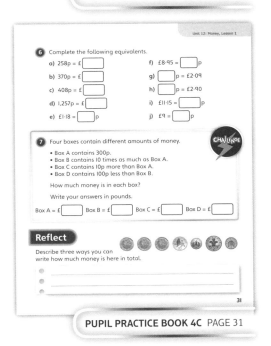

PUPIL PRACTICE BOOK 4C PAGE 31

After the lesson

- Can children add coins and record the total in pence, pounds and pence, and pounds?
- Do children know how and when to use '£', 'p' and '·'?
- Can children divide and multiply by 100 to convert from pence to pounds and vice versa?

Pounds, tenths and hundredths

Learning focus

In this lesson, children will focus on the place value of coins and amounts when recording in pounds. Children will make links between fractions of a pound and converting to decimals with two decimal places.

Small steps

→ Previous step: Pounds and pence
→ **This step: Pounds, tenths and hundredths**
→ Next step: Ordering amounts of money

NATIONAL CURRICULUM LINKS

Year 4 Measurement – Money
• Estimate, compare and calculate different measures, including money in pounds and pence.
• Solve simple measure and money problems involving fractions and decimals to two decimal places.

ASSESSING MASTERY

Children can count and write totals in pounds to two decimal places. Children understand that pence are made up of tenths and hundredths and can identify and record tenths and hundredths in totals they work out. They can explain the difference between each place value column in an amount and what each column is worth.

COMMON MISCONCEPTIONS

Children may not see the importance of 0 as a place holder and may incorrectly write amounts. Ask:
• *Have you remembered to use 0 as a place holder? Why is this important?*

STRENGTHENING UNDERSTANDING

Provide children with tens strips, hundredths grids and plastic coins to help them identify tenths and hundredths. To help children to identify which digit is the tenth or the hundredth, they may benefit from writing the amounts on a place value grid.

GOING DEEPER

To deepen understanding, ask children to explore and explain the relationships between pounds, tenths and hundredths. Ask children to look for different ways to make amounts, looking at how tenths and hundredths could be made using different coins.

KEY LANGUAGE

In lesson: pence (p), pounds (£), equal

Other language to be used by the teacher: amount, total, price, decimal point, tenth, hundredth, fraction

STRUCTURES AND REPRESENTATIONS

hundredths grids, tens strip

RESOURCES

Optional: plastic coins

 In the eTextbook of this lesson, you will find interactive links to a selection of teaching tools.

Before you teach

• Do children have an effective strategy for counting coins and finding totals?
• Can children record totals in pence, pounds and pence, and pounds?
• Do children know there is 100p in £1?

Discover

WAYS OF WORKING Pair work

ASK

- Question ❶ a): *What coins does Emma have? How many 1p coins does Emma have? What coins does Danny have? How many 10p coins does Danny have? Did you need to count each coin individually?*
- Question ❶ b): *Where are the coins showing heads on Emma's grid? Did you need to count each coin individually? Was there a quicker way? How many of Danny's coins are showing heads? How much are these coins worth altogether?*

IN FOCUS In question ❶ a), remind children that 100p is equal to £1 so they do not need to count each individual penny. Similarly, do children remember that ten 10p coins make £1? Question ❶ b) highlights children's understanding of place value and whether they are aware of pounds, tenths and hundredths when recording amounts.

PRACTICAL TIPS Provide children with a hundredths grid filled with 1p coins and a tens strip filled with 10p coins. Images of Emma's filled hundredths grid and Danny's filled tens strip may also be useful.

ANSWERS

Question ❶ a): Emma has 100p, which equals £1. Danny also has 100p, which equals £1.

Question ❶ b): Emma has £0·43 showing heads. Danny has £0·70 showing heads.

Share

WAYS OF WORKING Whole class teacher led

ASK

- Question ❶ a): *What do you know about 100 pennies? How are you going to record Emma's amount? What will be the quickest way to find the total of Danny's coins? How are you going to record Danny's amount?*
- Question ❶ b): *How can you work out how many coins there are showing heads? What is the worth of forty-three 1p coins? How do you record that in pounds? Are there any pounds? How much is there in pence?*
- Question ❶ b): *How many coins on Danny's grid are showing heads? What is the worth of seven 10p coins? How do you record this in pounds? What goes before the decimal point? What goes after the decimal point?*

IN FOCUS For question ❶ a), discuss the layout of both grids and how this can help children work out the totals for Emma and Danny. To work out the total of coins showing heads in question ❶ b), children may need to count the coins individually. Some children could be encouraged to use the layout of the hundredths grid – there are four full rows plus three, therefore 43 coins showing heads.

PUPIL TEXTBOOK 4C PAGE 44

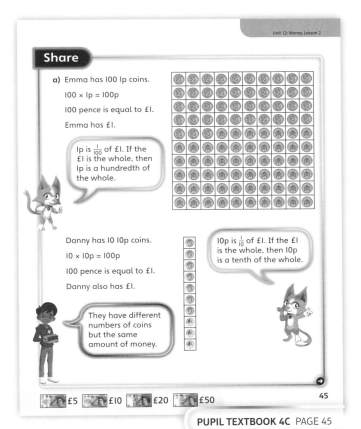

PUPIL TEXTBOOK 4C PAGE 45

Think together

Whole class teacher led (I do, We do, You do)

ASK

- Question **1** : *How many 1p or 10p coins are there? How can you count the number of coins on the grids? What is the worth of the 1p or 10p coins on the grid? How can you write the amount of coins as a fraction? What would these fractions look like as decimals? Where will the decimal points go?*
- Question **2** : *What coins are in each box? Are there any pounds? How many pounds? How much is there in pence? How many tenths? How many hundredths? What will they look like as decimals?*
- Question **3** b): *If $\frac{1}{100}$ is 1p, how much will $\frac{17}{100}$ be? How will you write this in pounds? Are there any whole pounds?*
- Question **3** c): *What coins will be used for $\frac{9}{100}$? How much is this equivalent to? If Mo loses this amount, what will the calculation be? How can you find the answer?*

IN FOCUS Question **2** requires children to find totals and write them correctly to two decimal places. Encouraging children to think carefully about the tenths and hundredths in terms of how many 10p coins and 1p coins they could have will aid them in correctly writing the amounts using decimal points.

STRENGTHEN For question **1** a), have coins available for children so they can get the relevant amount and count how many tens they can make. To help with writing the pence after the decimal point in question **2**, children may want to write the pence fractions to help with writing them correctly as decimals. When completing question **3**, children may need to use coins and make the given amounts on hundredths grids or tens strips.

DEEPEN For question **1** a), encourage children to find multiple strategies for working out how much money is on the grid. For questions **1** b) and **2**, ask children to show each amount as tenths or hundredths with hundred squares and tens strips. Deepen understanding further by encouraging children to mentally convert the fractions into amounts, using their knowledge of 1p coins and hundredths and 10p coins and tenths in question **3**.

ASSESSMENT CHECKPOINT Children should now be able to correctly write tenths and hundredths as a decimal and know that $\frac{1}{100}$ of £1 is 1p and that $\frac{1}{10}$ of £1 is 10p. Ensure children can use this knowledge to convert fractions into decimals or amounts.

ANSWERS

Question **1** a): There is £0·55.

Question **1** b): There is £0·30.

Question **2** : There is £3·30 in box A.
There is £3·03 in box B.
There is £0·03 in box C.
There is £0·36 in box D.

Question **3** a): Aki has £0·30.

Question **3** b): Lexi has £0·17.

Question **3** c): Mo has £0·91.

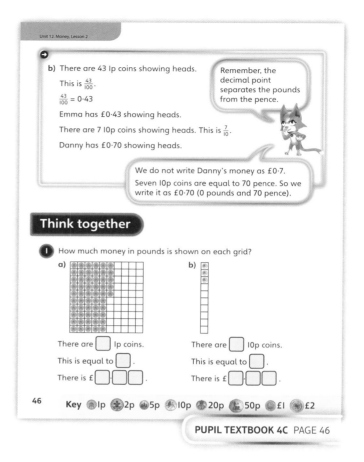

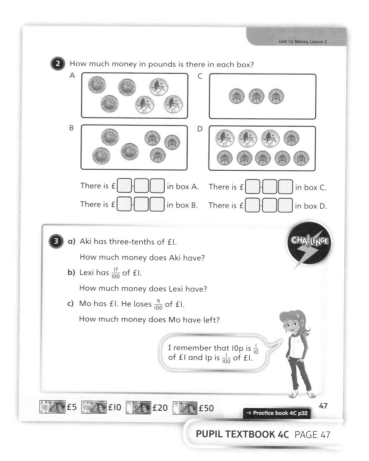

Practice

WAYS OF WORKING Independent thinking

IN FOCUS Question **6** a) allows children to see the relationships between tenths and hundredths and see how this changes the place value and how they record amounts. Question **6** b) requires children to use their prior knowledge of fractions to convert $\frac{3}{5}$ into tenths. Children may need prompting in order to realise they need to make the fraction into tenths or hundredths of £1.

STRENGTHEN Before starting to work out question **3**, encourage children to look for any coins that could be used together to make tenths. Provide hundredths grids, tens strips and plastic coins so children can accurately record the pence after the decimal point. Initially, children may need to work out the tenths first, followed by the hundredths.

DEEPEN Encourage children to find different ways to make the same amounts in question **4** and identify how many tenths and hundredths there are for each version.

ASSESSMENT CHECKPOINT Children should now be able to add coins together and identify whole pounds, tenths and hundredths in the amount to record the total correctly in pounds. Assess whether children can choose appropriate coins to make given pounds, tenths and hundredths. Do children understand the link between tenths and hundredths?

ANSWERS Answers for the **Practice** part of the lesson appear in the separate **Practice and Reflect answer guide**.

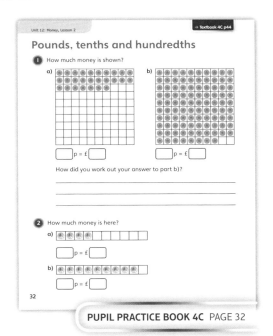

PUPIL PRACTICE BOOK 4C PAGE 32

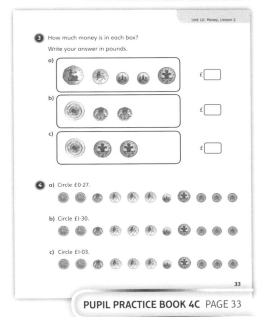

PUPIL PRACTICE BOOK 4C PAGE 33

Reflect

WAYS OF WORKING Independent thinking

IN FOCUS This question will highlight children's understanding of tenths and hundredths and how they relate to pence. Children should identify that both amounts have the same number of pounds but different tenths and hundredths.

ASSESSMENT CHECKPOINT Assess children's explanations of the difference in tenths and hundredths. Can children identify that the amounts have the same number of whole pounds but a different number of tenths and hundredths?

ANSWERS Answers for the **Reflect** part of the lesson appear in the separate **Practice and Reflect answer guide**.

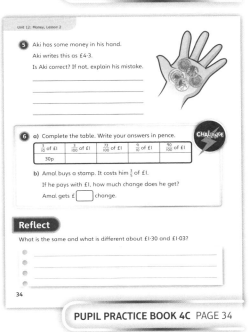

PUPIL PRACTICE BOOK 4C PAGE 34

After the lesson

- Do children recognise pence as tenths and hundredths?
- Can children record amounts correctly, thinking about the tenths and hundredths?
- Can children discuss the value of each digit in a given amount?

Ordering amounts of money

Learning focus

In this lesson, children will identify and put in order the most and least expensive items and amounts of money. Children will convert prices and amounts in a variety of notations into a common unit.

Small steps

→ Previous step: Pounds, tenths and hundredths
→ **This step: Ordering amounts of money**
→ Next step: Rounding money

NATIONAL CURRICULUM LINKS

Year 4 Measurement – Money
• Estimate, compare and calculate different measures, including money in pounds and pence.
• Solve simple measure and money problems involving fractions and decimals to two decimal places.

ASSESSING MASTERY

Children can convert a mixture of notations into a common unit and identify the most and least expensive item and the greatest and least amount of money. Children can order prices and amounts from greatest to least and from least to greatest.

COMMON MISCONCEPTIONS

When converting notations, children may mix up whether they are multiplying by 100 or dividing by 100 and so misidentify which is the most or least. Ask:
• *What calculation do you need to use? How do you know who has the most? How do you know who has the least?*

STRENGTHENING UNDERSTANDING

Having access to plastic coins so that children can make amounts, try different combinations of coins and visually compare what is the same and what is different about amounts, may make it easier for children to compare. When ordering totals, encourage children to set amounts out on a number line to make the order very visual.

GOING DEEPER

Encourage children to work between units rather than converting every amount into a common notation. Question children about their decisions, discussing their understanding of worth and order and giving explanations using correct mathematical vocabulary linked to ordering money.

KEY LANGUAGE

In lesson: convert, most, greatest, least, more than (>), less than (<), order

Other language to be used by the teacher: price, total, amount, units, common, ascending, descending

STRUCTURES AND REPRESENTATIONS

number lines

RESOURCES

Optional: plastic coins, place value grid

 In the eTextbook of this lesson, you will find interactive links to a selection of teaching tools.

Before you teach

• Can children read prices and amounts in various notations?
• Can children convert between units?
• Do children understand vocabulary linked to ordering?

Discover

WAYS OF WORKING Pair work

ASK

- Question ❶ a): *What does least and most expensive mean? Are you starting with the largest or smallest price? Are the prices recorded in the same way?*
- Question ❶ b): *How much does each item cost? How much does Isla have to spend? Which items cost less than £5? What are you looking for in each price?*

IN FOCUS In question ❶ a), children may look at the amount of pounds in each item and mentally use their knowledge of 100p = £1 to order the items. Some children may convert all of the prices into pounds or pence so that they can compare the items more easily.

PRACTICAL TIPS Set up the shop scenario using toys and price tags and provide children with a variety of plastic coins and notes.

ANSWERS

Question ❶ a): Notepad, pack of pencils, football, teddy bear, computer game and musical keyboard

Question ❶ b): Isla could buy the football, the pack of pencils or the notepad.

PUPIL TEXTBOOK 4C PAGE 48

Share

WAYS OF WORKING Whole class teacher led

ASK

- Question ❶ a): *Are these items priced in the same units? Can you convert them into the same units? How do you convert from pence to pounds? How do you write prices in pounds? How do you convert from pounds to pence? How do you write prices in pence?*
- Question ❶ b): *What is this note worth in pounds? What is this note worth in pence? Which items are less than £5 or 500p? Which items are the same as £5 or 500p? Which items are more than £5 or 500p?*

IN FOCUS In question ❶ b), some children may want to convert the £5 into pence and others may want to convert the items in pence into pounds. Discuss why both of these options would be possible and whether one is more efficient than the other. Encourage children to then explain why certain items can be eliminated.

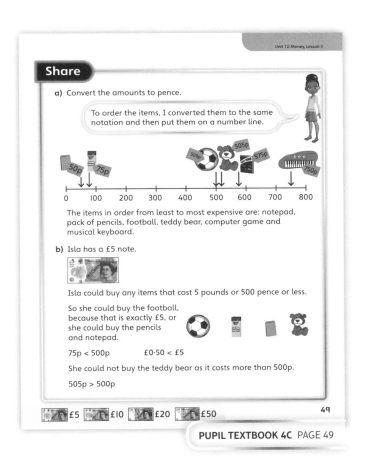

PUPIL TEXTBOOK 4C PAGE 49

Think together

WAYS OF WORKING Whole class teacher led (I do, We do, You do)

ASK

- Question **1**: *What are the prices of each of the items? What does cheapest mean? What does most expensive mean?*
- Question **2**: *How much are Isla's coins worth altogether? How do you write Isla's amount in pounds? How do you write Isla's amount in pence? Which items couldn't Isla buy?*
- Question **3**: *How much money does each child have? Why would Max think he has the most because he has a note? Why would Richard think he has the most because he has the most coins?*

IN FOCUS Question **3** will highlight children's understanding of a coin or note's worth, while highlighting possible misconceptions such as the bigger the coin, the more you have, or the more coins you have, the larger the amount.

STRENGTHEN For question **1**, encourage children to make prices with coins and notes in order to identify and compare how many pounds or pence each item costs. To strengthen understanding of question **2**, encourage children to write down the coins Isla has in pounds and then in pence. Children could also use individual coins to buy certain items, for example using the £1 for the comic or car.

DEEPEN Deepen understanding of question **2** by asking children what combinations of items Isla could buy with £5. Children could also calculate how much extra she would need if she wanted to buy all the items. Additionally, when looking at the misconceptions for question **3**, ask children to use examples of coins and notes to prove the misconceptions are incorrect.

ASSESSMENT CHECKPOINT Children should now be able to identify the most and least expensive by converting into the same notation and correctly order prices following set criteria. Ensure children can identify which items are more than, less than or the same as the total given. Children should also recognise common misconceptions related to money and be able to explain why the misconceptions are incorrect.

ANSWERS

Question **1** a): The cheapest item on the shelf is the comic.

Question **1** b): The most expensive item on the shelf is the train set.

Question **1** c): Comic, car, DVD, rag doll, train set.

Question **1** d): Train set, rag doll, DVD, car, comic.

Question **2**: Alex has £6·50. She could buy the comic, the rag doll, the car or the DVD.

Question **3**: Max is assuming he has the most because he has a note. Max is not taking into consideration that the other children could have coins that equal more than his note. Richard thinks he has the most because he has the most coins. Richard is correct on this occasion, but other children could have fewer coins that are worth more than Richard's.

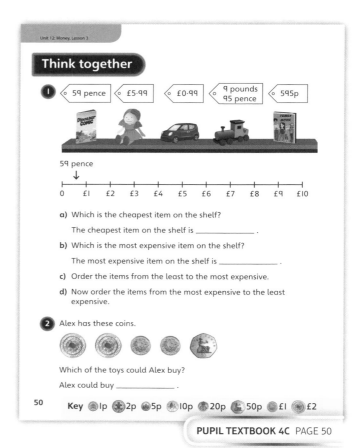

PUPIL TEXTBOOK 4C PAGE 50

PUPIL TEXTBOOK 4C PAGE 51

Practice

WAYS OF WORKING Independent thinking

IN FOCUS Question ① allows children to convert or compare mentally using their secure knowledge of 100p = £1. Children can show their understanding of the language and what a total is worth by explaining how they know which is the most or least expensive.

STRENGTHEN Encourage children to convert different amounts into the same units or to make them using plastic coins. Children may also find it beneficial to set amounts out on a number line in order to compare.

DEEPEN Deepen understanding of question ⑦ by asking children to explain how they knew which money bag belonged to which child after reading the clues. Children could also explain why specific money bags could not belong to other children based on the clues given. Ask children to write different clues that would reveal whose money bag was whose.

ASSESSMENT CHECKPOINT Children should have an understanding of the vocabulary 'most and least expensive' and be able to identify the most or least expensive from a list of totals and justify their choice. They should also be able to identify amounts greater than, less than, or equal to a given amount and to order prices to specific criteria.

ANSWERS Answers for the **Practice** part of the lesson appear in the separate **Practice and Reflect answer guide**.

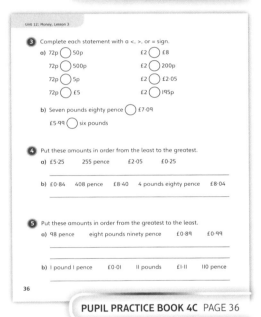

PUPIL PRACTICE BOOK 4C PAGE 35

PUPIL PRACTICE BOOK 4C PAGE 36

Reflect

WAYS OF WORKING Independent thinking

IN FOCUS In this part of the lesson, children reflect on their knowledge of place value, conversions and the inequality signs.

ASSESSMENT CHECKPOINT Children should identify that Isla is incorrectly showing £3 as 3p in the statement and be able to explain that £3 is 300p, which is larger than 257p, or that 257p is £2·57, which is less than £3.

ANSWERS Answers for the **Reflect** part of the lesson appear in the separate **Practice and Reflect answer guide**.

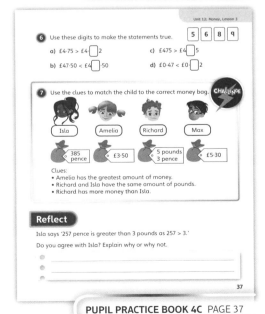

PUPIL PRACTICE BOOK 4C PAGE 37

After the lesson

- Can children identify and order amounts according to given criteria?
- Can children use the inequality signs to compare amounts?
- Can children identify and discuss common misconceptions related to ordering money?

Rounding money

Learning focus

In this lesson, children will round amounts of money to the nearest 10p and £1 using number lines. Children will explore the difference between given amounts and multiples of 10 and 100 in order to round correctly.

Small steps

→ Previous step: Ordering amounts of money
→ **This step: Rounding money**
→ Next step: Using rounding to estimate money

NATIONAL CURRICULUM LINKS

Year 4 Measurement – Money
- Estimate, compare and calculate different measures, including money in pounds and pence.
- Solve simple measure and money problems involving fractions and decimals to two decimal places.

ASSESSING MASTERY

Children can round to the nearest 10p and £1, use number lines to identify multiples of 10 and 100 and explain how they know a number rounds to a certain multiple. Children can identify prices that would round to a given multiple from a given list.

COMMON MISCONCEPTIONS

Children may not be confident about which digit to look at when deciding which way to round. Ask:
- *If you are rounding to the nearest 10p, which digit should you look at? If you are rounding to the nearest £1, which digit should you look at?*

STRENGTHENING UNDERSTANDING

Having a variety of completed, partially completed and blank number lines available may help children who are not confident working with digits alone. Place value grids can also give children a clearer visual representation of which digit will change when rounding and therefore which digit determines how the number changes.

GOING DEEPER

Ask children to create a rounding rule that focuses on the digits in each column. Encourage children who show a good understanding of multiples of 10 and 100 and rounding to the nearest 10p or £1 to round to other amounts and adapt the rule they previously created. Children could create their own problems that require the rounded amount to be in the middle of a number line.

KEY LANGUAGE

In lesson: round to the nearest, closer, between

Other language to be used by the teacher: far, estimate, difference, multiple, tens numbers, hundreds numbers

STRUCTURES AND REPRESENTATIONS

number lines

RESOURCES

Optional: plastic coins

 In the eTextbook of this lesson, you will find interactive links to a selection of teaching tools.

Before you teach

- Can children explain any rules they know for rounding?
- Do children know the multiples of 10 and multiples of 100?
- Can children accurately place numbers on a number line?

Discover

Pair work

ASK

- Question **1** a): *What does 'round' mean? If rounding to the nearest 10p, which digits will you need to look at?*
- Question **1** b): *If rounding to the nearest £1, which digits will you need to look at? Why do you need to think about multiples of 100 when rounding to the nearest pound?*

IN FOCUS Question **1** highlight children's understanding of rounding and multiples of 10 or 100. Question **1** b) will give a good indication of children's prior understanding of rounding, whether they know why we round numbers and if they can link this knowledge to money.

PRACTICAL TIPS Recreate the jumble sale with the same items and price tags. Create a large number line in the classroom for children to stand holding whiteboards for multiples of 10s and 100s and the given amounts.

ANSWERS

Question **1** a): The magazine (27p) rounded to the nearest 10p is 30p, the train (£4·32) rounded to the nearest 10p is £4·30 and the plane (£5·95) rounded to the nearest 10p is £6.

Question **1** b): The magazine rounds to £0 to the nearest pound, the train rounds to £4 to the nearest pound and the plane rounds to £6 to the nearest pound. Ebo and Zac might be rounding the prices to estimate how much the items cost altogether, quickly work out the difference between the prices of items or to estimate how much change they would get back.

Share

Whole class teacher led

ASK

- Question **1** a): *Can you show the multiples of 10 on a number line? Where would the price go on your number line? Which multiple of 10 is the price closest to? What is the difference between the price and each multiple of 10?*
- Question **1** b): *Can you show the multiples of 100 on a number line? Which multiple of 100 is each price closest to? What is the difference between each price and each multiple of 100?*
- Question **1** b): *How does rounding make it easier to work with money?*

IN FOCUS Model identifying the multiples of 10 or 100 on either side of the chosen price and writing these multiples on a number line. Encourage children to discuss and justify where the price would go on the number line. Work out the difference between the price and each multiple and identify which multiple the price is closest to. Children may begin to see patterns relating to the ones digit and whether they round up or down.

PUPIL TEXTBOOK 4C PAGE 52

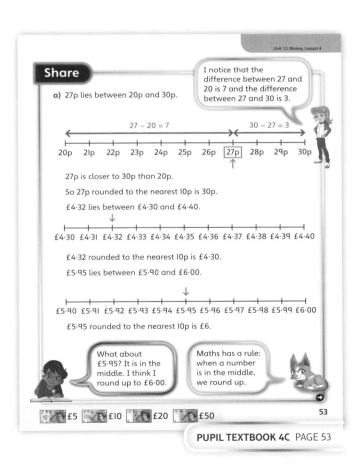

PUPIL TEXTBOOK 4C PAGE 53

Think together

WAYS OF WORKING Whole class teacher led (I do, We do, You do)

ASK

- Question **1**: *Which digits do you need to look at? Can you show the multiples of 10 or 100 on a number line? What would half way be? Which multiple is the price closest to?*
- Question **2**: *Do you need to think about multiples of 10 or 100 when you round? How do multiples of 10 and 100 link to rounding to the nearest 10p or £1?*
- Question **3**: *Which multiples need to be on either end of the number line if £3 is the answer when rounded to the nearest 10p? Which multiples need to be on either end of the number line if £3 is the answer when rounded the nearest £1? Which half of the number lines will round to £3?*

IN FOCUS Question **3** gives children the opportunity to approach rounding in a different way. Children must think about which hundredth digits would round to £3 and which tenth digits would round to £3.

STRENGTHEN Encourage children to mark increments of 1 or 10 on number lines to help them work out the differences between the prices and the multiples. For question **3**, children may find it easier to round each price to the nearest 10p and £1 and then look for those that have £3 as an answer.

DEEPEN Deepen understanding of questions **1** and **2** by asking children to identify what the hundredths would need to be to round to the other multiple of 10 and what the tenth would need to be to round to the other multiple of 100.

ASSESSMENT CHECKPOINT Assess whether children know which digits to focus on to work out which multiple they should round to. Children should be confident rounding to the nearest 10p and £1 using a number line.

ANSWERS

Question **1** a): £1·68 rounded to the nearest 10 pence is £1·70.

Question **1** b): £1·68 rounded to the nearest pound is £2·00.

Question **2** a): £3·25 rounded to the nearest 10 pence is £3·30.

Question **2** b): £3·25 rounded to the nearest pound is £3·00.

Question **3**: £3·04 and £2·99 round to £3 to the nearest 10p and pound.

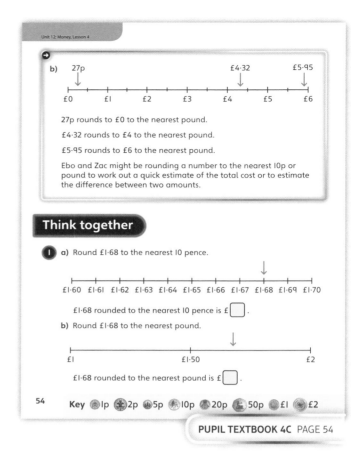

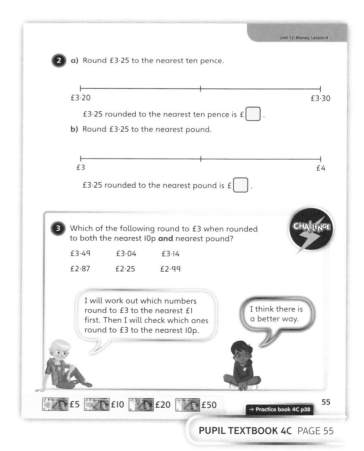

Practice

WAYS OF WORKING Independent thinking

IN FOCUS For question **3**, children need to identify which digit tells them whether to round up or down, using the rule 1 to 4 rounds down and 5 to 9 rounds up. For question **4**, children must think about which tenth digits would round to £5. For question **5**, encourage children to think about the boundaries for rounding to £2·50 to the nearest 10p and all of the prices within that boundary.

STRENGTHEN As the number lines in question **1** reduce in markings and labels, encourage children to work through set steps for each answer. As question **1** d) is more open-ended, children may benefit from a 'check list' of steps to complete based on previous questions, which can also be used for question **2**.

DEEPEN Deepen understanding of question **3** by asking children to add another column to the table and round the prices to the nearest 50p. As well, once question **6** is completed, ask children to investigate how many other prices they can find that are the same but round to different criteria.

THINK DIFFERENTLY Question **5** prompts children to explore the relationship between rounding and the possible price of an item. This question lends itself to the multiple being rounded to be labelled in the middle of a number line rather than at either end.

ASSESSMENT CHECKPOINT Assess whether children can correctly label information on a number line to aid rounding to 10 or 100. Can children work out and list possible prices when given a price rounded to the nearest 10p or £1?

ANSWERS Answers for the **Practice** part of the lesson appear in the separate **Practice and Reflect answer guide**.

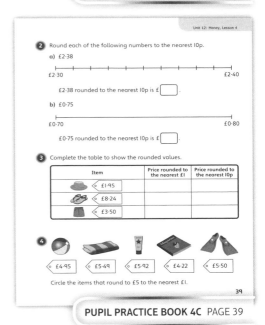

PUPIL PRACTICE BOOK 4C PAGE 38

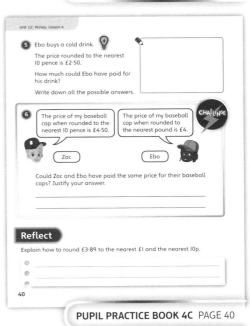

PUPIL PRACTICE BOOK 4C PAGE 39

Reflect

WAYS OF WORKING Independent thinking

IN FOCUS Children should be able to use their newly gained knowledge to create steps or rules for rounding to the nearest 10p or £1.

ASSESSMENT CHECKPOINT Assess whether children can provide a coherent set of steps or rules to follow when rounding. Do children know how to round £3·89 to the nearest 10p and £1? Have they explained these clearly?

ANSWERS Answers for the **Reflect** part of the lesson appear in the separate **Practice and Reflect answer guide**.

After the lesson

- Can children correctly round to the nearest 10p or £1?
- Can children give possible answers for rounding to a given multiple?
- Can children explain how to round to the nearest 10p or £1?

PUPIL PRACTICE BOOK 4C PAGE 40

Using rounding to estimate money

Learning focus

In this lesson, children will round amounts to estimate totals, look at differences between prices and work out how much money remains. Children will explore over and under estimates depending on how prices were rounded.

Small steps

→ Previous step: Rounding money
→ **This step: Using rounding to estimate money**
→ Next step: Problem solving – pounds and pence

NATIONAL CURRICULUM LINKS

Year 4 Measurement – Money

Estimate, compare and calculate different measures, including money in pounds and pence.

ASSESSING MASTERY

Children can confidently round amounts to the nearest 10p or £1, use estimated amounts to work out totals, find the difference between prices and determine if there is enough money to purchase given items. Children can also find possible prices for items that have been rounded to the nearest 10p or £1 and determine if an estimate is an over or under estimation.

COMMON MISCONCEPTIONS

Children may not understand that after rounding and calculating, the answer is not exact. Ask:
• *If rounding gives you an estimate, how can you find the exact answer?*

STRENGTHENING UNDERSTANDING

Providing children with a range of number lines with various scaffolds and place value grids will support any children who are still not confident rounding. When calculating with rounded amounts, children may benefit from using a blank number line, a number track of multiples of 10p or 100p or having the money to manipulate. Also getting children to make the exact price and the rounded price with play money will give them a good visual that, when rounding, they are working with a little more or a little less than the exact answer.

GOING DEEPER

With each question answered, some children may be able to calculate the exact amount and work out the difference between the exact answer and their estimated answer. Some children may also be able to work out where the difference came from.

KEY LANGUAGE

In lesson: round, nearest, estimate, **over estimate**, **under estimate**, 10p, £1, total, most, least

Other language to be used by the teacher: closest, approximately, different, more, less, left

STRUCTURES AND REPRESENTATIONS

number lines

RESOURCES

Optional: plastic coins

 In the eTextbook of this lesson, you will find interactive links to a selection of teaching tools.

Before you teach

• Are children confident rounding to the nearest 10p and £1?
• Do children know what estimate means?
• Can children confidently add multiples of 10 and 100?

Discover

Pair work

ASK

- Question **1** a): *Which digit do you need to look at to determine whether you round up or down?*
- Question **1** b): *Which hundredth digits round up and down to 70? Which is the highest price rounded to £1·70? Which is the lowest price rounded to £1·70?*

IN FOCUS Question **1** b) requires children to work out all of the possible prices that could be rounded to £1·70. Children will need to look at the prices as a whole when looking for the greatest and smallest prices rather than just the hundredth or tenth digit.

PRACTICAL TIPS Set up the supermarket scene with corresponding items and prices. Provide children with £1 notes and 10p coins to help them find totals once prices have been rounded.

ANSWERS

Question **1** a): The milk, oranges and bread round to £1 to the nearest pound.
The chocolate rounds to £2 to the nearest pound.
The cereal rounds to £4 to the nearest pound.
An estimate for the total cost of the items in the trolley is £9.

Question **1** b): The cost of the eggs has been rounded to the nearest 10p.
The most the eggs could cost is £1·74. The least the eggs could cost is £1·65.

Share

Whole class teacher led

ASK

- Question **1** a): *Which multiples are either side of each of the prices? Which multiple is each price closest to? How can you use the rounded prices to find an approximate total? Why is the total going to be an estimate and not exact?*
- Question **1** b): *How much would the eggs be if rounded to the nearest pound? What is the first number that could be rounded up to £1·70? What is the last number that could be rounded down to £1·70? What are the possible prices within this range?*

IN FOCUS For question **1** a), encourage children to explain how they knew to round the price up or down. Discuss what sort of calculation would be needed to find the total. Encourage children to compare adding the exact prices and adding multiples of 100p, then discuss which is quicker. In question **1** b), the rounded price is in the middle of the number line. Some children may be able to mentally work out all of the possible prices of the eggs, while others may feel more confident recording possibilities on a number line.

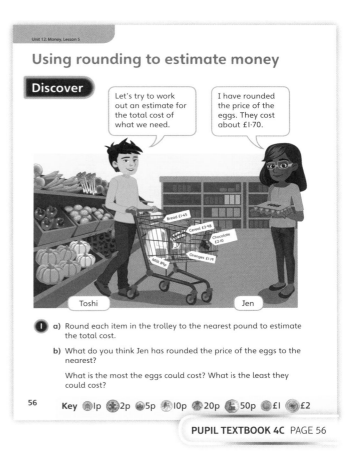

PUPIL TEXTBOOK 4C PAGE 56

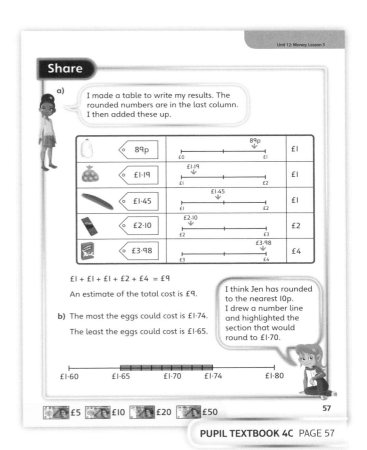

PUPIL TEXTBOOK 4C PAGE 57

Think together

Whole class teacher led (I do, We do, You do)

ASK

- Question **1**: *Which digits could change when rounding to the nearest 10p? How can you use the number line to help you work out the difference between the items?*
- Question **2** a): *How can you work out which multiple of 100p the items will round to? What sort of a calculation do you need to do to find the total cost?*
- Question **2** c): *If you round more of your prices up, how will that affect the total? Did you round all of the items the same way? Will your rounded total be more or less than the exact amount?*
- Question **3** a and b): *What do you need to do with the rounded prices to find the totals? How are you going to add these rounded prices?*

IN FOCUS In question **3**, children investigate the efficiency and accuracy of rounding to estimate. Discuss which form of rounding is quicker and more accurate, and why this is.

STRENGTHEN For question **2** c), encourage children to note how many prices they rounded up and how many they rounded down in order to work out whether their approximate total is an over or under estimate. This will give children a clear idea of whether they added or took away from the exact prices.

DEEPEN For questions **2** b) and c), ask children to calculate the exact cost and conclude how good their estimate was. Children could also round to the nearest 10p and estimate the total.

ASSESSMENT CHECKPOINT Children should now be able to round to the nearest £1 or 10p and be able to identify why an estimated answer is an over or under estimate. They should also be able to explain why rounding to the nearest £1 could be less accurate than rounding to the nearest 10p.

ANSWERS

Question **1**: £1·45 rounds to £1·50 to the nearest 10p. £3·98 rounds to £4·00 to the nearest 10p. The cereal costs about £2·50 more than the loaf of bread.

Question **2** a): The bunch of grapes rounds to £2. The jar of sweets rounds to £3. The orange juice rounds to £2. The estimated total cost is £7.

Question **2** b): The answer is a fairly good estimate. However, all of the items have been rounded down, so the exact cost will be higher than the estimation.

Question **2** c): It is an under estimation because the costs were rounded down.

Question **3** a): The butter rounds to £5. The potatoes round to £2. The crisps round to £1. An estimate for the total cost is £8.

Question **3** b): The butter rounds to £4·80. The potatoes round to £1·90. The crisps round to £0·90 to the nearest 10p. An estimate for the total cost is £7·60. Adding multiples of 100 is quicker. Adding multiples of 10 is more accurate.

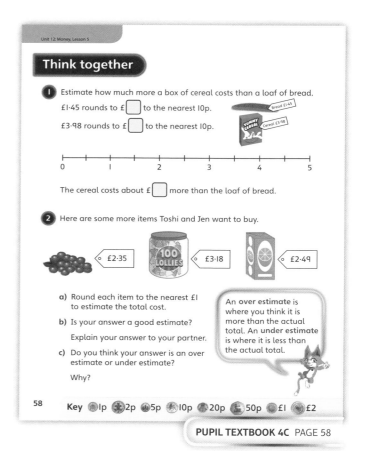

PUPIL TEXTBOOK 4C PAGE 58

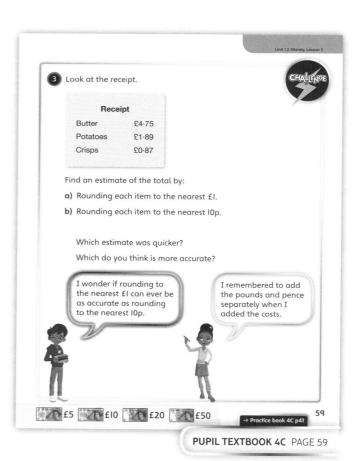

PUPIL TEXTBOOK 4C PAGE 59

Practice

WAYS OF WORKING Independent thinking

IN FOCUS In question **4**, ensure children understand that Holly is rounding to the nearest pound, therefore they need to think about what tenths would round up or down to £7.

STRENGTHEN Encourage the use of a number line to help children accurately add pounds and pence. Support children with questions **1** c) and **3** by encouraging them to record whether they rounded each item up or down in order to assess the accuracy of their estimation. Similarly, for question **6**, encourage children to work through the stages of rounding. This will make it clearer why Lexi doesn't have enough money for all the items.

DEEPEN Deepen understanding of question **6** by asking children to create all possibilities of the items Lexi could buy with £20 and explain why certain groups of items can and cannot be purchased when rounding and estimating the total. As well, challenge children to work out the exact cost of all the items and then find out how much extra Lexi would need to buy them all.

THINK DIFFERENTLY Question **5** allows children to use what they have learnt over previous lessons to help them find an approximate answer. Children need to make decisions about what they are going to round to and how accurate this will make their answer.

ASSESSMENT CHECKPOINT Responses to question **6** will identify whether children are confident identifying whether an approximate total will be an over or under estimate. Do children recognise that how prices are rounded will affect the total?

ANSWERS Answers for the **Practice** part of the lesson appear in the separate **Practice and Reflect answer guide**.

Reflect

WAYS OF WORKING Pair work

IN FOCUS This question allows children to explore why the skills covered in the lesson are useful and reasons why they may not always be helpful.

ASSESSMENT CHECKPOINT Children's answer to this section will highlight whether they truly understand rounding to estimate money or whether they have just learnt the procedure behind it. Can children explain why rounding to the nearest pound is useful? Can children explain why rounding to the nearest pound is not always useful?

ANSWERS Answers for the **Reflect** part of the lesson appear in the separate **Practice and Reflect answer guide**.

After the lesson ⏸

- Do children know that estimated prices will not be exact?
- Can children recognise an over or under estimation and explain why it has occurred?
- Do children understand when it is appropriate and useful to round to estimate money?

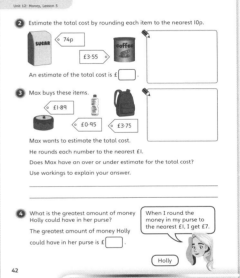

PUPIL PRACTICE BOOK 4C PAGE 41

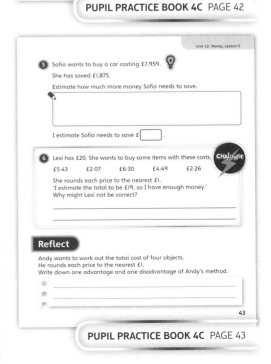

PUPIL PRACTICE BOOK 4C PAGE 42

PUPIL PRACTICE BOOK 4C PAGE 43

Problem solving – pounds and pence

Learning focus

In this lesson, children will solve problems involving pounds and pence. They will solve addition and subtraction problems and work out change.

Small steps

→ Previous step: Using rounding to estimate money
→ **This step: Problem solving – pounds and pence**
→ Next step: Problem solving – multiplication and division

NATIONAL CURRICULUM LINKS

Year 4 Measurement – Money

Estimate, compare and calculate different measures, including money in pounds and pence.

ASSESSING MASTERY

Children can find totals of coins and amounts by partitioning into pounds and pence. They can use a number line to find the difference and can work out change. Children can look at the structure of problems and identify multiple steps, relevant information and what given information fits into a pictorial representation and a calculation.

COMMON MISCONCEPTIONS

Children may not understand why they are recombining pounds and pence when finding totals. Ask:
• *Look at the pounds and pence answer individually. Why can they not be the final answers? How can you come to the final answer?*

STRENGTHENING UNDERSTANDING

Using plastic coins to find totals helps children to identify the pounds and pence within amounts and add like amounts together more easily. Having coins available to place in the jumps on the number lines will also benefit understanding of totalling up the jumps. Showing children calculations and problems as pictorial representations such as bar models or part-whole models allows children to examine and become familiar with the structure of questions, see what information is needed and understand the best method for finding it.

GOING DEEPER

Expose children to a variety of methods for adding and subtracting with money and investigate the suitability of certain methods for certain questions. Encourage children to create rules or guidance for when to use specific methods and ask them to explain and discuss their choices for and against methods depending on the numbers given or the structure of the question.

KEY LANGUAGE

In lesson: change, total, add, pounds, pence

Other language to be used by the teacher: count, altogether, partition, recombine, subtract, find the difference, nearest 10p, nearest £1

STRUCTURES AND REPRESENTATIONS

number lines, bar models

RESOURCES

Optional: plastic coins

 In the eTextbook of this lesson, you will find interactive links to a selection of teaching tools.

Before you teach

• Do children recognise and understand vocabulary linked to addition and subtraction?
• Do children have strategies for addition and subtraction?
• Do children know what change is?

Discover

Problem solving – pounds and pence

Discover

WAYS OF WORKING Pair work

ASK

- Question **1** a): *How much does each item cost? What are you going to do to find the total cost? What sort of calculation will you use to find the total cost? What method are you going to use to add?*
- Question **1** b): *How much did Alex spend? What is change? Why does Alex need some? What sort of calculation is finding change? What method are you going to use to subtract?*

IN FOCUS In question **1** b), ensure children understand the concept of change and that they are required to subtract. Some children may take away and others might find the difference. Watching children find the answers for questions **1** a) and **1** b) will give a good indication of their current understanding, confidence and strategies for adding and subtracting money.

PRACTICAL TIPS Place the items and corresponding price tags to match **Discover** at the front of the classroom and place a bowl of coins on each table in the classroom for children to use throughout the lesson.

ANSWERS

Question **1** a): Alex could use: a 20p coin for the book; 50p, 20p and 5p coins for the CD; 50p and two 20p coins for the t-shirt. Alex spends £1·85 in total.

Question **1** b): Alex gets £8·15 change.

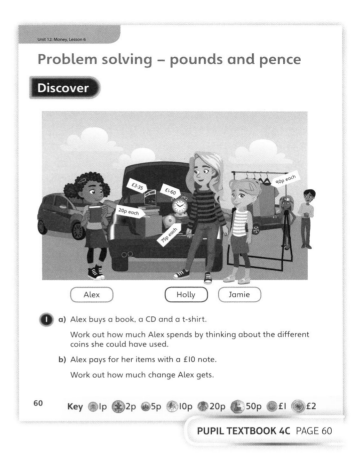

1 a) Alex buys a book, a CD and a t-shirt.

Work out how much Alex spends by thinking about the different coins she could have used.

b) Alex pays for her items with a £10 note.

Work out how much change Alex gets.

60   Key 〇1p ✱2p 〇5p 〇10p 〇20p 〇50p 〇£1 〇£2

PUPIL TEXTBOOK 4C PAGE 60

Share

WAYS OF WORKING Whole class teacher led

ASK

- Question **1** a): *What do you need to do with the coins Alex could have used? How are you going to add them together? Could you have also used the prices to work out how much Alex spends? Which method is the most efficient?*
- Question **1** b): *What did Alex pay with? Where does that amount go in your calculation? What method are you going to use to work out Alex's change? Are there any other methods for working out change?*

IN FOCUS Discuss children's various methods for adding and subtracting money as well as the vocabulary used in each question and how it gives an idea of what calculation is needed. In question **1** a), children are required to add coins together to make the prices of the items, then use these coins to find the total cost. Some children may choose to add the coins together to find the total cost, whereas others may add the prices of the items.

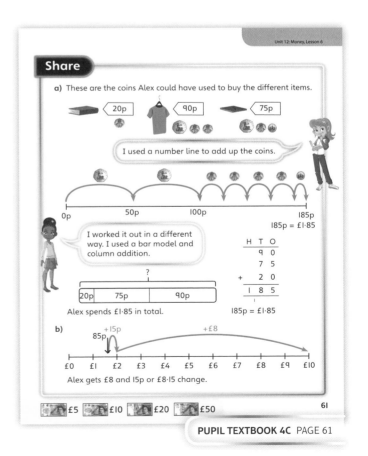

Share

a) These are the coins Alex could have used to buy the different items.

I used a number line to add up the coins.

I worked it out in a different way. I used a bar model and column addition.

Alex spends £1·85 in total.

b) Alex gets £8 and 15p or £8·15 change.

£5 £10 £20 £50   61

PUPIL TEXTBOOK 4C PAGE 61

Think together

WAYS OF WORKING Whole class teacher led (I do, We do, You do)

ASK

- Question **1**: *What sort of a calculation is total? Would it be easier to partition the prices into pounds and pence? How do you recombine the pounds and pence for your final answer?*
- Question **2**: *What sort of a calculation is change? Where does that amount go in your calculation? How do you get to £3 on the number line? How do you get from £3 to £10 on the number line? How do you combine these two amounts?*
- Question **3**: *Are the questions asking you to do the same thing? Which words in each question tell you what sort of a calculation it is? Where would the information you have been given go in a calculation?*

IN FOCUS In question **2**, discuss with children why they are counting up to find an answer, even though finding change is a subtraction calculation. Question **3** explores the structure of subtraction questions and how the context can affect what method is most efficient.

STRENGTHEN To help partition the prices into pounds and pence for question **1**, encourage children to make the amounts out of plastic coins. This will make it easier for children to see how many pounds or pence are in each price. In question **2**, children could place or draw coins onto the number line. This will also help them add the amounts together from the jumps.

DEEPEN Deepen understanding of question **2** by encouraging children to find as many different ways to make the change using notes and coins as possible. Then, ask children to explain what makes the problems different in question **3**.

ASSESSMENT CHECKPOINT Assess children's strategies for problem solving. Can children link totals or change to the correct mathematical calculations? Do children understand why partitioning into pounds and pence makes it easier to add? Can children recombine the pounds and pence?

ANSWERS

Question **1** a): The total cost is £4·95.

Question **1** b): The total cost is £4·15.

Question **2**: Zac will receive £7·65 change.

Question **3**: For example: Both questions are discussing change. The first question is a straight-forward calculation (£5 – £2·68 = ___), but the second is a missing number calculation (£5 – ___ = £3·46).

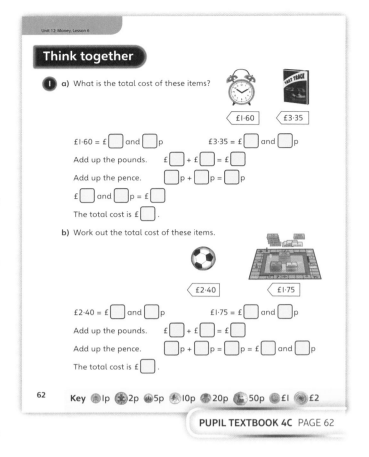

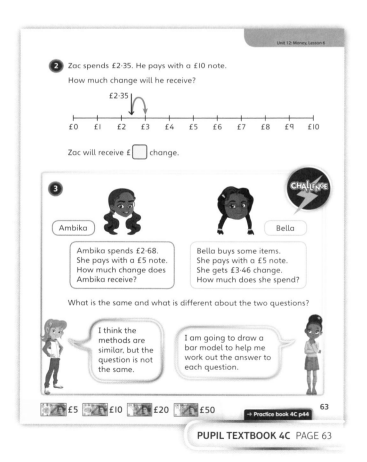

Practice

IN FOCUS In question **1**, children partition pounds and pence to find totals. Ensure children understand that question **1** c) requires them to partition the amounts found in questions **1** a) and **1** b) again and work out the total.

STRENGTHEN Provide plastic coins to pile up in pounds and pence to help children to partition and add together. Having the coins may allow children to spot any bonds to 100 and exchange coins for £1 coins. As well, blank number lines will help with addition and subtraction.

DEEPEN Deepen understanding by changing the information in question **6** slightly – Lexi could have a different amount of money, she may wish to buy more than one of each item, the change cannot contain any £1 coins, and so on. Challenge children to explore how this affects their current answer.

ASSESSMENT CHECKPOINT Ensure children can use appropriate methods to find totals and change. Children should now be confident partitioning and recombining amounts into pounds and pence in multi-step problems.

ANSWERS Answers for the **Practice** part of the lesson appear in the separate **Practice and Reflect answer guide**.

Reflect

IN FOCUS In this question, the information is not given in the order that children will need to use it. Children should demonstrate their understanding of adding amounts to find totals and work out change.

ASSESSMENT CHECKPOINT This question requires children to use different methods within one problem and will therefore show how secure they are with each individual method. Do children know which numbers need to be used in which calculation? Do children know what order the calculations need to be done in?

ANSWERS Answers for the **Reflect** part of the lesson appear in the separate **Practice and Reflect answer guide**.

After the lesson ⏸

- Can children find the total of coins and prices by partitioning into pounds and pence?
- Can the children decide on suitable jumps on a number line to count up or work out change?
- Can children move between methods within one problem or question?

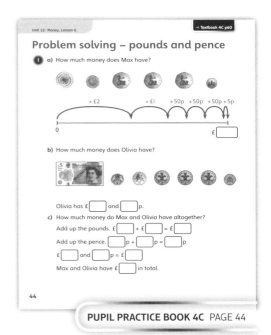

PUPIL PRACTICE BOOK 4C PAGE 44

PUPIL PRACTICE BOOK 4C PAGE 45

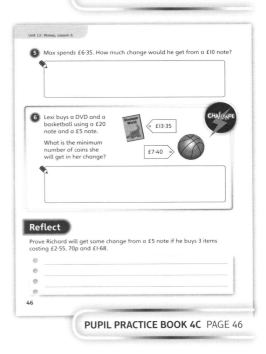

PUPIL PRACTICE BOOK 4C PAGE 46

Problem solving – multiplication and division

Learning focus

In this lesson, children will solve money problems with multiplication and division using the part-whole model.

Small steps

→ Previous step: Problem solving – pounds and pence
→ **This step: Problem solving – multiplication and division**
→ Next step: Solving two-step problems

NATIONAL CURRICULUM LINKS

Year 4 Measurement – Money
• Estimate, compare and calculate different measures, including money in pounds and pence.
• Solve simple measure and money problems involving fractions and decimals to two decimal places.

ASSESSING MASTERY

Children can multiply and divide amounts of money and prices by partitioning numbers using the part-whole model. Children can see how some methods are more suited to certain calculations or problems and can identify key language and structure of problems in order to create suitable pictorial representations and calculations.

COMMON MISCONCEPTIONS

To help children with partitioning, encourage the use of plastic coins to split amounts up into pounds and pence. Ask:
• *Where will you put the pounds? Where will you put the pence?*

STRENGTHENING UNDERSTANDING

Using plastic coins or pictorial representations alongside abstract calculations will help children understand what is happening when multiplying and dividing. It will allow them to spot patterns and trends they can use and apply in the future. Place value counters or base 10 equipment can also help children split numbers into parts that are easier to divide. Getting children to write out multiplication tables may also help them spot facts they can use and therefore split numbers accordingly.

GOING DEEPER

To give children a deeper understanding of multiplication and division with money, ask children to explore the use and benefits of different methods. This will encourage children to be flexible with their working and enable them to better understand which methods to choose and when and why to choose them.

KEY LANGUAGE

In lesson: divide, multiply, each, per item, pounds (£1), pence (p)

Other language to be used by the teacher: total, amount, price, more, each, partition, parts, whole

STRUCTURES AND REPRESENTATIONS

part-whole models, number lines, bar models

RESOURCES

Optional: plastic coins

 In the eTextbook of this lesson, you will find interactive links to a selection of teaching tools.

Before you teach

• Do children recognise and understand language related to multiplication and division?
• Do children have an understanding of what happens to a number when they multiply and divide?
• Do children currently have any methods for multiplication and division?

Discover

WAYS OF WORKING Pair work

ASK

- Question ❶ a): *Is there a bag containing 57 party poppers? How do you know how many bags would be needed for 57 party poppers? What calculation will tell you how much three bags cost?*
- Question ❶ b): *What calculation would you need to do to find the cost of one bouncy ball? How could you check the answer for one bouncy ball?*

IN FOCUS For question ❶ a), children could complete all steps with repeated addition or with multiplication. Discuss the different methods with children and which one they think is a suitable way to find the answer. Question ❶ b) requires children to divide. Watching how children divide £1·26 by 3 will highlight their current understanding and methods they are comfortable with.

PRACTICAL TIPS Provide children with items from **Discover**, matching price tags and a variety of plastic notes and coins for children to make amounts and practically multiply, share or group.

ANSWERS

Question ❶ a): Amal needs to buy 3 bags of party poppers. The total cost of 3 bags of party poppers is £7·50.

Question ❶ b): £1·26 (126p) ÷ 3 = £0·42 (42p) One bouncy ball costs 42p.

PUPIL TEXTBOOK 4C PAGE 64

Share

WAYS OF WORKING Whole class teacher led

ASK

- Question ❶ a): *How does the example work out the number of bags needed? Now you know how many bags you need, how will you work out the cost? How can you use the cost of one bag to work out the total cost?*
- Question ❶ b): *What do you need to do to find the price of one bouncy ball? What methods did you use to divide? How did converting the amount into pence help with the part-whole method? Why has 126 been split into 120 and 6?*

IN FOCUS For question ❶ a), discuss counting in 20s to work out the amount of bags needed, referring children to the number line. Introduce children to the part-whole method for multiplication. To solve question ❶ b), encourage children to feedback their ideas and the methods for finding the cost of one bouncy ball. Using the part-whole model for division, explain why the number has been split up in the way it has.

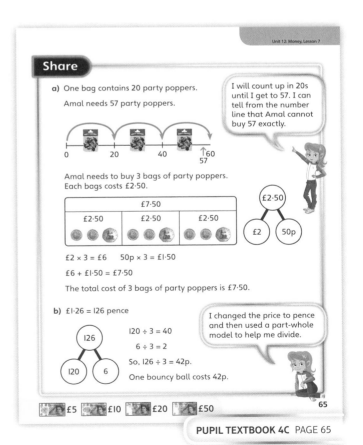

PUPIL TEXTBOOK 4C PAGE 65

Think together

WAYS OF WORKING Whole class teacher led (I do, We do, You do)

ASK

- Question **1** a): *What calculation do you need to get the price of 6 bags of yo-yos? What is £4·12 made up of?*
- Question **1** b): *What will you need to do to find the answer? Why can't this amount be split into pounds and pence and each part multiplied? What method is more appropriate?*
- Question **2**: *How is this different from question **1** b)? What do you need to do with £4·55 to find the cost of one puzzle? What methods do you know for division?*
- Question **3**: *What do you notice about the number of pounds for the number of packets of rice? What does this tell you roughly about each packet?*

IN FOCUS Question **1** b) alerts children to the fact that the part-whole method is not always suitable. Discuss why 4 × 97p does not lend itself to partitioning into pounds and pence. Question **3** a) encourages children to make links and reason about the cost and number of items without completing a calculation. For question **3** b), ask children why they created their calculations.

STRENGTHEN In questions **1** a) and **2**, encourage children to make amounts in the part-whole model with coins and find answers using repeated addition or long multiplication. Strengthen understanding of question **3** a) by encouraging children to make the total for the rice, decide how coins could be shared and then consider what the coins left over suggest about the price of each pack.

DEEPEN Deepen understanding of question **1** b) by asking children to explore different methods for multiplying by 4 such as double and double again. Extend question **3** a) by encouraging children to use the given information to make statements about other amounts and prices using the sentence starter 'If I know …'.

ASSESSMENT CHECKPOINT Assess whether children are confident multiplying and dividing pounds and pence. They should be able to recognise when a question requires a multiplication and when a question requires a division, and be able to use the most efficient method for each one.

ANSWERS

Question **1** a): 6 bags of yo-yos cost £24·72.

Question **1** b): 4 packs of pencils cost £3·88.

Question **2**: Each jigsaw puzzle costs 91p.

Question **3** a): There are 5 packets of rice and the total is over £6, so each packet will cost more than £1 because the pounds could be shared and there would still be £1 leftover, plus the 30p.

Question **3** b): 1 tin of beans costs 37p.
1 bread roll costs 42p.
1 packet of rice costs £1·26.

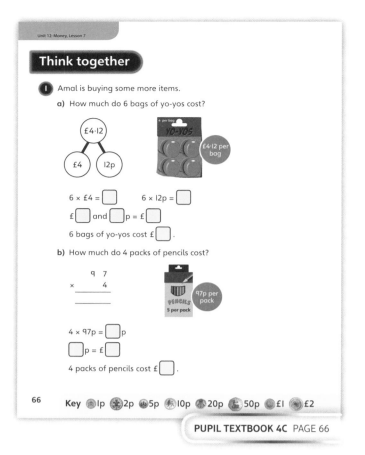

PUPIL TEXTBOOK 4C PAGE 66

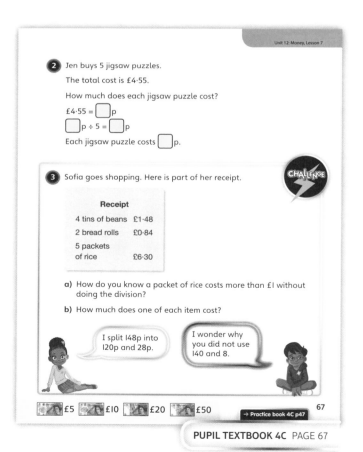

PUPIL TEXTBOOK 4C PAGE 67

Practice

WAYS OF WORKING Independent thinking

IN FOCUS For question **5**, encourage children to use the part-whole method but they may need some support splitting the number effectively. Question **7** encompasses multiplication and division so ensure children read the problem carefully in order to identify which information relates to which calculation.

STRENGTHEN As question **7** is a multi-step problem with two different types of calculation, children may find it useful to highlight or colour code related information. Children may also benefit from using bar models to set the information out clearly.

DEEPEN Encourage children to create word problems for calculations or conclude why certain methods were chosen for each type of multiplication. For question **4**, ask children to suggest reasons why 172 has been split into 160 and 12, or find alternative ways to split 172. Deepen understanding of question **7** by changing the information in the problem and asking children to solve it again. Double the amount of burgers needed, create a half-price sale on the bread buns, and so on.

THINK DIFFERENTLY Question **6** is a division question set out as a fraction. Children will need to use their knowledge of solving fractions or make the connection to division and continue with methods practised within this lesson.

ASSESSMENT CHECKPOINT Do children recognise problems that require them to multiply and problems that require them to divide? Can children partition prices into pounds and pence? Do children recognise the link between fractions and methods for division?

ANSWERS Answers for the **Practice** part of the lesson appear in the separate **Practice and Reflect answer guide**.

Reflect

WAYS OF WORKING Independent thinking

IN FOCUS Children here must establish what the question is asking them to do and in what order the calculations must be done. Encourage children to make the numbers or calculations as efficient as possible (making the amount £8 then subtracting 8p, double the amount three times, etc.). Ensure there is enough time given to compare methods.

ASSESSMENT CHECKPOINT Assess whether children can identify what sort of calculation is required and if they can use the information given in the correct way. Do children have any strategies to make the numbers or calculations easier to work with? Can children discuss their method and explain the choices they made?

ANSWERS Answers for the **Reflect** part of the lesson appear in the separate **Practice and Reflect answer guide**.

After the lesson ⏸

- Do children have methods for multiplying and dividing money?
- Can children identify and work through a series of steps in multi-step problems?
- Can children recognise why one method might be better than another for a specific calculation?

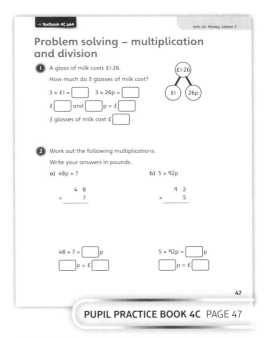

PUPIL PRACTICE BOOK 4C PAGE 47

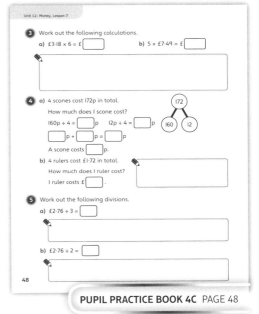

PUPIL PRACTICE BOOK 4C PAGE 48

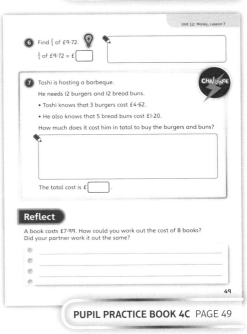

PUPIL PRACTICE BOOK 4C PAGE 49

Solving two-step problems

Learning focus

In this lesson, children will use their knowledge of money to solve problems. They will use different strategies to solve two-step word problems.

Small steps

→ Previous step: Problem solving – multiplication and division
→ **This step: Solving two-step problems**
→ Next step: Problem solving – money

NATIONAL CURRICULUM LINKS

Year 4 Measurement – Money
- Estimate, compare and calculate different measures, including money in pounds and pence.
- Solve simple measure and money problems involving fractions and decimals to two decimal places.

ASSESSING MASTERY

Children can use their knowledge of the four operations to apply strategies and methods to two-step problems. They recognise key information, problem structure and visual representations, and can link them to the correct operation. Children can apply previously learnt methods and break down two-step problems into smaller, manageable steps.

COMMON MISCONCEPTIONS

Children may not complete all steps of the problem and so get an incorrect answer. Ask:
- *Look back at the problem. Have you completed every step?*

STRENGTHENING UNDERSTANDING

Bar models are extremely beneficial when solving problems. Setting information out in a bar model helps children to make links and recognise the operations required. Ensuring plastic coins are available for children to use will also strengthen understanding. Using money alongside abstract calculations helps children to understand what is happening in each step.

GOING DEEPER

Children can really explore the concept of being flexible with their working in this lesson. Children have been exposed to a range of methods and they can apply these accordingly within the problems they are presented with. Having time to explore the idea of flexibility will allow children to come up with some 'rules' about when to use certain methods.

KEY LANGUAGE

In lesson: method, multiply, divide, add

Other language to be used by the teacher: problem, key information, structure, calculation, subtraction, find the difference, steps, bar model

STRUCTURES AND REPRESENTATIONS

bar models

RESOURCES

Optional: plastic coins

 In the eTextbook of this lesson, you will find interactive links to a selection of teaching tools.

Before you teach

- Can children find the difference between prices and work out change?
- Can children multiply and divide coins, prices and amounts?
- Can children solve two-step problems involving money?

Discover

WAYS OF WORKING Pair work

ASK

- Question ① a): *How can you work out the cost of 5 apples? How can you work out the cost of 5 oranges? What do you need to do with the totals to work out an overall price for the apples and oranges? How do you record this amount?*
- Question ① b): *Was your method quick and efficient? Would Holly be able to use your method for every sale? What other methods could have been used? Which methods are the quickest? Which methods are the most efficient?*

IN FOCUS Question ① b) gives children the opportunity to explore different possible methods. Encourage children to share the steps and methods they used and discuss the advantages and disadvantages of each method. Ask children whether these methods would be quick and efficient for Holly, a busy greengrocer, to use all day.

PRACTICAL TIPS Recreate **Discover** by displaying the fruit and vegetables with prices tags and giving children access to plastic coins.

ANSWERS

Question ① a): The total cost of 5 apples and 5 oranges is £2·50.

Question ① b): Holly quickly worked out the total by adding the cost of 1 apple and 1 orange together, then multiplying by 5.

PUPIL TEXTBOOK 4C PAGE 68

Share

WAYS OF WORKING Whole class teacher led

ASK

- Question ① a): *What do you need to do to work out the price of 5 apples, then 5 oranges? How could you make the numbers easier to multiply? How can you partition 26 and 24? Can you use any answers from the previous calculations? How can you make these numbers easier to add?*
- Question ① b): *What method did you use? Did anybody use a different method? Which method was quicker? Could the method Holly uses depend on what the prices are?*

IN FOCUS For question ① a), discuss the information children currently have and what the question requires them to do with it. Children should identify the different stages they need to work through and the best starting point. Show children the calculations in a bar model, with plastic coins alongside to aid their understanding. Record each multiplication step alongside the bar model or plastic coins and remind children about the importance of recombining the pounds and pence. Emphasise the importance of adding the two prices together as a final step.

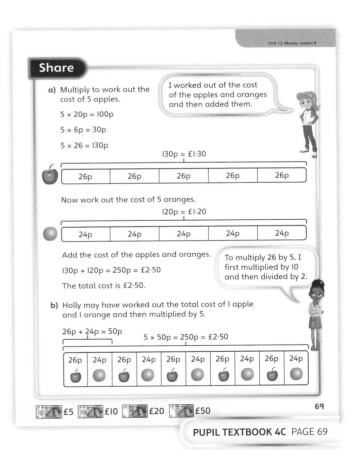

PUPIL TEXTBOOK 4C PAGE 69

Think together

Whole class teacher led (I do, We do, You do)

ASK

- Question **1**: *Do you know the individual price of anything? How could you work out the cost of the 2 bananas? If you know the cost of 2 bananas, can you work out the cost of 1 banana?*
- Question **2**: *What do you know the prices of? How can you work out the prices of types or pieces of fruit? How can you use the price of a mango to find the price of a pineapple?*
- Question **3**: *How does Luis know 1 mango and 1 pear costs 60p? Is he correct? Whose method has Luis used? Why has he multiplied by 5? Does this method work if there is an unequal amount of each item?*

IN FOCUS In question **2**, encourage children to think back to earlier lessons and use an appropriate method (counting up) for finding the difference, rather than just subtracting one amount from the other. Question **3** gives children the opportunity to see possible misconceptions and mistakes that could be made when using this method.

STRENGTHEN For question **1**, encourage children to look carefully at the bar model in order to visualise the problem. For questions **1** to **3**, creating the amounts with coins and putting them alongside the fruit may help children see the difference. Pairing the fruit up should allow children to see that multiplying by 5 does not work as there are not 5 pieces of each fruit.

DEEPEN Deepen understanding of question **1** by encouraging children to use the bar model to work out the cost of other items, such as 3 apples and 2 bananas, double the amount of apples, and so on. As well, once children have spotted Luis's mistake in question **3**, encourage them to explore ways to make that method fit the calculation given, such as adding 1 mango and 1 pear, then multiplying by 4, then adding on 2 extra mangos.

ASSESSMENT CHECKPOINT Can children use information in a problem to decide on the steps needed to solve that problem and the correct numbers to use in the calculations they create?

ANSWERS

Question **1**: A banana costs 34p.

Question **2**: A pineapple costs £1 and 19p.

Question **3** a): Luis cannot add one of each item together and multiply by 5, because there are not 5 pieces of each fruit. The price Luis has worked out is the cost for 5 mangoes and 5 pears, rather than 6 mangoes and 4 pears.

Question **3** b): The correct answer is £3·04. Luis will need to multiply 32p × 6 for the mangoes, then multiply 28p × 4 for the pears. He should then add the two prices together.

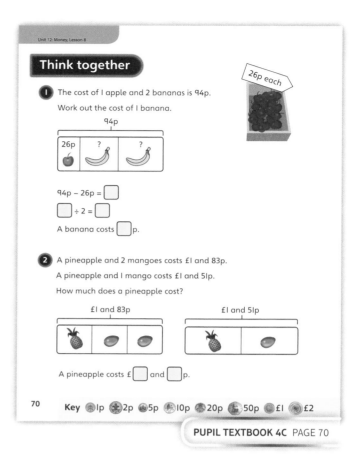

PUPIL TEXTBOOK 4C PAGE 70

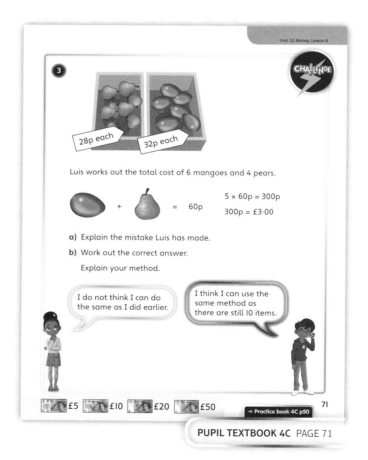

PUPIL TEXTBOOK 4C PAGE 71

Practice

WAYS OF WORKING Independent thinking

IN FOCUS Question **5** requires children to multiply and divide. The problem is less structured so children will need to link the relevant numbers to the correct operation and work out what numbers they need to work with and when.

STRENGTHEN Using plastic coins for questions **1** to **4** will give children a visual representation of what is happening at each step of the calculations. Using the coins will also highlight the similarities between the methods. For questions **2** and **4**, children may benefit from drawing and making a bar model. Children should look back at the steps in question **1** to check they are working through the method correctly. For question **3**, to find out whether Lexi has enough money, children could use a number line, hundredths grid or place value chart to compare the total with the money Lexi has.

DEEPEN After solving question **2**, encourage children to use the information given to work out different combinations of items. Similarly, in question **3**, challenge children to find a variety of combinations Lexi could buy with her £2. Children could also work out any change and the coins given for the change.

ASSESSMENT CHECKPOINT Assess whether children can complete the same calculation using different methods. Can children discuss and explain why they prefer one method over another?

ANSWERS Answers for the **Practice** part of the lesson appear in the separate **Practice and Reflect answer guide**.

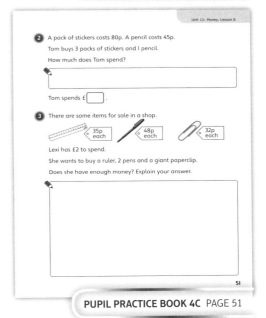

PUPIL PRACTICE BOOK 4C PAGE 50

PUPIL PRACTICE BOOK 4C PAGE 51

Reflect

WAYS OF WORKING Independent thinking

IN FOCUS This **Reflect** allows children to self-assess their learning journey within this lesson. Children can identify strengths and weakness and possibly set themselves targets.

ASSESSMENT CHECKPOINT Children's answers to this section will further help you decide whether to add extra support. Can children reflect on the strategies and methods they have learnt and practised? Can children identify areas for development and articulate what they found difficult?

ANSWERS Answers for the **Reflect** part of the lesson appear in the separate **Practice and Reflect answer guide**.

After the lesson ⏸

- Can children use key vocabulary and visual representations to recognise when to use specific calculations?
- Can children break a problem down into small steps?
- Can children use multiple methods within one problem?

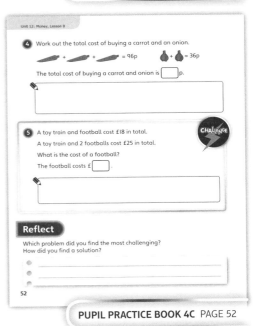

PUPIL PRACTICE BOOK 4C PAGE 52

Problem solving – money

Learning focus

In this lesson, children will use previously learnt strategies and methods to solve multi-step problems.

Small steps

→ Previous step: Solving two-step problems
→ **This step: Problem solving – money**
→ Next step: Units of time (1)

NATIONAL CURRICULUM LINKS

Year 4 Measurement – Money
• Estimate, compare and calculate different measures, including money in pounds and pence.
• Solve simple measure and money problems involving fractions and decimals to two decimal places.

ASSESSING MASTERY

Children can identify small steps within a larger problem, picking out key information or using the structure of the problem to work out what mathematical calculation is needed. Children can use previously learnt methods and strategies to find answers and use their working out to agree or disagree with statements.

COMMON MISCONCEPTIONS

Multi-step problems can cause confusion. Encourage children to mark up or highlight key information in the problem. Ask:
• *What information do you have? What information do you need to find the answer? How can you find this information?*

STRENGTHENING UNDERSTANDING

Using a range of bar models, part-whole models and number lines helps children visualise the amounts, make links and recognise the operations required. Using plastic coins to represent money and items or pictures to represent items will help strengthen understanding. Used against abstract calculations, coins and items help children to understand what is happening in each step.

GOING DEEPER

Children can explore a range of methods and structures in this lesson, allowing them to develop more flexibility with their working and apply the methods they feel are most suitable for each problem they are presented with. Building on the amount of flexibility enables children to independently develop their own 'rules' about when to use certain methods.

KEY LANGUAGE

In lesson: multiply, divide, explain, add, greater than (>)

Other language to be used by the teacher: problem, small steps, parts, key information, structure, calculate, subtract, find the difference, prove, less than (<)

STRUCTURES AND REPRESENTATIONS

bar models, part-whole models, number lines

RESOURCES

Optional: plastic coins

 In the eTextbook of this lesson, you will find interactive links to a selection of teaching tools.

Before you teach

• Can children solve addition, subtraction, multiplication and division calculations related to money?
• Can children move between methods?
• Can children break problems down into manageable steps?

Discover

WAYS OF WORKING   Pair work

ASK

- Question **1** a): *What does cheapest mean? What prices do you know? How can you work out the cost of 3 single buns?*
- Question **1** b): *What does 'best deal' mean? How else could Max buy 6 buns? How can you work out the cost of two packs of 3? How can you work out the cost of 6 individual buns?*

IN FOCUS   Question **1** a): requires children to multiply prices then compare amounts. Which option children choose for Kate to buy will highlight their understanding of the word 'cheapest' and what an amount is worth. In question **1** b) children need to find the three possibilities for purchasing 6 buns, multiply the relevant prices and compare them to decide whether Max could have paid less for the same items.

PRACTICAL TIPS   Display the food items to re-enact the stall in the **Discover** image. Have plastic coins available for children to use.

ANSWERS

Question **1** a): It is cheaper for Kate to buy the pack of 3 buns.

Question **1** b): Buying two packs of 3 buns is the best deal.

Problem solving – money

Discover

1 a) Kate wants to buy 3 buns at the cheapest price.

Should she buy a pack of buns for £1·50 or 3 single buns for 65p each?

b) Max buys one pack of 6 buns for £3·50.

Is this the best deal?

72   Key ●1p ✳2p ●5p ✱10p ●20p ●50p ●£1 ●£2

PUPIL TEXTBOOK 4C PAGE 72

Share

WAYS OF WORKING   Whole class teacher led

ASK

- Question **1** a): *How can you make 65 easier to multiply? How could you partition 65? What do you need to do with your partitioned answers? What do you need to do with the prices for a 3-pack and 3 single buns?*
- Question **1** b): *How will you know if Max got the best deal? Was there a cheaper option? Was the pack of 6 the most expensive?*

IN FOCUS   For question **1** b), discuss what 'best deal' means and ask children to give ideas of other ways Max could buy 6 buns. Children should identify what sort of a calculation this would be and offer their methods. For Max's other option, show children 2 packs of buns and discuss the easiest way to find the cost. Once the class has the cost of all 3 options, discuss whether buying the 6-pack was the best deal.

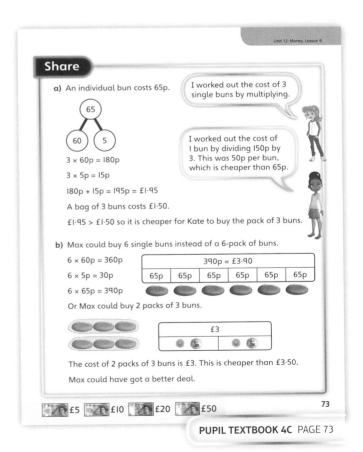

Share

a) An individual bun costs 65p.

> I worked out the cost of 3 single buns by multiplying.

> I worked out the cost of 1 bun by dividing 150p by 3. This was 50p per bun, which is cheaper than 65p.

3 × 60p = 180p
3 × 5p = 15p
180p + 15p = 195p = £1·95
A bag of 3 buns costs £1·50.
£1·95 > £1·50 so it is cheaper for Kate to buy the pack of 3 buns.

b) Max could buy 6 single buns instead of a 6-pack of buns.

6 × 60p = 360p
6 × 5p = 30p
6 × 65p = 390p

390p = £3·90

| 65p | 65p | 65p | 65p | 65p | 65p |

Or Max could buy 2 packs of 3 buns.

£3

The cost of 2 packs of 3 buns is £3. This is cheaper than £3·50.

Max could have got a better deal.

£5 £10 £20 £50   73

PUPIL TEXTBOOK 4C PAGE 73

Think together

WAYS OF WORKING Whole class teacher led (I do, We do, You do)

ASK

- Question **1**: *What method will you use to work out the price of three goes? What multiplication facts can you use to help you work out 3 × 60? What else do you need to work out to answer the question?*
- Question **2**: *What is the first thing you need to work out? What calculation will help you work out how much Bella spent? What is the second part of the problem asking you to solve?*
- Question **3**: *How can you compare 4 cookies and 6 cookies? How could you work out the cost of 1 cookie from each bag? What can you see about the prices of the single cookies? Does this mean that Lee is correct or incorrect?*

IN FOCUS For question **1**, encourage children to identify the two parts to the problem – finding the total Kate spent, then the change she would receive. To answer question **2** a), children must use a 'find the difference' method. To solve question **2** b), children need to use the answer to **2** a) and divide it by 10.

STRENGTHEN When using the number line in question **1**, some children may find it easier to record the coins in the jumps as well as the number. For question **2** a), encourage children to use plastic coins to make £6·60 and then investigate what other coins they need to reach £10. For question **2** b), encourage children to set the information out in a bar model as it will make the need to divide more obvious. To aid children in recognising the division element of question **3**, encourage children to show the information in a bar model.

DEEPEN Once children have worked out Kate's change in question **1**, encourage them to calculate how many more goes on hook-a-duck Kate could afford. In question **2**, challenge children to use the information they have worked out to reason about other amounts. For example, 'If 10 tickets cost £3·40, I know that 5 tickets would cost £1·70' or 'If I know 1 ticket costs 34p and 10 tickets cost £3·40, I know that 11 tickets would cost £3·74'.

ASSESSMENT CHECKPOINT Assess whether children recognise each step in a multi-step problem. Can children link information to the correct operation? Can children use appropriate methods and strategies to find answers?

ANSWERS

Question **1**: Kate receives £2·93 change from £5.

Question **2** a): Bella spent £3·40 on 10 raffle tickets.

Question **2** b): £3·40 ÷ 10 = 34p. Each raffle ticket costs 34p.

Question **3**: Lee is incorrect.
£2·40 ÷ 4 = 60p
£3·36 ÷ 6 = 56p
The price per cookie in the bag of 6 is cheaper than in the bag of 4.

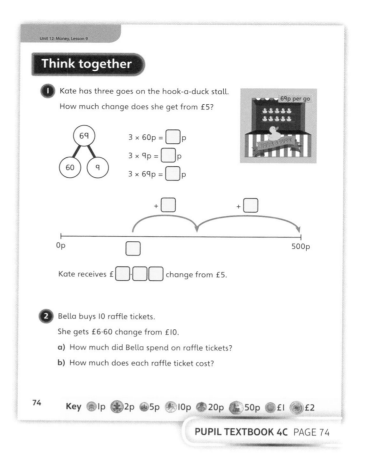

PUPIL TEXTBOOK 4C PAGE 74

PUPIL TEXTBOOK 4C PAGE 75

Practice

WAYS OF WORKING Independent thinking

IN FOCUS Question ❶ requires children to multiply an amount, then find the change using a 'find the difference' method. For question ❷ a), children need find the difference to work out how much Max spent. Questions ❸ and ❹ require children to solve calculations with multiplication and division, then compare their answers to find the cheapest options.

STRENGTHEN For questions ❶ and ❷, using plastic coins and creating bar models will show children the amounts and required calculations more clearly. For questions ❸ and ❹, prompt children to work out both calculations before making any claims. A bar model will highlight the division element of question ❻.

DEEPEN Before finding the exact answer to question ❺, challenge children to create a list of solutions that would not be possible and give reasons why.

THINK DIFFERENTLY Question ❺ assesses children's understanding of place value and ability to add.

ASSESSMENT CHECKPOINT Assess whether children can identify what operations are necessary and break a problem up into more manageable steps. Can children use answers from previous questions or earlier parts of the problem to find answers? Can children prove or disprove theories using information they have worked out?

ANSWERS Answers for the **Practice** part of the lesson appear in the separate **Practice and Reflect answer guide**.

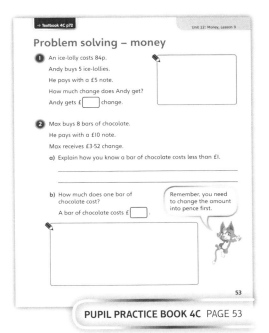

→ Textbook 4C p72

Problem solving – money

❶ An ice-lolly costs 84p.
Andy buys 5 ice-lollies.
He pays with a £5 note.
How much change does Andy get?
Andy gets £ ☐ change.

❷ Max buys 8 bars of chocolate.
He pays with a £10 note.
Max receives £3·52 change.

a) Explain how you know a bar of chocolate costs less than £1.

b) How much does one bar of chocolate cost?
A bar of chocolate costs £ ☐ .

Remember, you need to change the amount into pence first.

53

PUPIL PRACTICE BOOK 4C PAGE 53

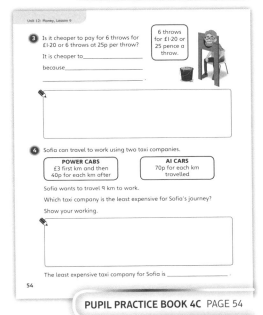

Unit 12: Money, Lesson 9

❸ Is it cheaper to pay for 6 throws for £1·20 or 6 throws at 25p per throw?

6 throws for £1·20 or 25 pence a throw.

It is cheaper to _____
because _____ .

❹ Sofia can travel to work using two taxi companies.

POWER CABS	AI CARS
£3 first km and then 40p for each km after	70p for each km travelled

Sofia wants to travel 9 km to work.
Which taxi company is the least expensive for Sofia's journey?
Show your working.

The least expensive taxi company for Sofia is _____ .

54

PUPIL PRACTICE BOOK 4C PAGE 54

Reflect

WAYS OF WORKING Independent thinking

IN FOCUS This question is open-ended and children can give a wide range of answers as long as they can explain their reasons and back up their thinking. Children need to realise that for a pack to be cheaper, they need to charge less than 55p × 4.

ASSESSMENT CHECKPOINT The question will highlight children's understanding of comparative language. Do children understand that cheaper means a lower price? Can children work out the cost of 4 single bread rolls by multiplying? Can children clearly explain why they have chosen a lower price than the answer they calculated?

ANSWERS Answers for the **Reflect** part of the lesson appear in the separate **Practice and Reflect answer guide**.

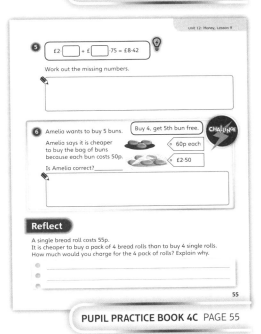

Unit 12: Money, Lesson 9

❺ £2· ☐ + £ ☐ ·75 = £8·42

Work out the missing numbers.

❻ Amelia wants to buy 5 buns.
Amelia says it is cheaper to buy the bag of buns because each bun costs 50p.

Buy 4, get 5th bun free.
60p each
£2·50
CHALLENGE

Is Amelia correct? _____

Reflect

A single bread roll costs 55p.
It is cheaper to buy a pack of 4 bread rolls than to buy 4 single rolls.
How much would you charge for the 4 pack of rolls? Explain why.

55

PUPIL PRACTICE BOOK 4C PAGE 55

After the lesson

- Can children break a problem up into small steps?
- Can children use their information to reason?
- Can children explain and use working out to agree or disagree with theories?

End of unit check

> Don't forget the *Power Maths* unit assessment grid on p26.

PUPIL TEXTBOOK 4C PAGE 76

WAYS OF WORKING Group work adult led

IN FOCUS

- Question **1** assesses whether children can find how much money is shown. Encourage children to count in pounds and pence separately. Children should give their answer in terms of £s. In question **2**, children are asked to write an amount that is less than £1 in £s to check their understanding of what is one of the most difficult concepts in this unit.
- In question **4**, children are given the amount of change and asked to work out a cost. Show children that working out the change if they are given the amount something costs is the same as working out the amount something costs if they are given the amount of change. This can be shown by counting on using a number line or bar model.
- In the SATS-style questions, children use their knowledge of multiplication and division to solve problems. In question **8**, children first need to find the cost of the pear by noticing that on the top line there is an extra pear. They can then use the cost of the pear to work out the cost of the apple.

ANSWERS AND COMMENTARY

Children who have mastered the concepts in this unit will be able to record money using the £·p notation, understand that a decimal point separates pounds and pence and will know how to convert between pounds and pence. They will be able to round amounts to the nearest 10p and £1 to help them estimate totals, they will be able to compare amounts of money and to order them to work out the cheapest and most expensive items and they will be able to solve multi-step money problems.

PUPIL TEXTBOOK 4C PAGE 77

Q	A	WRONG ANSWERS AND MISCONCEPTIONS	STRENGTHENING UNDERSTANDING
1	D	A suggests children have just counted the number of coins. C suggests children think that the £2 is the same as £1.	Encourage children to use coins and notes to help them count out the amounts. A number line can be used to help children find the total of some coins and notes given. Children should be told to start with the greatest notes or coins first.
2	D	A suggests children have just put £s in front. C suggests children have not written the correct notation.	
3	A	D suggests children think that £12·50 is less than £12·43, because 43 is greater than 5.	
4	A	C suggests children have added £2 to make £5, then added 85p and so make £6 in total.	For adding and subtracting amounts of money, children may use coins and place value equipment alongside the abstract calculation. Encourage children to convert amounts to pence before adding and then convert back to pounds at the end.
5	D	Children may think that £8·50 rounds to £8 to the nearest £1.	
6	B	C suggests children forgot to use the decimal point.	
7	£3·47	Children may forget that they then need to subtract 17 × 9 from £5 to find the change.	
8	35p	Children may divide the price by the number of fruit without considering the pear and apples cost different amounts.	

My journal

WAYS OF WORKING Independent thinking

ANSWERS AND COMMENTARY The answer is £2·06. This activity asks children to add two amounts of money. The question raises the issues that children cannot add together decimals at this moment. Children should be confident with changing these amounts to pence and then using column addition or other methods to add two 3-digit numbers. Once children have added the amounts, remind them about the final step. It is important children convert their final answer to pounds. Some children may want to explore the method of adding the pounds first and then adding the pence.

Power check

WAYS OF WORKING Independent thinking

ASK

- *Do you feel confident finding how much money is shown in notes and coins?*
- *Can you write amounts of money in pounds using £·p?*
- *Can you confidently round amounts of money to the nearest 10p and £1 and understand when it might be useful to do this?*
- *Do you feel confident when adding and subtracting amounts of money?*
- *Can you find change by counting on or subtracting?*

Power puzzle

WAYS OF WORKING Independent thinking

IN FOCUS This final activity brings together children's work on problem solving with their knowledge of money. Encourage children to extract the relevant information. For the first problem, children have been given a bar model. Ask children to explain why the bar model represents the situation. *What do you know the total is? How many parts do you have altogether? What do you know about each part? How can you find the value of each part?*

For each of the subsequent problems, encourage children to draw similar bar models to help them determine the steps they need to take to solve the problem. The problems get increasingly more complicated.

ANSWERS AND COMMENTARY

1 : A toaster costs £24. A kettle costs £48.

2 : The radio costs £85.

3 : A pair of speakers costs £51.
A pair of headphones costs £17.
A camera costs £87.

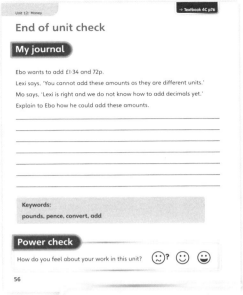

PUPIL PRACTICE BOOK 4C PAGE 56

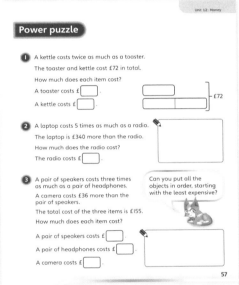

PUPIL PRACTICE BOOK 4C PAGE 57

After the unit ⏸

- Can children convert between pounds and pence?
- Can children round money to the nearest 10p and £1?
- Can children compare and order amounts of money?

Strengthen and **Deepen** activities for this unit can be found in the *Power Maths* online subscription.

Unit 13
Time

Don't forget to watch the Unit 13 video!

Mastery Expert tip! "I found that this unit was a great opportunity to introduce several clocks into the classroom – a 12-hour and a 24-hour digital clock as well as the existing analogue clock on the wall. Seeing the time represented in these different ways throughout the school day helped children to build natural connections between them."

WHY THIS UNIT IS IMPORTANT

This unit will develop children's ability to convert between units of time. Children will apply their knowledge of existing facts (for example, the number of minutes in an hour) when expressing a period of time using a different unit of measurement. Children will also be introduced to the concept of the 24-hour clock, learning to state the time as both a 12- and 24-hour clock time. Children will solve problems using these new concepts and prior learning, including word problems.

WHERE THIS UNIT FITS

→ Unit 12: Money
→ **Unit 13: Time**
→ Unit 14: Statistics

This unit builds on the concepts of time learned in Year 3 Unit 11, particularly when telling time to the minute. Children will link their prior knowledge of facts to bar models that will help them convert between units.

Before they start this unit, it is expected that children:
• can read and write times to the nearest minute
• know the number of seconds in a minute, minutes in an hour and hours in a day
• understand how to express 12-hour times digitally, including using the terms am and pm.

ASSESSING MASTERY

Children who have mastered this unit will be able to convert between seconds and minutes, and between minutes and hours. They will also be able to convert between longer periods of time expressed in days, weeks, months and years. They will confidently use these different units of measurement in their description of times. They will be able to express times in both analogue and digital forms, including 24-hour clock times. Children will apply these elements to confidently solve mathematical problems.

COMMON MISCONCEPTIONS	STRENGTHENING UNDERSTANDING	GOING DEEPER
Children may consider only the numerical value of periods of time without understanding the significance of their units (for example: 1 week and 4 days equals 1 + 4 = 5 days).	Display calendars and year planners in the classroom. Ask questions relating a week on the calendar to the number of days or the year on the year planner to the number of months.	Challenge children to make up problems using the calendar and/or the year planner. Encourage them to use as many different units of time as they can.
Children may confuse the numbers on a digital time with those on an analogue clock face, thinking that 04:11 will have the hands pointing to the numbers 4 and 11.	Label five-minute intervals around a clock face to show the number of minutes in digital form (:00, :05, :10 and so on). Display three different types of clocks (analogue, 12-hour digital and 24-hour digital). Refer to the three clocks over the course of daily routines in order to build connections between these different ways of representing the time.	Challenge children to express times in different ways throughout the day. For example, only one of the three clocks could be shown and children asked to give the time as it would be shown on the other clocks.

Unit 13: Time

WAYS OF WORKING

Use these pages to introduce the unit focus to children. Use the characters to discuss concepts and phrases that children have not heard before.

STRUCTURES AND REPRESENTATIONS

Analogue clock and digital clock: Pictures of clock faces (both analogue and digital) are used regularly to represent times. They are used to demonstrate times as well as forming the basis of problems to solve. Children will be encouraged to use these representations themselves, completing them to represent different times.

Bar model: This model will help children to represent the equivalence between different units of time. The upper bar can be split into one unit and the lower bar used to show the equivalent parts expressed in another unit. Children can then see the calculation that they need to do to convert one unit into another.

1 minute	1 minute	1 minute
60 seconds	60 seconds	60 seconds

KEY LANGUAGE

There is some key language that children will need to know as part of the learning in this unit.

→ seconds, minutes, hours

→ days, weeks, months, years

→ units of time

→ convert, equal to (=), compare

→ 12-hour, 24-hour, am, pm

→ analogue, digital

→ bar model

PUPIL TEXTBOOK 4C PAGE 78

PUPIL TEXTBOOK 4C PAGE 79

Units of time ❶

Learning focus

In this lesson, children will revise their understanding of the equivalences between different units of time. They will apply their knowledge to convert between units.

Small steps

→ Previous step: Problem solving – money
→ **This step: Units of time (1)**
→ Next step: Units of time (2)

NATIONAL CURRICULUM LINKS

Year 4 Measurement – Time

Convert between different units of measure [for example, kilometre to metre; hour to minute].

ASSESSING MASTERY

Children can express 1 hour in minutes and 1 minute in seconds. Children can confidently convert measurements given in these units and apply this skill in problem-solving contexts.

COMMON MISCONCEPTIONS

Children may add the numbers in measurements without considering the units or converting them. For example, they might write 1 minute 20 seconds as 1 + 20 = 21 seconds. Ask:
• *What is 2 minutes in seconds? What is 2 minutes and 10 seconds in seconds? What did you do to find the answer?*

STRENGTHENING UNDERSTANDING

To strengthen understanding, use stopwatches to time short activities (slightly more than 1 minute). Ask children to observe what happens when the timer goes beyond 59 seconds. With each time, ask children how they could write the time in seconds. Use bar models to support the equivalence of 1 minute = 60 seconds.

GOING DEEPER

Provide children with results tables that show Olympic race times in minutes and seconds (for example, the 800 metre running race) or in hours and minutes (the marathon). Challenge children to convert these into the lesser unit (for example, converting hours and minutes into simply minutes). They can use these new times to devise their own quiz questions to ask each other.

KEY LANGUAGE

In lesson: unit of time, convert, minute, second, hour

Other language to be used by the teacher: measure

STRUCTURES AND REPRESENTATIONS

bar model

RESOURCES

Optional: digital timers/stopwatches

 In the eTextbook of this lesson, you will find interactive links to a selection of teaching tools.

Before you teach ⏸

• Can children recall equivalences of different units of time confidently?
• How could you help them to remember these?

Discover

Unit 13: Time, Lesson 1

WAYS OF WORKING Pair work

ASK

- Question **1** a): *What is the difference between the two timers?*
- Question **1** a): *What will the next time shown on each timer be?*
- Question **1** a): *What fact do you know about minutes and seconds that you can use to help compare the times?*

IN FOCUS Ensure that children are given the opportunity to explain their answer to question **1** a). Encourage children to use reasoning to justify their understanding.

PRACTICAL TIPS Provide children with stopwatches to revise the concept of minutes and seconds, particularly observing how their stopwatches behave when 60 seconds is reached. Use timers to illustrate the concept of counting down.

ANSWERS

Question **1** a): 3 minutes 20 seconds = 200 seconds, so both timers show the same time until launch.

Question **1** b): In one minute's time, the controller's timer will show 2 minutes 20 seconds. The astronaut's timer will show 140 seconds.

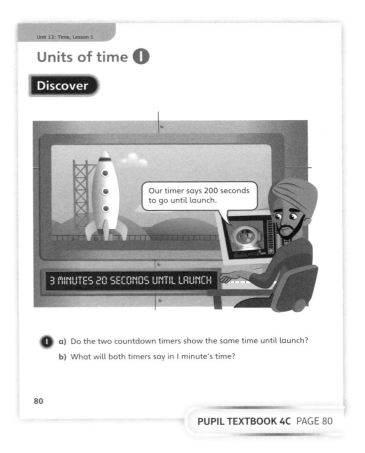

Units of time 1

Discover

1 a) Do the two countdown timers show the same time until launch?

b) What will both timers say in 1 minute's time?

80

PUPIL TEXTBOOK 4C PAGE 80

Share

WAYS OF WORKING Whole class teacher led

ASK

- Question **1** a): *Why do you think you need to convert times into the same unit to compare them?*
- Question **1** a): *How does the bar model represent the controller's and the astronaut's timers? What would you expect to see if the times are the same?*
- Question **1** a): *Dexter mentions using the 6 times-table to help multiply by 60. How can this help?*
- Question **1** b): *Is there a quicker way to find the answer? How can you use subtraction?*

IN FOCUS Ensure that children are able to explain how the bar models have been used to solve the problem, noting how 1 minute is visually shown to be equivalent to 60 seconds. Ask where the answer is shown on the bar model, and what calculation is needed to find the total.

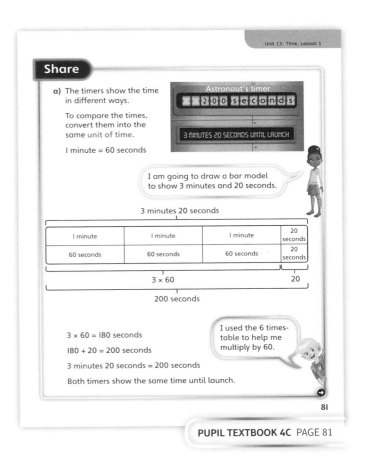

Share

a) The timers show the time in different ways.

To compare the times, convert them into the same unit of time.

1 minute = 60 seconds

I am going to draw a bar model to show 3 minutes and 20 seconds.

3 minutes 20 seconds

1 minute	1 minute	1 minute	20 seconds
60 seconds	60 seconds	60 seconds	20 seconds

3 × 60 ... 20

200 seconds

3 × 60 = 180 seconds

180 + 20 = 200 seconds

3 minutes 20 seconds = 200 seconds

Both timers show the same time until launch.

I used the 6 times-table to help me multiply by 60.

81

PUPIL TEXTBOOK 4C PAGE 81

Think together

WAYS OF WORKING Whole class teacher led (I do, We do, You do)

ASK
- Question ❶: *Explain the question using your own words. How does the bar model help you to answer the problem?*
- Question ❶: *What is the same and what is different about the bars in the bar model?*
- Question ❷: *How would you complete the bar model?*
- Question ❷: *How do you know how many 60 second bars are equal to 280 seconds? Is there a quick way to find this out?*
- Question ❷: *Why do you think this bar model has seconds on the top and minutes on the bottom?*

IN FOCUS In question ❸, children apply their knowledge of bar models to the new units of time. Ask them to describe what is the same and what is different about the question and about the bar model they could to draw to solve it. Ensure that children are able to explain *why* converting hours into minutes is similar to converting minutes into seconds as well as *how* (because there are 60 minutes in 1 hour as well as 60 seconds in 1 minute).

STRENGTHEN To emphasise the equivalence between 1 minute and 60 seconds, provide children with base 10 equipment and ask them to group them in sixes (with each group of 6 tens representing 1 minute). These can be used in both questions ❶ and ❷ to support children's understanding of the two units of time.

DEEPEN In question ❷, ask children how they would draw the bar model if the correct timer was the one on the left. Challenge children to solve this type of problem without drawing a bar model.

ASSESSMENT CHECKPOINT Use questions ❶, ❷ and ❸ to assess whether children can convert between minutes and seconds and between hours and minutes. Look for clear explanations of how they are using the bar models to represent their conversions.

ANSWERS

Question ❶: 2 minutes = 2 × 60 seconds = 120 seconds
120 seconds + 50 seconds = 170 seconds
The two timers do not show the same time.

Question ❷: 280 seconds is the same as 4 minutes + 40 seconds.
The timer on the left should show 4 minutes 40 seconds.

Question ❸: 5 hours and 10 minutes = 310 minutes
This is similar to converting minutes into seconds because there are the same number of minutes in 1 hour as there are seconds in 1 minute (60).

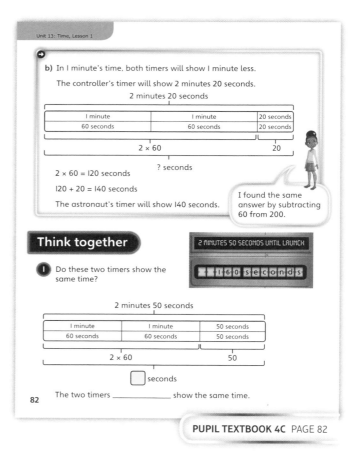

PUPIL TEXTBOOK 4C PAGE 82

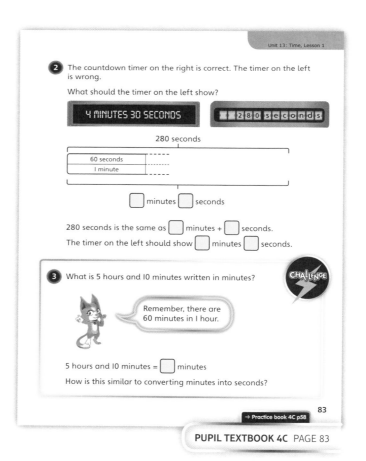

PUPIL TEXTBOOK 4C PAGE 83

Practice

WAYS OF WORKING Independent thinking

IN FOCUS Question **1** scaffolds children's understanding of the equivalence of hours and minutes through the use of bar modelling. These bar models become progressively less complete, requiring children to draw most of the final model themselves.

STRENGTHEN For children finding it difficult to convert one unit into the other, it may be beneficial to get them to make their own bar models out of pieces of coloured card. They could write 1 minute on the front of each piece and 60 seconds on the reverse (or 1 hour on the front and 60 minutes on the reverse). Having formed a bar model that matches their known information, they could turn all the cards over to find the answer.

DEEPEN In question **5**, children are given a problem where they are required to calculate the number of seconds in 1 hour. Give children similar problems, for example, to find the number of hours in a week. Ask them to explain whether they could find the number of hours in a month from the number of weeks in a month.

THINK DIFFERENTLY Question **3** asks children to use a different method to apply their knowledge of converting between minutes and hours. Encourage children to use subtraction to work out each film length in terms of hours and minutes. Challenge them to investigate the duration of their own favourite films as these are usually shown in minutes.

ASSESSMENT CHECKPOINT Use questions **1** and **3** to assess whether children can convert between units of time. Check whether they are confident using different methods; they should be able to apply both times-tables facts (6 times-tables to help identify multiples of 60) and subtraction methods (repeatedly subtracting 60).

ANSWERS Answers for the **Practice** part of the lesson appear in the separate **Practice and Reflect answer guide**.

Reflect

WAYS OF WORKING Independent thinking

IN FOCUS Use this question to check children's methodology. Pay attention to the way that children approach the conversion. Some may look for the nearest multiple of 60 to find the number of hours, others may repeatedly subtract 60. Ask children to share their working and ask whether it matters which method they used. Ask how they would have converted if they had been given the number of hours and minutes and asked to give the time in minutes.

ASSESSMENT CHECKPOINT Check that children are able convert the given time accurately and explain their method.

ANSWERS Answers for the **Reflect** part of the lesson appear in the separate **Practice and Reflect answer guide**.

After the lesson ⏸

- Were children confident explaining their reasoning in this lesson?
- In the next lesson, children will continue to convert between units of time (days, weeks, months and years). Do they have the confidence to apply what they have learnt in this lesson to convert between different units of time?

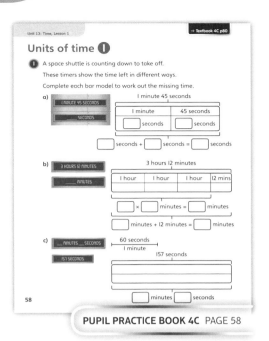

PUPIL PRACTICE BOOK 4C PAGE 58

PUPIL PRACTICE BOOK 4C PAGE 59

PUPIL PRACTICE BOOK 4C PAGE 60

Units of time ②

Learning focus

In this lesson, children will revise their understanding of the equivalences between days, weeks, months and years, applying their knowledge to convert between units of time.

Small steps

→ Previous step: Units of time (1)
→ **This step: Units of time (2)**
→ Next step: Converting times (1)

NATIONAL CURRICULUM LINKS

Year 4 Measurement – Time

Convert between different units of measure [for example, kilometre to metre; hour to minute].

ASSESSING MASTERY

Children can express 1 week in days and 1 year in months. Children can confidently convert measurements given in these units and apply this skill in problem-solving contexts.

COMMON MISCONCEPTIONS

Children may add the numbers in measurements without considering the units or converting them. For example, 1 week 4 days might be written as 1 + 4 = 5 days. Ask:

• *What is 2 weeks in days? What is 2 weeks and 3 days in days? What did you do to find the answer?*

Children may think of the larger unit of measurement as being worth 10, so they may consider 4 years and 3 months as being equivalent to 43 months. Ask:

• *How many months are in 1 year? How many months are in 2 years? How many months are in 2 years and 1 month?*

STRENGTHENING UNDERSTANDING

Reinforce children's knowledge of multiples of 7 and 12 (useful when converting between days and weeks, and between months and years respectively). Display an unmarked number line split into 50. Choose one group of children to count along the line from 1 to 50. A second group should call out '1', '2' and so on for each group of 7 that is counted. Use the same method to practise identifying multiples of 12.

GOING DEEPER

Give children problems where they need to use their knowledge of months of the year to convert to days. For example, ask: *Kate has a book out of the library for the whole of January and February. How many days is this? How many weeks and days is this?*

KEY LANGUAGE

In lesson: unit of time, convert, day, week, month, year

Other language to be used by the teacher: measure

STRUCTURES AND REPRESENTATIONS

bar model

RESOURCES

Optional: pieces of string

 In the eTextbook of this lesson, you will find interactive links to a selection of teaching tools.

Before you teach

• How could you use concrete representations (clocks, calendars) to support children?
• Can children recall equivalences of different units of time confidently?

Discover

WAYS OF WORKING Pair work

ASK

- Question ❶: *What sorts of things do we measure in weeks/ months/years?*
- Question ❶: *We use clocks and timers to measure hours, minutes and seconds. What do we use to measure days, weeks, months and years?*
- Question ❶: *What facts do you know about days, weeks, months and years that you can use to convert between these units?*

IN FOCUS Discuss the different units of time that are shown in the picture. Children sometimes do not see weeks, months and years as units of time like hours, minutes and seconds because they are not used in telling the time from a clock. Ensure that they understand that these are still units of time, but used for longer periods of time. Ask them how they might measure these units (for example, using dates on a computer screen, calendars, wall planners and so on).

PRACTICAL TIPS One way to model additions between times is to use a timeline. Give children a piece of string and ask them to use sticky labels to create a timeline that labels the information they know of the two dogs' ages. At the left-hand end should be 3 years and 8 months (Lexi's dog's age), then a jump of 1 year and 7 months, followed by 'Max's dog's age' at the other end of the timeline.

ANSWERS

Question ❶ a): The new play area will open in 28 days.

Question ❶ b): Max's dog is 5 years and 3 months old.

Share

WAYS OF WORKING Whole class teacher led

ASK

- Question ❶ a): *What fact do you need to use to convert a period of weeks into days?*
- Question ❶ a): *Would you rather work out 4 × 7 or 7 + 7 + 7 + 7 to find the answer?*
- Question ❶ b): *Is this an addition or subtraction question?*
- Question ❶ b): *The bar model is used for part of the working out. How does it help you?*

IN FOCUS Ensure that children can explain how the bar models have been used to solve each problem. In question ❶ a) they should note how 1 week is visually equivalent to 7 days. Children should understand that bar models provide a useful way of modelling equivalences. In question ❶ b), check that children understand that the bar model is being used for *part* of the question (to split up 15 months into years and months), not the whole question.

PUPIL TEXTBOOK 4C PAGE 84

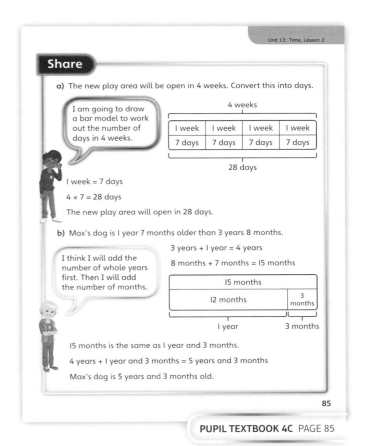

PUPIL TEXTBOOK 4C PAGE 85

Think together

WAYS OF WORKING Whole class teacher led (I do, We do, You do)

ASK

- Question **1** a): *How is this question similar to question* **1** *b) in* **Discover**?
- Question **1** a): *How does the bar model help you to answer the problem?*
- Question **1** a): *Why could the answer not just be '8 years 14 months'?*
- Question **2**: *How do you know how many 7-day bars are equal to 35 days? Is there a quick way to find this out?*
- Question **2**: *Why do you divide by 7 to find the answer, not any other number?*

IN FOCUS In question **1** a), make sure that children understand why the bar model is used to convert 14 months into years and months. Ask them to explain why the bar model shows 14 months split into 12 months and 2 months, not 7 and 7 or 13 and 1, for example.

STRENGTHEN In question **2**, encourage children to use strips of paper to build up various bar models, exploring the different numbers of days that are formed by blocks of 7 days (1 week). Ask how many weeks are the same as 7 days, 14 days, 21 days … Link this to times-tables facts and guide children towards a quicker way to find the answer – dividing 35 by 7.

DEEPEN Deepen children's conceptual understanding of question **3** by challenging them to teach the correct way of converting years and months into months to someone who has never converted units of time before. Ask how they could help them to avoid making the kind of mistake Amelia made and what resources or pictures they could use.

ASSESSMENT CHECKPOINT Use questions **1**, **2** and **3** to assess whether children can convert between months and years and between weeks and days, supporting their reasoning with pictorial representations (bar models). Look for children who use the bar model to recognise the different operations they can use when converting between units of time: division for smaller units into larger ones and multiplication for larger units into smaller ones.

ANSWERS

Question **1** a): Andy is 9 years and 2 months old.

Question **1** b): Mo is 10 years and 9 months old.

Question **2**: 35 ÷ 7 = 5
5 weeks are the same as 35 days.

Question **3**: Amelia is wrong because she thinks that the number of years and months are the same as tens and ones. 4 years are worth 4 × 12, not 4 × 10. 4 years and 3 months = 51 months

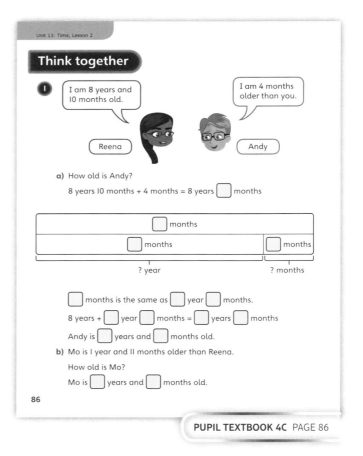

PUPIL TEXTBOOK 4C PAGE 86

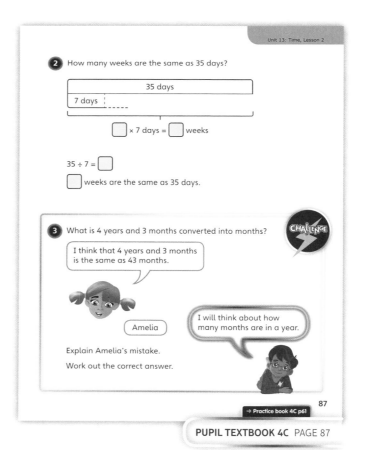

PUPIL TEXTBOOK 4C PAGE 87

Practice

WAYS OF WORKING Independent thinking

IN FOCUS Question ❶ scaffolds children's understanding of the equivalence of days, weeks, months and years through the use of bar modelling. These bar models become progressively less complete, requiring children to draw most of the final model themselves.

STRENGTHEN In question ❷, children may need reminding that there are 365 days in a year.

If children are finding it difficult to calculate abstractly in question ❹, point out the part of the question that may need converting (in both cases, the second period of time). Then encourage them to use pictorial representations (bar models) to convert the units of time. Ask children to explain how they used their bar models to help work out the calculations.

DEEPEN In question ❻, ask children whether all years have 365 days. Discuss how their calculation needs to change to take account of leap years. Challenge children to devise their own investigations similar to question ❻, for example working out the number of weeks they have been attending school. This requires converting from the number of years and months, so prompting a discussion about how many weeks are in a year and a month and whether this is a precise number.

ASSESSMENT CHECKPOINT Use questions ❶ and ❷ to assess whether children are confident in converting between days and weeks, and between months and years. Look for children using pictorial representations (bar models) to support their reasoning. Use question ❺ to check whether they are able to explain which operation to use when converting between different units.

ANSWERS Answers for the **Practice** part of the lesson appear in the separate **Practice and Reflect answer guide**.

Reflect

WAYS OF WORKING Independent thinking

IN FOCUS Explain to children that this sort of conversion is one that people need to do regularly in real life, as babies' ages are often given in months only, even after a year. Ask them to explain how they will use unit conversion to find the answer.

ASSESSMENT CHECKPOINT Children should explain clearly how to convert 20 months into 1 year and 8 months by finding the number of groups of 12 (1 year) in 20 months. This may involve using a pictorial representation, choosing to use subtraction or division.

ANSWERS Answers for the **Reflect** part of the lesson appear in the separate **Practice and Reflect answer guide**.

After the lesson ⏸

- Are children confident converting between days, weeks, months and years?
- What opportunities can you give for children to continue to practise these skills in meaningful, real-life contexts?

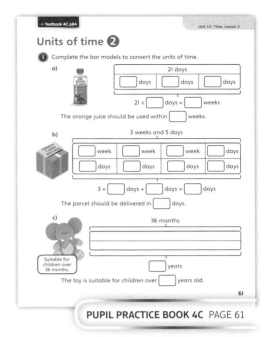

PUPIL PRACTICE BOOK 4C PAGE 61

PUPIL PRACTICE BOOK 4C PAGE 62

PUPIL PRACTICE BOOK 4C PAGE 63

Converting times

Learning focus

In this lesson, children will convert between analogue and digital times.

Small steps

→ Previous step: Units of time (2)
→ **This step: Converting times (1)**
→ Next step: Converting times (2)

NATIONAL CURRICULUM LINKS

Year 4 Measurement – Time

Convert between different units of measure [for example, kilometre to metre; hour to minute].

ASSESSING MASTERY

Children can confidently convert between analogue and digital 12-hour times to the nearest minute. They apply this skill when problem solving.

COMMON MISCONCEPTIONS

Children may misunderstand the relationship between the numbers on a digital clock face and the numbers on an analogue clock face. For example, they may represent the digital time 6:10 as one hand pointing to the number 6 and the other hand pointing to the number 10. Similarly, children may represent the analogue time ten past 7 as 7:02 because these are the two numbers the hands are pointing to. Ask:

• *What do the numbers on each side of the colon in a digital time represent? How would you show this time on an analogue clock face?*

STRENGTHENING UNDERSTANDING

To help children build connections between analogue and digital times, consider times to the nearest five minutes. Provide children with large analogue clock faces and ask them to place number cards next to each number to show the digital equivalent minutes. For example, the number 1 on the clock face represents 5 past and so is represented by :05 in a digital time. Turn this into a quick-fire question and answer game where children point to the correct part of the clock for minutes given in a digital time (such as :45).

GOING DEEPER

Show children different 'minutes to' analogue times. Challenge them to write the time in three different ways. For example, three minutes to four might be written as '3:57', 'fifty-seven minutes past 3' or 'three minutes to 4'. This will further consolidate children's understanding of the links between digital and analogue times.

KEY LANGUAGE

In lesson: unit of time, convert, **analogue**, **digital**, **am**, **pm**, hour, minute, 12-hour

STRUCTURES AND REPRESENTATIONS

analogue clock, digital clock

RESOURCES

Optional: analogue clocks, digital clocks, number cards

 In the eTextbook of this lesson, you will find interactive links to a selection of teaching tools.

Before you teach

• How confident are children when reading analogue times to the nearest minute?
• What opportunities are there for you to refer to both analogue and digital times throughout the school day to embed the concepts learnt in this lesson?

Discover

WAYS OF WORKING Pair work

ASK

- Question ❶ a): *Look at the two types of clock face shown. What is the same? What is different?*
- Question ❶ a): *How does Sofia know that her watch is wrong? Is it too fast or too slow?*
- Question ❶ a): *What time does the park clock say it is?*
- Question ❶ b): *How far will the minute hand move in an hour and a half? How far will the hour hand move?*

IN FOCUS When considering question ❶ b), encourage children to discuss how both methods of showing the time will change over the course of an hour (for example, the minute hand on the analogue clock moving once around the clock face, or the hours digit on the digital watch increasing by 1). Extend the question to consider how the clocks will change over the course of one and a half hours.

PRACTICAL TIPS Provide children with practice clock faces with movable hands and with number cards for modelling digital watches. Call out different times and challenge them to set their clocks to the correct time as quickly as possible. Move from times to the nearest five minutes to times to the nearest minute.

ANSWERS

Question ❶ a): The time on the watch should say 3:07 pm.

Question ❶ b): Analogue:

Digital: 4:37 pm.

Share

WAYS OF WORKING Whole class teacher led

ASK

- Question ❶ a): *What do the letters am and pm mean? The digital watch shows that it is a pm time – how else can you tell this fact?*
- Question ❶ b): *What happens to both types of clock when the time crosses into a new hour?*
- Question ❶ b): *How would you show the time 1:56 on an analogue clock? Or the time sixteen minutes to 4 on a digital watch?*
- Question ❶ b): *If Sofia presses the SET button on her watch once for every minute it needs to change, how many times will she need to press it to alter it by one and a half hours?*

IN FOCUS When answering question ❶ b), ensure that children recognise that the number of minutes past the hour increases by 30 as half an hour equals 30 minutes. Give examples that cross the hour boundary. For example: *What time will the spies need to meet if the time now is 3:50 pm?* In these cases, children will need to partition 30 and complete two additions – one to get to 4 o'clock (+ 10) and one to add the remainder of the 30 minutes (+ 20).

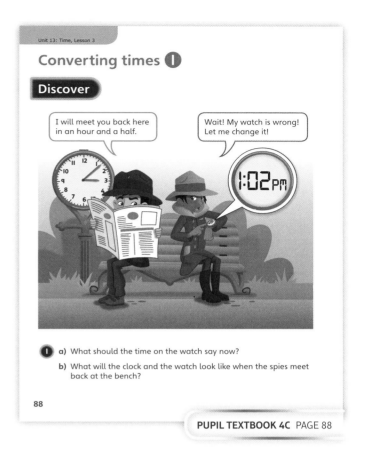

PUPIL TEXTBOOK 4C PAGE 88

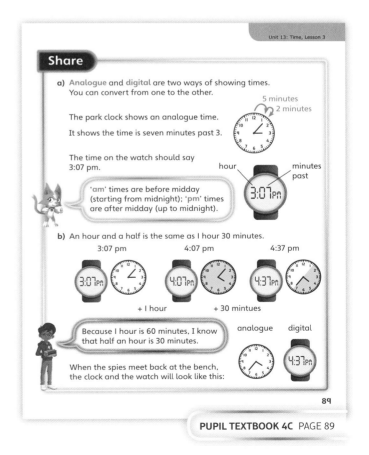

PUPIL TEXTBOOK 4C PAGE 89

Think together

Whole class teacher led (I do, We do, You do)

ASK

- Question **1**: *How could you say twenty to 9 in a different way? Why is this important?*
- Question **1**: *Why doesn't the digital version of twenty to 9 have the number 20 or 9 in it?*
- Question **2**: *There are two ways to say the time on the first clock. What are they? Which one is the most helpful when finding the correct digital clock that goes with it?*
- Question **2**: *Do the am or pm letters make a difference to how you answer the question?*

IN FOCUS The times in question **2** test children's understanding of the two numbers in a digital time. For example, the analogue clock showing twenty-one minutes past 5 might be matched incorrectly to the digital time 4:05 am because children believe that the numbers on the clock face towards which the hands are pointing should be the same as the ones in the digital time.

STRENGTHEN In questions **1** and **2**, provide children with digit cards and analogue clock faces with movable hands. These will enable children to physically model the times as both analogue and digital.

DEEPEN Question **3** requires children to convert a digital time to analogue and use reasoning to explain incorrect answers that are based on common misconceptions. The key error here is that children may not be able to recognise the meaning of each number either side of the colon in a digital time. Challenge children to think of other common misconceptions. They could make up similar problems to question **3**, with one correct match and two mismatches, and swap with a partner to explain the mistakes.

ASSESSMENT CHECKPOINT Use question **2** to assess whether children can convert digital times to analogue and vice versa. They should be able to express digital times in different ways, particularly being able to describe times that are both minutes past and minutes to the hour (for example, 4:50 as 'fifty minutes past 4' and 'ten to 5').

ANSWERS

Question **1**: Twenty to 9 is the same as forty minutes past 8.

analogue   digital

 8:40 am

Question **2**: a) 7:51 pm, b) 5:21 pm, c) 8:10 am, d) 4:05 am

Question **3**: Alex's clock face matches the digital time.
Jamilla thinks 6:10 am means six minutes past 10 and has drawn this time instead.
Bella has mixed up the minute and the hour hands.

PUPIL TEXTBOOK 4C PAGE 90

PUPIL TEXTBOOK 4C PAGE 91

Practice

WAYS OF WORKING Independent thinking

IN FOCUS In question **2**, the analogue clock shows two minutes to 11 and so the first misconception is that the numbers being pointed to on the clock face are the same as the numbers in a digital time. The second mistake is that, as the hour hand looks closest to the 11, the time is 11:58. Ask children how they would help Emma and Max so that they do not make the same mistakes again.

STRENGTHEN To support children as they attempt to convert each written time in question **3** into analogue and digital, suggest that they underline the important words in the message. Provide analogue clock faces for them to model each time before copying onto the blank clock face provided. If necessary, ask questions to guide them to the relevant information on the clock face needed to make each part of the digital time.

DEEPEN Use question **5** to deepen children's understanding and reasoning skills. Ask children whether there are any incorrect digital times that they can make using the given digits. These may be those that are formatted incorrectly (63:5) or those that refer to impossible times (3:65). Give children different sets of number cards to make possible times, including sets of four cards where two are 0, 1 or 2.

THINK DIFFERENTLY In question **4**, children revise what the digits in a digital time represent by considering a time where the same number has different meanings in the analogue and digital representations. Ask children whether they can think of any other examples where one of the hands on a clock face points to a digit in the digital time, but they both represent different things.

ASSESSMENT CHECKPOINT Use questions **1** and **3** to assess whether children can convert between analogue and 12-hour digital times. They should recognise what both sets of digits either side of the colon in a digital time represent and be able to express 'minutes to' digital times in different ways (for example, 6:42 as 'eighteen minutes to 7').

ANSWERS Answers for the **Practice** part of the lesson appear in the separate **Practice and Reflect answer guide**.

Reflect

WAYS OF WORKING Independent thinking

IN FOCUS Children need to explain what the numbers in a digital time represent. Children should be able to describe how to look for the hour of the clock that the time is (which will give the first number in the digital time) and then the number of minutes *past* the hour (which will give the second number). Ask them to give an example.

ASSESSMENT CHECKPOINT Look for children who are able to describe accurately how to convert an analogue time into a digital time.

ANSWERS Answers for the **Reflect** part of the lesson appear in the separate **Practice and Reflect answer guide**.

After the lesson ⏸

- In the next lesson children will convert between 24-hour digital times and analogue times. Do children have the confidence to apply what they have learnt in this lesson in a new context?

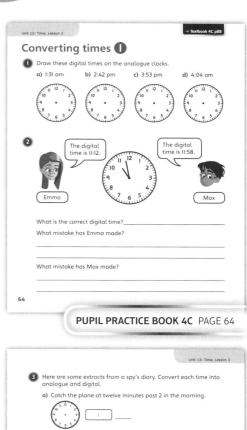

PUPIL PRACTICE BOOK 4C PAGE 64

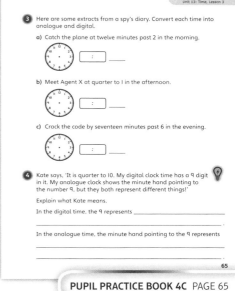

PUPIL PRACTICE BOOK 4C PAGE 65

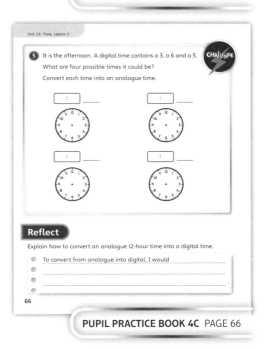

PUPIL PRACTICE BOOK 4C PAGE 66

123

Converting times ②

Learning focus

In this lesson, children will convert between 12-hour and 24-hour times expressed on analogue and digital clocks.

Small steps

→ Previous step: Converting times (1)
→ **This step: Converting times (2)**
→ Next step: Problem solving – units of time

NATIONAL CURRICULUM LINKS

Year 4 Measurement – Time

Convert between different units of measure [for example, kilometre to metre; hour to minute].

ASSESSING MASTERY

Children can confidently convert between analogue and digital 24-hour times to the nearest minute. They apply this skill when problem solving.

COMMON MISCONCEPTIONS

Children may think, because 17:00 can be said as 17 hundred hours, there are 100 minutes in an hour. Ask:
• *How many hours go by between 13:00 and 14:00? How many minutes is this?*

Children may interchange minutes and hours from digital times. For example, they may read 16:05 as sixteen minutes past 5 – this error is often because analogue times are said in this order (minutes past hour). Ask:
• *If a clock shows 13:07, what time is it? Can you make this time on an analogue clock?*

STRENGTHENING UNDERSTANDING

To support children's understanding of 24-hour clock times in different contexts, present times in different ways (clock on computer, times in different parts of the world, times shown on timetables). Discuss the way that these 24-hour times are formatted. Choose individual times and ask children to say these times and to represent them on an analogue clock.

GOING DEEPER

Explore possible misconceptions and encourage children to consider the advice they would give to someone making that particular error. For example, show children an analogue clock displaying twenty-five past 3. Explain that this is an afternoon time. Ask children to think what wrong answers someone might give if asked to write this time as a 24-hour digital time and how they would correct the mistakes.

KEY LANGUAGE

In lesson: convert, analogue, digital, 12-hour time, **24-hour time**, hour, minute, am, pm

STRUCTURES AND REPRESENTATIONS

analogue clock, digital clock

RESOURCES

Optional: analogue clocks, digital clocks, number cards, examples of 24-hour clock times from everyday life (computer clock, timetables etc.)

 In the eTextbook of this lesson, you will find interactive links to a selection of teaching tools.

Before you teach

• Are children confident when relating 12-hour digital times to analogue times?
• Can children recall what is meant by a 24-hour time and why they are used?

Discover

WAYS OF WORKING Pair work

ASK

- Question **1** a): *Compare these digital times with the ones in the last lesson. What is the same? What is different?*
- Question **1** a): *How can a digital time show more than 12 hours when there are only 12 hours on a clock face?*
- Question **1** b): *How could you say each time a different way?*

IN FOCUS Ensure that the picture provides an opportunity for children to revise the characteristics of 24-hour times and to explore the differences between 24-hour digital times and the 12-hour digital times they used in the previous lesson. Check that children understand what is meant by a '24-hour time'.

PRACTICAL TIPS Provide digital clocks (or use online digital clocks) for children to practise exploring 24-hour clock times. Ask children to make the different times in the picture. As they move from one time to the other, children should notice how the 24-hour clock behaves (for example, the hours go to 00 when moving on from 23).

ANSWERS

Question **1** a): The first two digits show the hour (from 00 up to 23). The last two digits show the number of minutes past (from 00 up to 59).

Question **1** b): The correct watch shows 15:52.

PUPIL TEXTBOOK 4C PAGE 92

Share

WAYS OF WORKING Whole class teacher led

ASK

- Question **1** a): *Look at the table. What do you notice about the way that the digital times are written?*
- Question **1** a): *How would you write each time as a 12-hour time?*
- Question **1** b): *What advice would you give someone looking at an analogue clock to convert it into a 24-hour digital time?*
- Question **1** b): *What would each digital time look like on a clock face? Which one is the same as the clock in the picture?*

IN FOCUS Use both analogue and digital clocks (or number cards) for children to model both sets of times. The physical acts of moving the hands of the clock and altering the digits in a digital time will ensure that children build connections between the two formats. It is particularly important to spend time considering times after 12 pm (where the hour digits will be more than 12) and where the number of minutes are after half past (where the digital time uses the number of minutes *past* even though the time would normally be read as a number of minutes *to*).

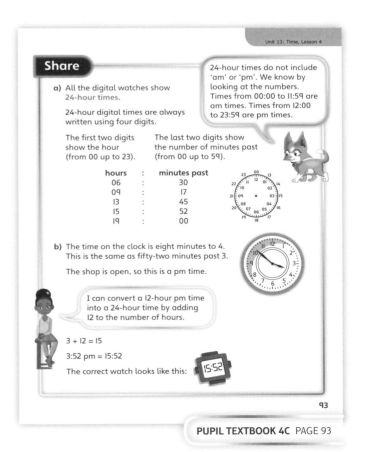

PUPIL TEXTBOOK 4C PAGE 93

Think together

WAYS OF WORKING Whole class teacher led (I do, We do, You do)

ASK

- Question **1**: *What do you need to find out from an analogue time to convert it into a digital time?*
- Question **1**: *Explain how to convert a 12-hour am or pm time into a 24-hour digital time.*
- Question **2**: *Why do you think this question gets you to focus on the number of minutes past the hour, rather than the number of minutes to?*

IN FOCUS In question **2**, ask children what they notice about the answer boxes given for the 24-hour time. Children should identify that there is no space for am/pm and also that there are spaces for four digits (both of which are features of 24-hour times). Ask how their answer would differ if this time was in the afternoon.

STRENGTHEN Provide analogue clocks with movable hands and number cards for children to model their answers. Emphasise the 'minutes to' elements of a clock face and also how 'to' times can also be said as 'minutes past' times. If helpful, use flash cards to reinforce children's understanding of these two ways of expressing times (for example, showing 'twenty to 5' and expecting children to respond with 'forty minutes past 4').

DEEPEN After children have identified the mistake in question **4**, ask them to give further mistakes that could be made when converting between different formats of times in real life. Ask: *What mistakes might you make if you were looking at the time on your 24-hour digital watch and wanting to adjust the time on your analogue clock in the kitchen to match it? What if you wanted to set your digital watch by looking at the analogue clock in your classroom?*

ASSESSMENT CHECKPOINT Use questions **1** and **2** to assess whether children can convert between analogue and 24-hour digital times.

ANSWERS

Question **1** a): The clock shows twelve minutes past 8.
As a 12-hour time, this is written as 8:12 am.
As a 24-hour time, this is written as 08:12.

Question **1** b): The clock shows thirteen minutes to 12.
As a 12-hour time, this is written as 11:47 pm.
As a 24-hour time, this is written as 23:47.

Question **2**: Quarter to 5 is the same as forty-five minutes past 4.
Analogue: 24-hour digital: 04:45

Question **3** a): Mo's watch would show 06:35.

Question **3** b): Mo's watch would show 18:35.

Question **4**: Isla has treated it as a pm time. It is the morning, so she does not need to add 12 to the number of hours. To convert 7:28 am into a 24-hour time, Isla needs to write a 0 at the start of the time so it has four digits and to remove the letters 'am' as these are not needed. The 24-hour time is 07:28.

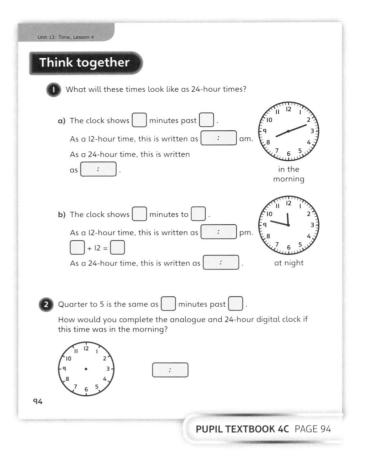

PUPIL TEXTBOOK 4C PAGE 94

PUPIL TEXTBOOK 4C PAGE 95

126

Practice

WAYS OF WORKING Independent thinking

IN FOCUS Question ① challenges children to convert a variety of times – expressed in both words and as 12-hour digital times – into both analogue and 24-hour digital formats. Ask children how each time shows what part of the day it is describing. Ask them to explain why this is important when writing the time on an analogue or 24-hour digital clock.

STRENGTHEN As question ④ is more abstract in nature, ask children what they might do to help visualise the current time and then the time $1\frac{1}{2}$ hours later. Ask them what they could use to count on one and a half hours from 2:17. Provide access to analogue and digital clocks for children to model the question.

DEEPEN Use the open-ended task in question ⑤ to deepen children's understanding of converting between 24-hour and 12-hour times. Ask questions about the times they make: whether it is before or after midday, and how this affects how they will work out the 12-hour time. Challenge children to come up with examples of times that are not correct and then explain why not (for example, 24:11 because 24-hour clock times go to 00 after 23, or 4:40 because all 24-hour times need four digits).

ASSESSMENT CHECKPOINT Use questions ① and ② to assess whether children can convert between analogue and 24-hour digital times as well as between 12-hour and 24-hour digital times. They should be able to use their understanding of the digital format to identify what each set of numbers means, applying this knowledge when moving between analogue and digital times. Children should be confident when representing am and pm times using 24-hour notation.

ANSWERS Answers for the **Practice** part of the lesson appear in the separate **Practice and Reflect answer guide**.

Reflect

WAYS OF WORKING Independent thinking

IN FOCUS Give children the opportunity to consider the different representations of time they have worked with. Ask them to describe the features of 12-hour times and 24-hour times, and how they would convert between them. Children may find it useful to refer back to previous pages in the Textbook to help explain their ideas.

ASSESSMENT CHECKPOINT Look for children who are able to explain that they need to identify whether the 12-hour time is an am or pm time and how to convert each of these into 24-hour times. Children's reasoning should make mention of the concepts they have covered so far, for example the 24-hour clock times always contain four digits.

ANSWERS Answers for the **Reflect** part of the lesson appear in the separate **Practice and Reflect answer guide**.

After the lesson ⏸

- Have children made connections between the past two lessons when converting using digital times?
- How will you reinforce these connections during the next lesson when problem solving?

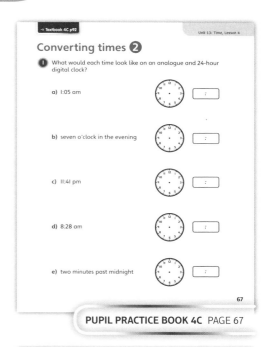

→ Textbook 4C p92

Unit 13: Time, Lesson 4

Converting times ②

① What would each time look like on an analogue and 24-hour digital clock?

a) 1:05 am

b) seven o'clock in the evening

c) 11:41 pm

d) 8:28 am

e) two minutes past midnight

67

PUPIL PRACTICE BOOK 4C PAGE 67

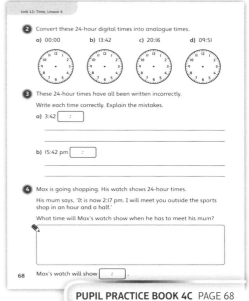

Unit 13: Time, Lesson 4

② Convert these 24-hour digital times into analogue times.

a) 00:00   b) 13:42   c) 20:16   d) 09:51

③ These 24-hour times have all been written incorrectly. Write each time correctly. Explain the mistakes.

a) 3:42 [:]

b) 15:42 pm [:]

④ Max is going shopping. His watch shows 24-hour times.

His mum says, 'It is now 2:17 pm. I will meet you outside the sports shop in an hour and a half.'

What time will Max's watch show when he has to meet his mum?

68   Max's watch will show [:].

PUPIL PRACTICE BOOK 4C PAGE 68

Unit 13: Time, Lesson 4

⑤ Write down ten 24-hour times where the four digits add up to 8 each time.   **CHALLENGE**

Convert your times into 12-hour times.

For example, 05:21 → 5:21 am

	24-hour time	12-hour time		24-hour time	12-hour time
1			6		
2			7		
3			8		
4			9		
5			10		

Reflect

Explain how to change between 12-hour and 24-hour clock times.

69

PUPIL PRACTICE BOOK 4C PAGE 69

Problem solving – units of time

Learning focus

In this lesson, children will apply their knowledge of units of time to problem-solving contexts. They will use mathematical reasoning, choosing when and how to convert between units of time or between analogue and digital times in order to solve problems.

Small steps

→ Previous step: Converting times (2)
→ **This step: Problem solving – units of time**
→ Next step: Charts and tables (1)

NATIONAL CURRICULUM LINKS

Year 4 Measurement – Time

Convert between different units of measure [for example, kilometre to metre; hour to minute].

ASSESSING MASTERY

Children can solve time-based problems confidently, where they are required to convert between units of time and/or between times shown on analogue and digital clocks.

COMMON MISCONCEPTIONS

Children may think that 24-hour times in a problem are not correct because there are only 12 numbers on a clock face. Ask:
• *Why might the time 16:10 look unusual to some people? Is it written correctly? What does it mean?*

Children may think that – because two pieces of information in a problem are given using different units of time – they are unconnected. Ask:
• *Can you highlight the units of time mentioned in this problem? How can you make them easier to compare?*

STRENGTHENING UNDERSTANDING

To strengthen understanding, ensure that children use the structures and representations that they have been using throughout the unit. Suggest that they underline the parts of the problem that are most important. Ask whether they can say the problem in a different way. Provide blank bar models and analogue/digital clocks to help children model each problem.

GOING DEEPER

Provide children with data that shows the number of hours/days/weeks/months that it has taken various explorers to complete their journeys. Challenge children to devise their own problems based on these. The simplest form of question may be a straightforward conversion from one unit into another. Encourage children, however, to come up with more complicated multi-step questions including information of their own.

KEY LANGUAGE

In lesson: convert, seconds, minutes, hours, days, weeks, months, years, analogue, digital, 12-hour, 24-hour, compare

Other language to be used by the teacher: unit of time, measure, slower, quicker

STRUCTURES AND REPRESENTATIONS

bar model, analogue clock, digital clock

RESOURCES

Optional: calendars/year planners, flash cards, analogue clocks, digital clocks, number cards

 In the eTextbook of this lesson, you will find interactive links to a selection of teaching tools.

Before you teach

• Are children confident converting between units of time?
• Are children confident problem solving and reasoning?

Discover

ASK

- Question **1**: *Why is it important for the explorers to be able to convert times accurately? Can you think of another example when it might be important?*
- Question **1**: *What different units of time can you see in the picture?*
- Question **1**: *What facts do you know about these units of time? How many days are in 1 week? How many days/weeks are in 1 month? (How does it depend on the month?) How many days/weeks/months are in 1 year?*

IN FOCUS Explore the different units of time mentioned in the picture. Ask children to list them and then revise the equivalence of each unit. Use the opportunity to discuss the different lengths of months and how this affects the answer. Encourage children to suggest when different units of time might be important when going on an expedition. Can they think of one example for each unit of time?

PRACTICAL TIPS Provide pairs with calendars/year planners and encourage them to role-play the parts of the explorers. For example, they can use the calendars to mark the current date and then when they might expect to run out of woolly socks! It does not matter which month they use as the questions do not specify this information. Using calendars in this way should help children visualise the equivalence between 7 days and 1 week (or 1 row down on the calendar) and between 12 months and 1 year (or 1 whole calendar!).

ANSWERS

Question **1** a): The explorers have been training for $2\frac{1}{2}$ years.

Question **1** b): Toshi does have enough socks to make it to the North Pole, because three weeks (or 21 days) of socks is greater than the 20 days left of travelling.

Share

ASK

- Question **1**: *Describe what each question is asking you to do in as few words as possible.*
- Question **1**: *It is easier to compare two periods of time if they are converted so that they are the same unit. Does it matter which unit you choose to convert?*
- Question **1** b): *Dexter and Flo give two different methods. Explain how they reach the same answer.*

IN FOCUS Both questions employ bar models in order to represent the problem visually. Ask children to explain how the bar models have been used to help solve the problem. Ask them whether they could work out the answer without using a bar model.

PUPIL TEXTBOOK 4C PAGE 96

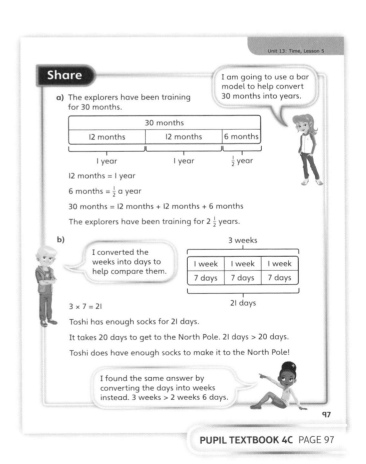

PUPIL TEXTBOOK 4C PAGE 97

Think together

WAYS OF WORKING **WAYS OF WORKING** Whole class teacher led (I do, We do, You do)

ASK

- Question **1**: *Why is the bar model useful?*
- Question **1**: *Is the quicker time the one with the larger or smaller number of seconds?*
- Question **1**: *Flo mentions a different way to convert the times. What do you think it is?*
- Question **2**: *What is the difference between the two methods of finding the answer?*
- Question **2**: *Is the tin that needs to be used first the one with the longer or shorter 'Use by' date?*

IN FOCUS Question **2** takes children through two methods of finding the answer (by converting either the tin A or tin B label so that the chosen label is expressed in the same units of measurement as the other). Show children the problem initially without revealing the structured responses and ask how they would work out the answer. This may reveal themselves in children's initial responses and can then be used for discussion.

STRENGTHEN To strengthen children's understanding of the connections between units of time, use flash cards with equivalent times on each side (for example, 1 minute on the front and 60 seconds on the back). Children could then use these flash cards to form their own bar models.

DEEPEN The problems in this section all allude to two ways of finding the answer (i.e. converting either of the two times so that it is the same as the other and can then be compared more easily). Ask whether it matters which unit they decide to convert. Some children may find it easier to go from large units to small units as the operation used is multiplication rather than division. Give children several pairs of times to investigate.

ASSESSMENT CHECKPOINT Use questions **1**, **2** and **3** to assess whether children are confident in solving problems that involve conversion and comparison. Ensure children are able to explain clearly why and how they are using bar models to help solve each problem.

ANSWERS

Question **1**: $(3 \times 60) + 14 = 180 + 14 = 194$ seconds
194 seconds < 203 seconds
3 minutes 14 seconds is a quicker time than 203 seconds.
Jen is quicker than Toshi.

Question **2** a): Tin A = Use by 4 weeks 2 days
Tin B = Use by 4 weeks
Tin B needs to be used first.

Question **2** b): Tin A = Use by 30 days, B = Use by 28 days
Tin B needs to be used first.

Question **3**: Answers will vary but should involve converting one of the given measurements so that the unit of time is the same.

Question **3** a): 3 hours and 45 minutes is 225 minutes, so it is longer than 200 minutes.

Question **3** b): $4\frac{1}{2}$ years is 54 months, so it is longer than 50 months.

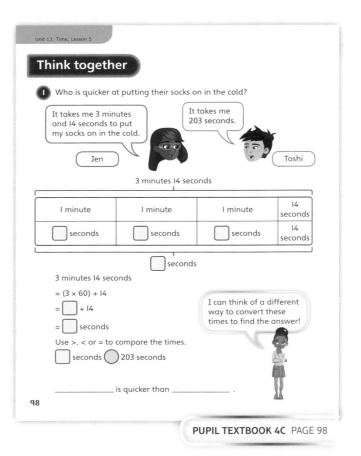

PUPIL TEXTBOOK 4C PAGE 98

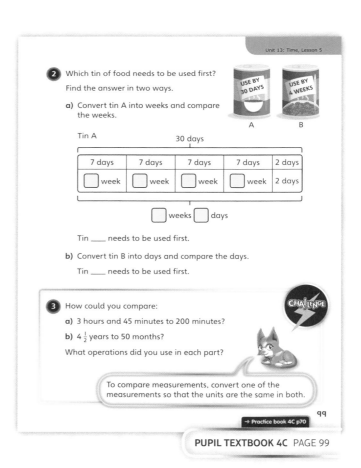

PUPIL TEXTBOOK 4C PAGE 99

Practice

WAYS OF WORKING Independent thinking

IN FOCUS In question **1**, children explore the relationship between weeks and days in the context of a mountain climb. The climb consists of four stages, the times for which are given in tabular form. Spend time asking children questions about the data in the table – time taken to complete a stage, time taken to complete two or three consecutive stages, etc. – so that they become familiar with what is being represented.

STRENGTHEN With children who need further support for question **2**, begin by asking them to look at the third column of the table – what unit of time does it ask for the answer to be given in? Children should then work backwards and look at the second column. If children are unsure how to convert between seconds, minutes and hours, encourage them to look back at the bar models they used in the **Textbook**.

DEEPEN Ask children to make up similar questions to question **5**. They could use the times of the school buses to ask questions about when they need to collect from different places for children to get to school in time for lessons. Encourage them to solve problems using both 12-hour and 24-hour times.

THINK DIFFERENTLY In question **4**, children are presented with four ages of babies. The ages are given for the first two babies (using different units of time) and related clues are given for the remaining two. Children are expected to both convert one of the first two babies' ages and then solve the clues so that each age is now given in the same unit of time.

ASSESSMENT CHECKPOINT Use questions **1**, **2** and **3** to assess whether children are confident when approaching and solving time-based problems where they are required to convert between units of time and/or between times shown on analogue and digital clocks. They should display reasoning skills, explaining appropriate methods and thinking with confidence.

ANSWERS Answers for the **Practice** part of the lesson appear in the separate **Practice and Reflect answer guide**.

Reflect

WAYS OF WORKING Pair work

IN FOCUS This activity provides an opportunity to check children's methodology. They should begin by thinking individually and deciding on a method they would use. Then they should explain this method to their partner. In their explanation, children should include the equivalence of 1 year and 12 months and describe how they would use this information to help. Ask children whether they used the same method as their partner, and whether their answers were the same.

ASSESSMENT CHECKPOINT Look for children who describe clearly and accurately how to convert 108 months into years.

ANSWERS Answers for the **Reflect** part of the lesson appear in the separate **Practice and Reflect answer guide**.

After the lesson ⏸

- How did children respond mathematically to the problems and how did the mathematical processes flow and develop during the lesson?
- Do you feel that children are ready to move on?

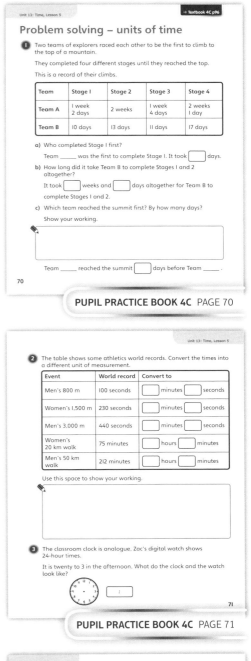

PUPIL PRACTICE BOOK 4C PAGE 70

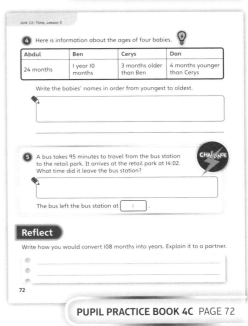

PUPIL PRACTICE BOOK 4C PAGE 71

PUPIL PRACTICE BOOK 4C PAGE 72

End of unit check

> Don't forget the *Power Maths* unit assessment grid on p26.

WAYS OF WORKING Group work adult led

IN FOCUS

- Questions ❶ and ❷ assess children's ability to convert measurements of time: seconds into minutes and weeks into days.
- Questions ❸ and ❹ assess children's ability to convert and compare times represented in different ways (including analogue clocks and 12-hour and 24-hour digital clocks).
- Question ❺ assesses children's ability to convert between units of time in a problem-solving context.
- Question ❻ is a SATs-style question where conversion between units of time (minutes and seconds) is necessary to solve the problem.

ANSWERS AND COMMENTARY

Children who have mastered the concepts in this unit will be able to convert between seconds, minutes and hours, and between days, weeks, months and years. They will confidently use these units of measurement in their description of times. They will be able to express times in both analogue and digital forms, including 24-hour clock times. Children will apply these elements to confidently solve mathematical problems.

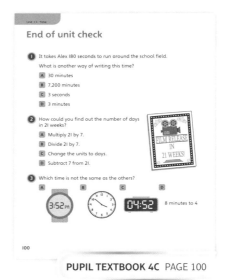

PUPIL TEXTBOOK 4C PAGE 100

PUPIL TEXTBOOK 4C PAGE 101

Q	A	WRONG ANSWERS AND MISCONCEPTIONS	STRENGTHENING UNDERSTANDING
1	D	A suggests the child has divided by 6 instead of 60. B suggests the child has multiplied instead of divided. C suggests the child has correctly calculated the answer, but confused the units of time.	Play matching pairs games using flashcards, where children are required to match times expressed in different units. Provide three different types of clocks in the classroom (analogue, 12-hour digital and 24-hour digital). Use the following activities to build connections between the three ways of showing the time: • At various times during the school day, ask children to express the time in these three different ways. • Cover up one or two of the clocks and encourage children to predict what they show. • Alter one of the clocks so that it shows the wrong time. Ask children to identify which clock is wrong and what it should show.
2	A	B or D suggest the child has used the incorrect operation. C suggests the child does not understand that a calculation is needed to convert between units of time.	
3	C	A, B or D suggests the child has incorrectly identified the common time.	
4	B	A suggests the child does not realise that 24-hour clock times revert to 00:00 after reaching 23:59. C suggests the child has added 12. D suggests the child is not aware that 24-hour times must have four digits.	
5	B	A or C suggests the child has incorrectly converted the units of time before comparing them. D suggests the child has chosen the largest number.	
6	1 minute 19 seconds	Some may get the right answer in seconds, but then not manage to convert it correctly.	

My journal

WAYS OF WORKING Independent thinking

ANSWERS AND COMMENTARY

Children's answers will vary depending on their age (which may be more, equal to or less than 100 months). Their responses should show one of the following methods:

- Children should convert 100 months into years and months and then compare this with their own age. For example: *I know I have been alive less than 100 months because 100 months is the same as 8 years and 4 months (100 divided by 12 is 8 remainder 4). I am 8 years and 2 months old, so I have been alive less than 100 months.*
- Children should convert their own age into months and then compare this with 100 months. For example: *I know that I have been alive less than 100 months because I am 8 years and 2 months old. This is the same as 98 months (8 multiplied by 12 is 96 plus another 2 months equals 98).*

To help children work out how to answer the question, ask:
- *Write your age down. Is it written in the same units as the number you want to compare it to? How can you convert either your age or the number in the question so that they are written in the same units?*

Power check

WAYS OF WORKING Independent thinking

ASK
- *What did you know about converting between different units of time before you began this unit?*
- *Do you think you would be able to convert between an analogue time and a 12-hour or 24-hour digital time on your own?*

Power puzzle

WAYS OF WORKING Independent thinking or pair work

IN FOCUS The purpose of this puzzle is for children to move seamlessly between different units of time, finding equivalent pairs until there is one square left. Children should colour each pair using a different colour. When they reach the final square, a final challenge might be to invent a match that could go with it.

ANSWERS AND COMMENTARY

The pairs are as follows:

06:56 matched with 6:56 am
3 hours 46 minutes matched with 226 minutes
60 months matched with 5 years
Analogue clock showing four minutes to 6 matched with 17:56
8 weeks 4 days matched with 60 days
4 years 11 months matched with 59 months
Analogue clock showing ten past 1 matched with 13:10

The remaining, unmatched square is: 01:02

After the unit

- How did children respond to the materials and approaches used during the unit?
- How do you feel that the unit assessment went?

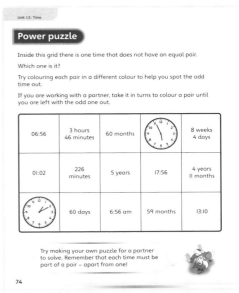

PUPIL PRACTICE BOOK 4C PAGE 73

PUPIL PRACTICE BOOK 4C PAGE 74

Strengthen and **Deepen** activities for this unit can be found in the *Power Maths* online subscription.

Unit 14
Statistics

Mastery Expert tip! "My class really enjoyed it when we made cross-curricular links to other subjects, collecting our own data to analyse. This helped them make real connections between the data and its presentation; it was particularly effective when introducing them to continuous data and line graphs for the first time."

Don't forget to watch the Unit 14 video!

WHY THIS UNIT IS IMPORTANT

This unit exposes children to a range of ways in which information and data can be presented and interpreted. Children explore pictograms, bar charts and tables in more detail than they have before. Children begin exploring the use of a wider range of scales and interpreting quarter symbols in pictograms, as well as reading from bars which are a quarter of the way between two marked points on a bar chart.

Children are shown data presented in line graphs for the first time and are introduced to the distinction between continuous and discrete data. They are also exposed to a range of more complex, multi-step problems, which use information presented in a range of charts and tables.

WHERE THIS UNIT FITS

→ Unit 13: Time
→ **Unit 14: Statistics**
→ Unit 15: Geometry – angles and 2D shapes

In this unit, children build on the work from Year 3 on statistics, where they were introduced to basic pictograms, bar charts and tables. Children are encouraged to explore the range of information which they can get from the data that is presented to them. Children will explore how the structure of line graphs, and data presented within them, differs from bar charts. Children should then be able to apply this knowledge through the remaining units in Year 4.

Before they start this unit, it is expected that children:
• know how to interpret a basic pictogram and bar graph
• are confident in carrying out addition, subtraction, multiplication and division calculations
• can recall the 1–12 times-tables and related division facts.

ASSESSING MASTERY

Children who have mastered this unit can interpret data that is presented in a range of ways, including pictograms, bar charts, line graphs and tables. Children can use this data to answer a range of questions, including comparison, ordering and total questions. They can also make their own statements based on the data presented to them and are beginning to compare linked data which is presented across multiple sources. Children can answer more complex multi-step problems, which use information presented in a chart, table or graph.

COMMON MISCONCEPTIONS	STRENGTHENING UNDERSTANDING	GOING DEEPER
Children may miscount the number of pictogram symbols (and their value) or misread the value on the vertical axis when a point falls between two marked values on the axis.	Represent the pictogram and/or bar chart physically using counters, cubes or other objects. Encourage children to physically count each object, and to use the key in a pictogram, or vertical axis in a bar chart to work out the total value. You can also link the vertical axis to a vertical number line.	Encourage children to make their own increasingly complex statements based on data, including data presented across multiple types of charts and tables. Ask: *What else can you tell me based on this data? How do you know? What questions could you ask someone else based on this data?*
Children may identify the incorrect operation when answering questions and carrying out calculations based on the data presented to them.	Ask: *What is the question asking you to do? What operation could this involve?* Encourage children to consider the different steps they need to take to solve multi-step problems.	Encourage children to think about whether a statement is true or false in relation to the data being presented.

Unit 14: Statistics

Use these pages to introduce the unit focus to children. You can use the characters to explore how data can be presented.

STRUCTURES AND REPRESENTATIONS

Children are presented with a range of ways in which to represent data, including:

Pictograms:

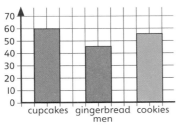

	Number
cupcakes	⊙⊙⊙⊙⊙
gingerbread men	⊙⊙⊙⊙
cookies	⊙⊙⊙⊙◖

Each ⊙ represents 10 items.

Bar charts:

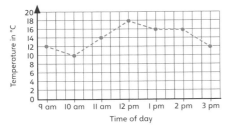

Line graphs:

Tables:

	Class 4T	Class 4A	Class 4S
Raisin	16	10	6
Chocolate	5	18	19
Rainbow	9	14	22

Children may also benefit from using the structures and representations introduced in Year 3 to support their calculations, including the number line.

KEY LANGUAGE

There is some key language that children will need to know as part of the learning in this unit.

→ table, line graph, bar chart, pictogram

→ discrete data, continuous data

→ operation

→ altogether, more than, greatest, smallest

→ compare

PUPIL TEXTBOOK 4C PAGE 102

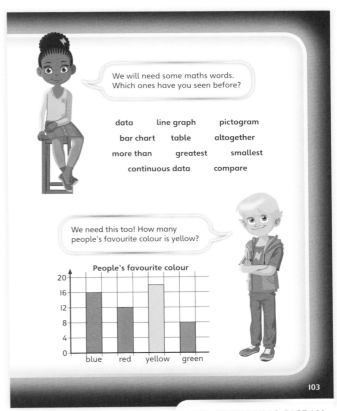

PUPIL TEXTBOOK 4C PAGE 103

135

Charts and tables ❶

Learning focus

In this lesson, children will extend their knowledge of bar charts, tables and pictograms to interpret data with larger numbers and a wider range of scales.

Small steps

→ Previous step: Problem solving – units of time
→ **This step: Charts and tables (1)**
→ Next step: Charts and tables (2)

NATIONAL CURRICULUM LINKS

Year 4 Statistics

Interpret and present discrete and continuous data using appropriate graphical methods, including bar charts and time graphs.

ASSESSING MASTERY

Children can read data and values from a range of bar charts and pictograms which have various scales and symbol values, including half and quarter values. Children can interpret data from tables and use this to complete charts and pictograms, as well as answer simple comparison questions.

COMMON MISCONCEPTIONS

Children may misread the scales on a bar chart, assuming that each square always stands for one. Ask:
• *What do you notice about the scale on the vertical axis of this chart? What does it increase in?*

Children may also assume that each symbol in a pictogram has a value of 1. Draw children's attention to the key on a pictogram and ask:
• *What can you look at to identify the value of each symbol? Is this always the same for every pictogram?*

STRENGTHENING UNDERSTANDING

Strengthen understanding of bar charts by asking children to recreate the bars using multilink cubes. This will help children compare the heights of each bar.

GOING DEEPER

Encourage children to make statements based on the data presented to them in different charts. For example, ask: *What can you tell me based on this bar chart/pictogram?*

KEY LANGUAGE

In lesson: bar chart, half, between, **pictogram**, symbol, table, row, column, vertical, horizontal

Other language used by the teacher: most, altogether

STRUCTURES AND REPRESENTATIONS

number lines, bar chart, pictogram

RESOURCES

Mandatory: rulers

Optional: multilink cubes

 In the eTextbook of this lesson, you will find interactive links to a selection of teaching tools.

Before you teach ⏸

• Are children confident finding numbers that lie half-way between two numbers?
• Can children interpret data given in tables?

Discover

WAYS OF WORKING Pair work

ASK

- Question **1**: *What types of chart are shown here?*
- Question **1**: *What can you tell from the charts?*
- Question **1** a): *What do you think half a symbol stands for?*

IN FOCUS This activity re-introduces children to pictograms and bar charts, which they last saw in Year 3. Children read a range of data, including where half values are used, and make simple comparisons.

PRACTICAL TIPS Use multilink cubes to interpret data on the bar chart and pictogram to check children can make connections between the data being presented in different ways. Use a number line to help with the understanding of scales.

ANSWERS

Question **1** a): Class 4T made 45 cookies. Class 4A made 55 cookies.

Question **1** b): Class 4A made more cupcakes than any other item. Class 4A made 60 cupcakes.

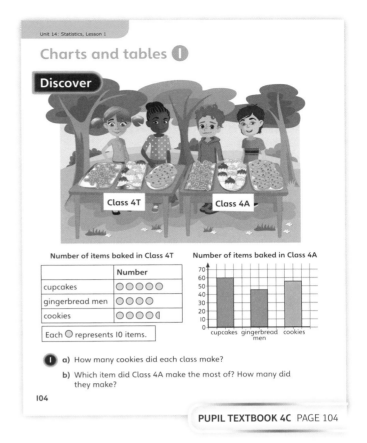

PUPIL TEXTBOOK 4C PAGE 104

Share

WAYS OF WORKING Whole class teacher led

ASK

- Question **1** a): *How can you work out how many cookies were made from the pictogram?*
- Question **1** a): *How can you work out the value of a bar half-way between two points?*
- Question **1** a): *How can you make sure you read the correct value on the vertical axis of the bar chart?*
- Question **1** a): *Is there more than one way to work out the value for items on a pictogram?*
- Question **1** b): *Can you work out which is the most popular item without working out the value of each bar?*

IN FOCUS In this part of the lesson, children must interpret information from pictograms and bar charts, where there are half symbols in a pictogram and the bar is half-way between two marked values on a bar chart. When working out the total value of an item on a pictogram, draw children's attention to the two different ways of working (repeated addition and multiplication) and the link between the two.

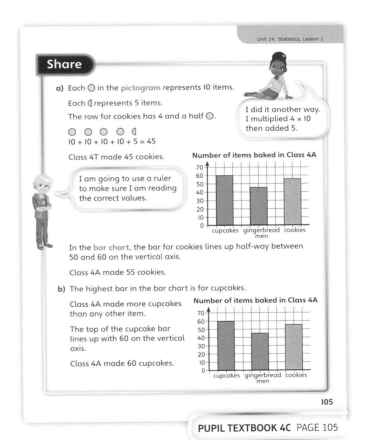

PUPIL TEXTBOOK 4C PAGE 105

137

Think together

WAYS OF WORKING Whole class teacher led (I do, We do, You do)

ASK

- Question **1** a): *How can you work out how many cupcakes each class has sold?*
- Question **1** b): *How can you work out the value of the $\frac{1}{4}$ of a symbol?*
- Question **2**: *How can you fill in the missing information?*

IN FOCUS In question **1**, children are introduced to $\frac{1}{4}$ pictogram symbols for the first time, and so need to extend their knowledge of how to calculate the value of $\frac{1}{2}$ symbols to calculating the value of $\frac{1}{4}$ symbols.

STRENGTHEN To strengthen understanding of the value of quarter symbols, represent a pictogram symbol using a set of 4 interconnecting cubes (in a 2 by 2 arrangement). You can then discuss what each quarter of the symbol would be worth, physically splitting up the symbol.

DEEPEN Deepen understanding by encouraging children to justify their responses to each question within question **3**. As this is the first time children have come across quarters, ask: *How could you work out the value of the bar that is $\frac{1}{4}$ of a way between two marked values?*

ASSESSMENT CHECKPOINT Use question **1** to assess whether children can independently read values from a bar chart and pictogram, including where the height of the bar is in between two marked numbers on the vertical axis on a bar chart and when there are part symbols on a pictogram.

ANSWERS

Question **1** a): Class 5T sold 28 cupcakes.
　　　　　　　Class 5A sold 45 cupcakes.

Question **1** b): Class 5T sold 26 gingerbread men.

Question **2**: Class 4C raised the most money (£36).

Question **3** a): £650

Question **3** b): Olivia is wrong, it should be 3 quarters of the way up between £600 and £700.

Question **3** c): £2,200

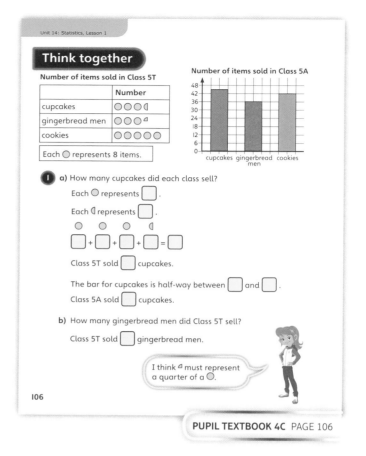

PUPIL TEXTBOOK 4C PAGE 106

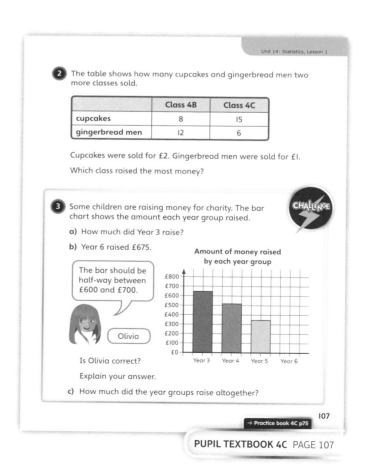

PUPIL TEXTBOOK 4C PAGE 107

Practice

WAYS OF WORKING Independent thinking

IN FOCUS In question ❸, children must construct a pictogram using the information provided in the table and in the key.

STRENGTHEN To support children with question ❶, encourage children to think carefully about the information provided in the key and how they can work out the value of a quarter symbol by halving and then halving again, or by dividing by 4.

DEEPEN Children should begin to solve more complex problems involving charts and tables including where they need to compare different sources of data in order to complete the chart, and where there are missing pieces of information. Question ❺ encourages children to do this, and relies on children having a deep understanding of how each type of chart is constructed. Ask: *How can you work out what the scale on the vertical axis is? How can you work out what value each symbols has? What information can you use to help you?*

ASSESSMENT CHECKPOINT Use questions ❷ and ❸ to assess whether children can correctly interpret data from a table and transfer this to another way of presenting data (in this case a pictogram).

ANSWERS Answers for the **Practice** part of the lesson appear in the separate **Practice and Reflect answer guide**.

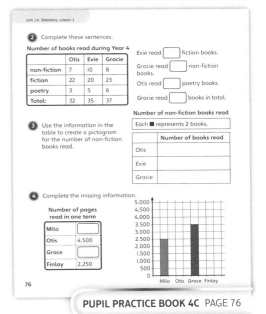

PUPIL PRACTICE BOOK 4C PAGE 75

PUPIL PRACTICE BOOK 4C PAGE 76

Reflect

WAYS OF WORKING Independent thinking

IN FOCUS This activity compares the benefits and similarities of each way of presenting data. Encourage children to discuss whether the type of data and values impact their choice.

ASSESSMENT CHECKPOINT Use this activity to assess whether children are able to identify the benefits of using each different type of representation.

ANSWERS Answers for the **Reflect** part of the lesson appear in the separate **Practice and Reflect answer guide**.

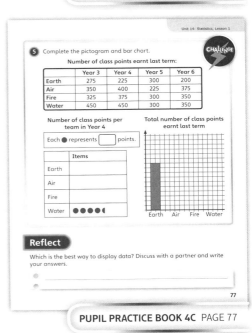

PUPIL PRACTICE BOOK 4C PAGE 77

After the lesson ⏸

- Are children secure at reading data from bar charts, tables and pictograms?
- Can children confidently interpret $\frac{1}{2}$ and $\frac{1}{4}$ symbols in a pictogram?

Charts and tables ②

Learning focus

In this lesson, children will use their knowledge of bar charts, tables and pictograms to answer increasingly complex problems, including those which involve differences and totals.

Small steps

→ Previous step: Charts and tables (1)
→ **This step: Charts and tables (2)**
→ Next step: Line graphs (1)

NATIONAL CURRICULUM LINKS

Year 4 Statistics

Solve comparison, sum and difference problems using information presented in bar charts, pictograms, tables and other graphs.

ASSESSING MASTERY

Children can read data and values from different bar charts and pictograms which have a range of scales and symbol values, and use these to calculate sums and differences. Children can also make direct comparisons between data and draw conclusions from data presented in different ways.

COMMON MISCONCEPTIONS

Children may choose the wrong operation when finding the total or difference. Ask:
• *What is the question asking you to find? Is this an addition or subtraction question?*

STRENGTHENING UNDERSTANDING

Help children interpret the scales on a bar chart where the bar is part-way between marked values. Link the scale on the vertical axis to a number line. Rotate the bar chart to help children see this connection. Ask: *What does this look like? How is it similar or different to a number line?* Help children identify the difference between each marked section, before writing what $\frac{1}{4}$, $\frac{1}{2}$ and $\frac{3}{4}$ of this difference is.

GOING DEEPER

Encourage children to draw their own conclusions based on the data that is presented to them. For example, ask: *Why do you think people spend more on chocolate in April than January?*

KEY LANGUAGE

In lesson: total, sum, difference, altogether, bar chart, half, between, pictogram, symbol, table, row, column, vertical, horizontal

Other language used by the teacher: most, quarter

STRUCTURES AND REPRESENTATIONS

number lines, bar charts, pictograms

RESOURCES

Mandatory: rulers

Optional: multilink cubes

 In the eTextbook of this lesson, you will find interactive links to a selection of teaching tools.

Before you teach ⏸

• Are children confident interpreting bar charts, pictogram and tables?
• Can children find $\frac{1}{4}$ and $\frac{1}{2}$ values on a number line?

Discover

WAYS OF WORKING Pair work

ASK

- Question ❶: *What are these charts called?*
- Question ❶: *What operations do you need to use to solve these problems?*
- Question ❶ a): *How can you work out the difference in the number of tickets?*
- Question ❶ b): *What operation do you need to use to work out the total number of tickets sold?*

IN FOCUS This activity extends the learning from Lesson ❶ and encourages children to find a difference and total, using information drawn from two different representations of data.

PRACTICAL TIPS Use a number line or ruler to help find values along the vertical axis on the bar chart. Use multilink cubes to help children visualise multiples of 12 as well as half and quarter values of 12.

ANSWERS

Question ❶ a): The farm sold 19 more child tickets on Saturday.

Question ❶ b): The farm sold 109 adult tickets altogether over the weekend.

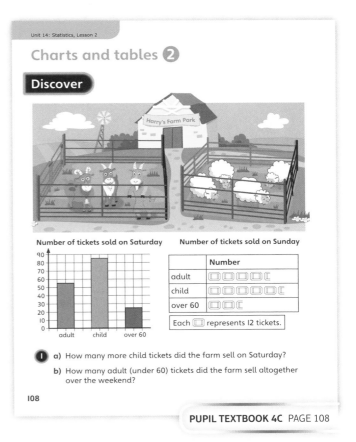

PUPIL TEXTBOOK 4C PAGE 108

Share

WAYS OF WORKING Whole class teacher led

ASK

- Question ❶: *How did you know how much each symbol represents on the pictogram?*
- Question ❶: *How can you make sure you read the correct value on the vertical axis of the bar chart?*
- Question ❶: *How can you work out the value of the bar if it is in between two numbers on the vertical axis?*
- Question ❶: *Is there more than one way to work out the value for items on a pictogram?*

IN FOCUS In this part of the lesson, children identify the information they need from each chart and the operation they need to calculate the difference and total. Discuss the choice of operation with children, encouraging them to justify and explain their decisions.

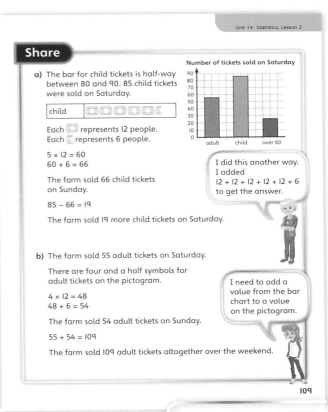

PUPIL TEXTBOOK 4C PAGE 109

Think together

WAYS OF WORKING Whole class teacher led (I do, We do, You do)

ASK

- Question **1** a): *How can you work out if more children or adults fed the lambs?*
- Question **1** b): *What operation do you need to use to find out how many people fed the foals altogether?*
- Question **2**: *How do you know which row and column you need to look at to answer the question?*
- Question **3** a): *How can you use the information we have to complete the table?*

IN FOCUS In question **1** a), children are asked to complete a direct comparison between two values first, refreshing their knowledge of the less than (<) sign.

STRENGTHEN Use a bar model to represent the structure of both sum and difference problems. This will help children identify the correct operation to use in order to solve each problem.

DEEPEN Children should be able to extend their learning and begin to draw their own conclusions based on the data that is presented to them. For example, in question **3**, children should be able to make a range of statements comparing single values, finding the totals and comparing sets of values. They can then be invited to draw conclusions from these statements. For example, ask: *Do people generally like their visit to the farm? How do you know?*

ASSESSMENT CHECKPOINT Use question **1** b) and questions **2** a) and b) to assess whether children can identify the correct operations needed to answer sum and difference questions.

ANSWERS

Question **1** a): 16 more children than adults fed the lambs.

Question **1** b): 75 people fed the foals altogether.

Question **2** a): On Sunday, the café made £600 from hot meals.

Question **2** b): The café made £75 more from cold children's meals on Saturday than Sunday.

Question **3** a): 33 more visitors rated the farm OK on Saturday (69) than Sunday (36).

Question **3** b): More people rated the farm on Saturday (148) than on Sunday (134).

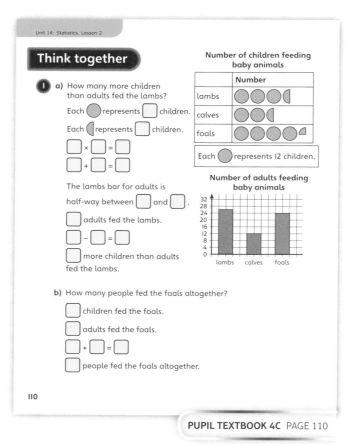

PUPIL TEXTBOOK 4C PAGE 110

PUPIL TEXTBOOK 4C PAGE 111

Practice

WAYS OF WORKING Independent thinking

IN FOCUS In question **3**, children's reasoning skills are developed further, as they are asked to interpret the information given in order to calculate the missing pieces of information from a table and then use this to populate a bar chart.

STRENGTHEN To support children with question **3** it may be useful to break down the task further. Encourage children to consider the relationships between the values in the table and the information given; for example, ask: *How many points did Tom score on Vault Explorer? We know that Mark scored 450 more than Tom, so how do we work out Mark's score?* Once children have correctly filled in the missing information from the table, look at the features of a bar chart. Review the scale provided, identifying what half and a quarter of 100 are, before inviting children to mark the values on the chart.

DEEPEN Children should begin to solve more complex logic-style questions that involve charts, tables and pictograms. Question **4** provides children with the opportunity to develop these skills. Challenge children to create their own logic-style clues for other charts and tables, including those presented elsewhere in this lesson.

ASSESSMENT CHECKPOINT Use question **2** to assess whether children can use the relationship between individual pieces of data and the total; for example, can they work out the value of one piece of data if they know the total and the other data values?

ANSWERS Answers for the **Practice** part of the lesson appear in the separate **Practice and Reflect answer guide**.

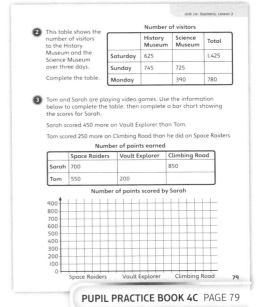

PUPIL PRACTICE BOOK 4C PAGE 78

PUPIL PRACTICE BOOK 4C PAGE 79

Reflect

WAYS OF WORKING Independent thinking

IN FOCUS In this part of the lesson, children reflect on the different types of graph that they know.

ASSESSMENT CHECKPOINT Use this activity to assess whether children are able to describe different ways of presenting and identifying data and to provide coherent reasoning as to which method they prefer over others.

ANSWERS Answers for the **Reflect** part of the lesson appear in the separate **Practice and Reflect answer guide**.

After the lesson ⏸

- Are children secure at interpreting data from bar charts, table and pictograms?
- How can you provide opportunities for children to further use and develop these skills during day-to-day school life?

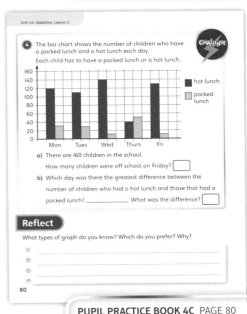

PUPIL PRACTICE BOOK 4C PAGE 80

143

Line graphs ❶

Learning focus

In this lesson, children will read values from a line graph.

Small steps

→ Previous step: Charts and tables (2)
→ **This step: Line graphs (1)**
→ Next step: Line graphs (2)

NATIONAL CURRICULUM LINKS

Year 4 Statistics

Interpret and present discrete and continuous data using appropriate graphical methods, including bar charts and time graphs.

ASSESSING MASTERY

Children can read data from line graphs, including where values lie in between two marked points on an axis. Children can identify which axis to read the data from and read the value from any point on the line. They can make simple statements about the values.

COMMON MISCONCEPTIONS

Children may think they can only read data from the marked points on the x-axis. Draw children's attention to the type of data displayed. Discuss how this is continuous and that the line graphs help us to estimate values in between two marked points. Ask:

• *What do you notice about the type of data shown in this graph? How is it the same as or different from the types of data we were looking at in our last lesson?*

STRENGTHENING UNDERSTANDING

To help children interpret the continuous scales on a line graph link the scales on both axes to a number line, rotating the chart so that the vertical axis is horizontal to help make the connection.

Children may also benefit from recording data and re-creating a line graph so that they are able to understand the connection between the marked points and the continuous sets of data. Consider linking data collection to a real-life context. Discuss how the measurement is still changing in between marked values.

GOING DEEPER

Encourage children to begin to consider the benefits of a line graph over other ways of presenting data. Ask: *Why is the line graph better at presenting this data compared to a bar graph, pictogram, or table?*

KEY LANGUAGE

In lesson: line graph, axis, vertical, horizontal

Other language to be used by teacher: most, least, longest, shortest, continuous data, bar chart

STRUCTURES AND REPRESENTATIONS

line graphs

RESOURCES

Mandatory: rulers

Optional: number lines, squared paper

 In the eTextbook of this lesson, you will find interactive links to a selection of teaching tools.

Before you teach ❶❶

• Are children confident at reading values from the vertical axis of bar charts, including when the bar height is in between two marked values?
• Have children been exposed to continuous data before in other subject areas?

Discover

Unit 14: Statistics, Lesson 3

WAYS OF WORKING Pair work

ASK

- Question **1**: *How is this chart the same as / different from the charts you have seen so far?*
- Question **1** a): *How can you find out what the temperature was at a given time?*

IN FOCUS This is the first time children have been exposed to line graphs so encourage them to explore the graph, including the title and axes. Discuss how this graph is different from other graphs they have explored in previous lessons.

PRACTICAL TIPS Use rulers to interpret continuous values on a line graph, reading across from both the horizontal and vertical axes. Use a number line to help understanding of in between values on a continuous scale.

ANSWERS

Question **1** a): The temperature at 11 am is 14 °C.

Question **1** b): The temperature decreases by 5 °C between 12:30 pm and 3 pm (from 17 °C to 12 °C).

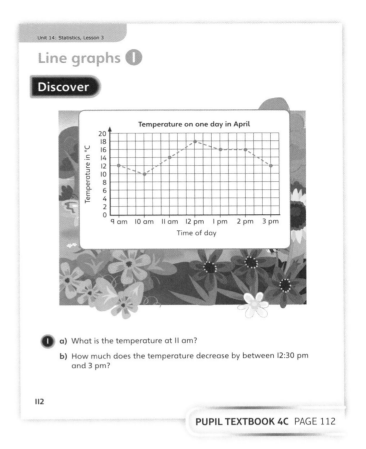

Line graphs ❶

Discover

1 a) What is the temperature at 11 am?

b) How much does the temperature decrease by between 12:30 pm and 3 pm?

112

PUPIL TEXTBOOK 4C PAGE 112

Share

WAYS OF WORKING Whole class teacher led

ASK

- Question **1**: *How is the data shown here different to the data shown on bar charts?*
- Question **1** a): *Where can we find 11 am on the graph? How can you work out the temperature at 11 am?*
- Question **1** a): *What could you use to help you read the times and temperatures accurately?*
- Question **1** b): *Is 12:30 pm marked on the horizontal axis? Where do you think 12:30 pm would be?*
- Question **1** b): *How can you work out a value that falls in between two marked points on the vertical axis?*

IN FOCUS In this part of the lesson, children read information from a line graph, starting from a given value for the horizontal axis and then reading the corresponding value from the vertical axis. Ensure children understand that a line graph shows continuous data, which means that you can read values that are in between marked values on the horizontal axis and use the line to find the approximate corresponding value on the vertical axis. In comparison, bar charts and pictograms show categorical, discrete data.

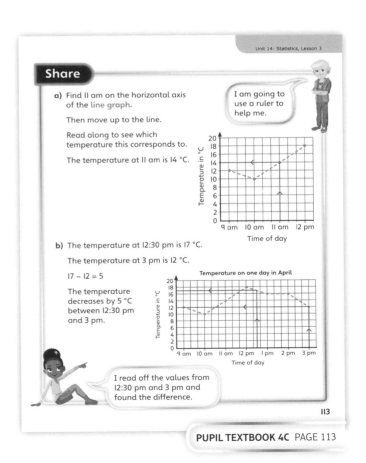

Share

a) Find 11 am on the horizontal axis of the line graph.

Then move up to the line.

Read along to see which temperature this corresponds to.

The temperature at 11 am is 14 °C.

I am going to use a ruler to help me.

b) The temperature at 12:30 pm is 17 °C.

The temperature at 3 pm is 12 °C.

17 − 12 = 5

The temperature decreases by 5 °C between 12:30 pm and 3 pm.

I read off the values from 12:30 pm and 3 pm and found the difference.

113

PUPIL TEXTBOOK 4C PAGE 113

Think together

WAYS OF WORKING Whole class teacher led (I do, We do, You do)

ASK

- Question **1** a): *How can you work out the temperature at a given time?*
- Question **1** c): *2:30 pm is not marked on the horizontal axis. How can you find the temperature at 2:30 pm?*
- Question **1** d): *How can you use the shape of the line to help you find out when it was warmest inside?*
- Question **3**: *Which axis do you need to read from in order to complete each of these sentences?*

IN FOCUS In this part of the lesson, children are introduced to reading values from a line graph from both the horizontal and vertical axes. Discuss how the continuous nature of the graph makes it possible to read values from either axis, including from points which lie in between marked values. In question **1** d), children determine the highest values by looking at the highest points of the line graph and begin to make statements based on the graph.

STRENGTHEN To help children read accurately from the horizontal or vertical axis, encourage them to use a ruler to draw a horizontal or vertical line from a given point on the axis to the line. They can then draw a horizontal or vertical line from this point to the other axis and read the required value.

DEEPEN Children should be able to extend their learning to interpret more complex line graphs, including where multiple sets of data are plotted as two or more lines. Question **3** provides an opportunity for children to explore this. Ask children to explain why they think there may be two lines on the same graph. They should begin to consider how they can use this to help them compare the two sets of data. Ask: *How can you use this line graph to help you compare the data for October and December?*

ASSESSMENT CHECKPOINT Use question **1** to assess whether children are able to accurately read values from a line graph, when they have to read values for a given point on the horizontal axis.

ANSWERS

Question **1** a): The temperature was 24 °C at 11 am.

Question **1** b): The temperature was 25 °C at 1 pm.

Question **1** c): The temperature was 25 °C at 2:30 pm.

Question **1** d): It was warmest at 2 pm.

Question **1** e): The temperature was 21 °C at 10:15 am.

Question **2**: It is above 24 °C for approximately $2\frac{1}{2}$ hours (from 12:30 pm to 3 pm).

Question **3** a): The temperature was 11 °C.

Question **3** b): The difference is 2 °C.

Question **3** c): For example:
Same: It was warmest at 12 pm on both days.
Different: It was warmer at 8 am than it was at 2 pm on 1 October, but the opposite is true of 1 December (warmer at 2 pm than at 8 am).

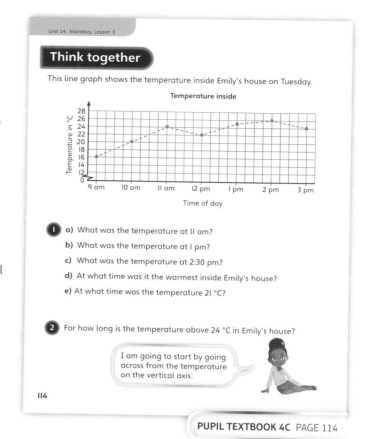

PUPIL TEXTBOOK 4C PAGE 114

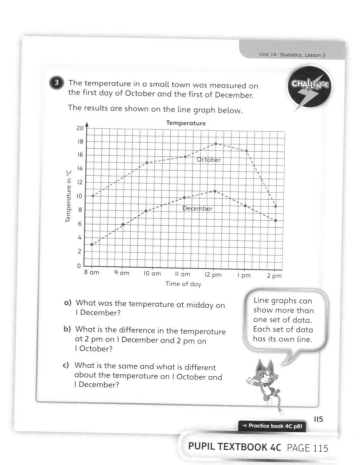

PUPIL TEXTBOOK 4C PAGE 115

Practice

WAYS OF WORKING Independent thinking

IN FOCUS Questions ❶, ❷ and ❸ help children practise reading from both the horizontal and vertical axis of a line graph. In question ❸, children make simple statements based on the line graph. For example, they must work out when the shadow is shortest and longest by looking at the height of the line at various points.

STRENGTHEN To support children in correctly identifying which axis to read from, ask children to consider which piece of information they 'know'. For example, in question ❸, ask: *Do you know the time or the length of the shadow?* Encourage children to ask themselves this question every time they are reading information from a line graph.

DEEPEN Children should begin to explore how line graphs can be developed and used to show more complex sets of information. Question ❺ exposes children to line graphs which have more than one set of data. Ask children about the benefits of presenting data this way. Ask: *Why could it be useful to show the results for both these cars on one graph, rather than on two separate graphs?*

ASSESSMENT CHECKPOINT Use questions ❸ and ❹ to assess whether children can correctly interpret data from a line graph and transfer this to another way of presenting data, such as in a table.

ANSWERS Answers for the **Practice** part of the lesson appear in the separate **Practice and Reflect answer guide**.

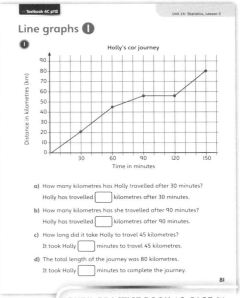

PUPIL PRACTICE BOOK 4C PAGE 81

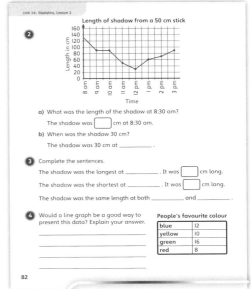

PUPIL PRACTICE BOOK 4C PAGE 82

Reflect

WAYS OF WORKING Independent thinking

IN FOCUS Children reflect on when it is appropriate to use a line graph.

ASSESSMENT CHECKPOINT Use this activity to assess whether children are able to identify the key feature of a line graph, and when a bar chart would be the more efficient option.

ANSWERS Answers for the **Reflect** part of the lesson appear in the separate **Practice and Reflect answer guide**.

After the lesson ⏸

- Are all children secure at reading continuous data from a line graph?
- Are children able to make connections when looking at the same data presented differently?

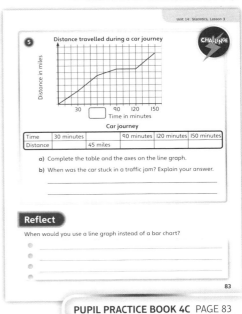

PUPIL PRACTICE BOOK 4C PAGE 83

Line graphs ②

Learning focus

In this lesson, children will continue to explore line graphs, and will make statements and comparisons based on data presented in line graphs.

Small steps

→ Previous step: Line graphs (1)
→ **This step: Line graphs (2)**
→ Next step: Problem solving – graphs

NATIONAL CURRICULUM LINKS

Year 4 Statistics

Solve comparison, sum and difference problems using information presented in bar charts, pictograms, tables and other graphs.

ASSESSING MASTERY

Children can read and compare data from both axes on a line graph, including where values lie in between two marked points on an axis, and use this to make comparisons and find the difference between two points. They can also use the shape and structure of a line graph to make statements about the rate of change and the highest and lowest values.

COMMON MISCONCEPTIONS

Children may think that the highest and lowest values are always the first and last points of a graph. Ask:
• *Where would you find the highest and lowest value on the vertical axis? Which point of the graph is at the highest and lowest point?*

STRENGTHENING UNDERSTANDING

To help children make statements about the rate of change, encourage them to collect data and create their own graph. Ask: *What does the steepness of the line between each set of points say about the rate of change?*

GOING DEEPER

Encourage children to make deeper and more hypothetical statements based on data presented to them in line graphs. For example, if presented with the timings of a race, encourage children to consider which athlete they think is the best and why.

KEY LANGUAGE

In lesson: line graph, **continuous data,** axis, vertical, horizontal, comparison

Other language to be used by the teacher: most, least, longest, shortest

STRUCTURES AND REPRESENTATIONS

line graph

RESOURCES

Mandatory: rulers

Optional: number lines, squared paper

 In the eTextbook of this lesson, you will find interactive links to a selection of teaching tools.

Before you teach

• Are children confident reading line graphs?
• How could children collect data as part of your wider curriculum coverage?

Discover

WAYS OF WORKING Pair work

ASK

- Question **1** a): *How can you work out how far Sofia travelled between two different times?*
- Question **1** b): *How can you work out how long it took Sofia to travel a certain distance?*

IN FOCUS In this part of the lesson, children are expected to apply their knowledge of how to read information from line graphs, which they have developed in the previous lesson, to answer comparison questions based on information presented in a line graph.

PRACTICAL TIPS Use a ruler to draw lines up from the horizontal axis to the graph line to find the corresponding vertical axis value. Remind children of the subtraction method to find out the difference between two values.

ANSWERS

Question **1** a): Sofia cycled 25 km between 11 am and 12 pm.

Question **1** b): It took Sofia 1 hour and 15 minutes to travel the next 40 km.

PUPIL TEXTBOOK 4C PAGE 116

Share

WAYS OF WORKING Whole class teacher led

ASK

Question **1** b): *Which axis should you look at first?*

IN FOCUS In part b), children read first from the vertical axis and build on the skill of identifying which axis to read from, which was developed in the previous lesson.

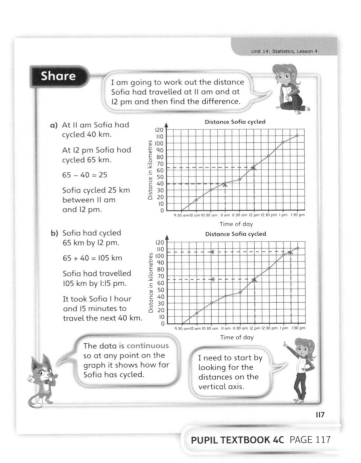

PUPIL TEXTBOOK 4C PAGE 117

Think together

WAYS OF WORKING Whole class teacher led (I do, We do, You do)

ASK

- Question ❶ b): *11:15 am is not marked on the horizontal axis. How can you work out the distance at 11:15 am?*
- Question ❷: *Which axis do you need to start to read from to solve this question?*
- Question ❸ a): *How can you use the two lines to help you make comparisons between the athletes?*
- Question ❸ a): *How does the shape of the two lines and their relationship to each other help you work out when both athletes had run the same distance?*

IN FOCUS In question ❷, children read first from the vertical axis, and build on the skill of identifying which axis to read from, which was developed in the previous lesson of this unit.

STRENGTHEN In question ❸, to help children differentiate between the two different sets of data shown on one graph, encourage them to focus on one set of data at a time. Break the questions down into narrower ones based on each data set. For example, ask: *Which line shows how far Ian has run? How far has Ian run after 60 minutes?*

DEEPEN Children should be able to use line graphs in order to make their own statements. They should also be able to extend this to drawing more detailed conclusions or hypotheses, giving reasons to support their ideas. For example, in question ❸, ask: *Who do you think is the best athlete?* and ask children to use the graph to help justify their answers.

ASSESSMENT CHECKPOINT Use question ❶ to assess whether children can accurately answer simple comparison questions based on information presented in a line graph. Question ❸ assesses whether children can make simple statements about data.

ANSWERS

Question ❶ a): Toshi travelled 25 km between 12:30 pm and 1:30 pm.

Question ❶ b): Toshi travelled 50 km between 11:15 am and 12:45 pm.

Question ❶ c): The race started at 9:30 am.

Question ❶ d): This could be the same race that Sofia took part in as they both cycled the same distance, and started and ended at the same times.

Question ❷: Toshi took $1\frac{1}{2}$ hours to travel between 20 km and 70 km.

Question ❸ a): After 60 minutes, Ian had run 16 km and Jo had run 14 km.
It took Jo 140 minutes and Ian 130 minutes to run 34 km.
Before the end of the race, Ian and Jo had both run exactly the same distance after 100 minutes.
The length of the running race was 42 km.

Question ❸ b): Any statements that are correct based on the graph presented in this question.

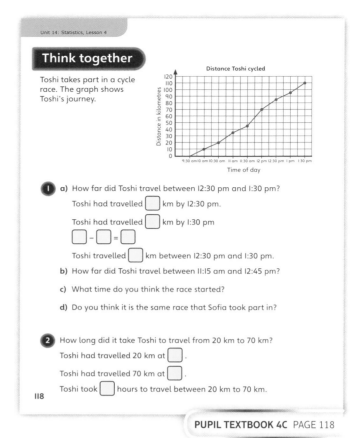

Think together

Toshi takes part in a cycle race. The graph shows Toshi's journey.

Distance Toshi cycled

❶ a) How far did Toshi travel between 12:30 pm and 1:30 pm?

Toshi had travelled ☐ km by 12:30 pm.

Toshi had travelled ☐ km by 1:30 pm

☐ – ☐ = ☐

Toshi travelled ☐ km between 12:30 pm and 1:30 pm.

b) How far did Toshi travel between 11:15 am and 12:45 pm?

c) What time do you think the race started?

d) Do you think it is the same race that Sofia took part in?

❷ How long did it take Toshi to travel from 20 km to 70 km?

Toshi had travelled 20 km at ☐ .

Toshi had travelled 70 km at ☐ .

Toshi took ☐ hours to travel between 20 km to 70 km.

118

PUPIL TEXTBOOK 4C PAGE 118

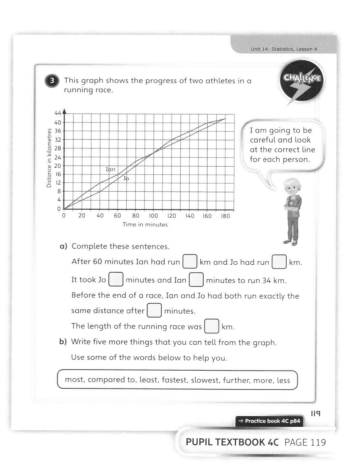

CHALLENGE

❸ This graph shows the progress of two athletes in a running race.

I am going to be careful and look at the correct line for each person.

a) Complete these sentences.

After 60 minutes Ian had run ☐ km and Jo had run ☐ km.

It took Jo ☐ minutes and Ian ☐ minutes to run 34 km.

Before the end of a race, Ian and Jo had both run exactly the same distance after ☐ minutes.

The length of the running race was ☐ km.

b) Write five more things that you can tell from the graph.

Use some of the words below to help you.

most, compared to, least, fastest, slowest, further, more, less

119

→ Practice book 4C p84

PUPIL TEXTBOOK 4C PAGE 119

Practice

WAYS OF WORKING Independent thinking

IN FOCUS For question **1** c), ensure children understand that the period during which it did not rain at all will be the period when the depth of water in the container does not change. It is important for children to make the link between the horizontal line and no change in the data.

STRENGTHEN To support children in making their own statements as part of question **4**, discuss the sentence structures as a group and ask questions together to decide on the information needed. For example, ask: *Between which times does the graph change the most? Could you use these times as the period you are comparing against?*

DEEPEN Encourage children to make comparison statements between multiple sets of data presented on the same line graph. Question **4** provides the ideal stimulus for this; you could ask: *What statements could you make that compare the temperatures in July and December?* Challenge children to create stories around data to demonstrate a deeper understanding of what the data is telling us.

THINK DIFFERENTLY Question **3** encourages children to make their own statements based on the line graph. Scaffolding is gradually reduced so that the final sentence structures are more open ended. This will help to develop children's reasoning skills and their knowledge of the different features and structures of a line graph. Children are also expected to deduce that the steeper the line between two points, the greater the rate of change between those points.

ASSESSMENT CHECKPOINT Use question **3** to assess whether children understand the structure of a line graph and can use it to make statements about the data presented.

ANSWERS Answers for the **Practice** part of the lesson appear in the separate **Practice and Reflect answer guide**.

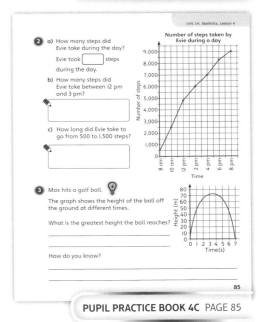

PUPIL PRACTICE BOOK 4C PAGE 84

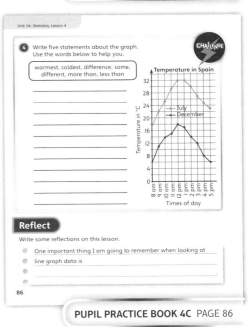

PUPIL PRACTICE BOOK 4C PAGE 85

Reflect

WAYS OF WORKING Independent thinking

IN FOCUS This activity encourages children to consider the type of data that can be represented with a line graph. Discussion about the difference between line and bar graphs should lead children to think about discrete and continuous data.

ASSESSMENT CHECKPOINT Use this activity to assess if children are able to verbalise the importance of line graphs. Do they understand continuous data?

ANSWERS Answers for the **Reflect** part of the lesson appear in the separate **Practice and Reflect answer guide**.

PUPIL PRACTICE BOOK 4C PAGE 86

After the lesson ⏸

- Are children secure at interpreting data and making comparisons from a line graph?
- Can children answer questions about data using inference and deduction?

Problem solving – graphs

Learning focus

In this lesson, children will apply their data interpretation and analysis skills, developed over the past four lessons, to a range of increasingly challenging problems.

Small steps

→ Previous step: Line graphs (2)
→ **This step: Problem solving – graphs**
→ Next step: Identifying angles

NATIONAL CURRICULUM LINKS

Year 4 Statistics

Solve comparison, sum and difference problems using information presented in bar charts, pictograms, tables and other graphs.

ASSESSING MASTERY

Children can read data from line graphs, bar charts, pictograms and tables, and use this data to solve a range of complex problems involving multiple steps and different operations. Children can analyse what other information is available from the data, as well as the benefits and drawbacks of how the data is presented.

COMMON MISCONCEPTIONS

Children may incorrectly identify the number of steps needed to solve a problem, and therefore leave a problem incomplete. Ask:

• *Can you answer this question using information just from the graph/chart? What else do you need to do to the information in order to answer the question?*

STRENGTHENING UNDERSTANDING

To help children solve more complex problems, it can be helpful to break down a problem into steps. Steps could be provided in 'help envelopes' when children need support.

GOING DEEPER

Encourage children to create their own more complex questions for others based on data presented in a range of different ways.

KEY LANGUAGE

In lesson: line graph, bar chart, pictogram, table, axis, vertical, horizontal, comparison

Other language to be used by the teacher: operations, steps, addition, subtraction, multiplication, division

STRUCTURES AND REPRESENTATIONS

line graphs, pictograms, bar charts

RESOURCES

Mandatory: rulers

Optional: number lines, squared paper, help envelopes

 In the eTextbook of this lesson, you will find interactive links to a selection of teaching tools.

Before you teach

• Are children confident answering simple questions about data which is presented in different ways?
• Do children have any weaknesses in calculation methods that need support?

Discover

WAYS OF WORKING Pair work

ASK

- Question ❶ a): *How can you work out the difference between Year 3 and 4 compared to Year 5 and Year 6?*
- Question ❶ b): *How can you use the information you have to help you work out how many cards Year 4 sold? Is there more than one way?*

IN FOCUS In this activity, children apply their knowledge of bar charts to answer more complex questions which involve comparisons across groups of data and carrying out further calculations. These skills will continue to be developed, using a range of data presentation, throughout this lesson.

PRACTICAL TIPS Remind children of the division method to find out how many cards Year 4 used. Use a number line to demonstrate the division method for numbers divisible by 2.

ANSWERS

Question ❶ a): Years 3 and 4 raised £30 more than Years 5 and 6.

Question ❶ b): Year 4 sold 60 cards in total.

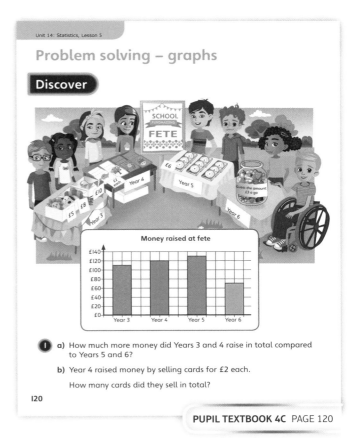

PUPIL TEXTBOOK 4C PAGE 120

Share

WAYS OF WORKING Whole class teacher led

ASK

- Question ❶ a): *How did you work out the difference between Years 3 and 4 compared to Years 5 and 6?*
- Question ❶ a): *How many steps did you have to take in order to solve this problem? What operations did you have to use?*
- Question ❶ b): *How did you work out how many cards Year 4 sold? What information did you use from the graph?*
- Question ❶ b): *What operation did you need to use to help you work out how many cards were sold? How could you check your answer?*

IN FOCUS The focus in this part of the lesson is on children using the data presented in the bar chart to answer more complex, multi-step problems. The skill of reading from a bar chart is not covered in this section, as this should be a secure skill from work earlier on in the unit. Instead, the focus is on how the data can be used to find out a wider range of information.

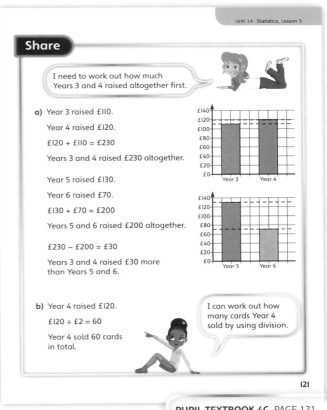

PUPIL TEXTBOOK 4C PAGE 121

Think together

Whole class teacher led (I do, We do, You do)

ASK

- Question **1** a): *Will you need to use more than one operation?*
- Question **1** b): *How can you work out the total amount raised?*
- Question **1** c): *How can you use the fact that each child raised £5 to help you work out how many children there are?*
- Question **2** a): *Is there more than one way to solve this problem?*
- Question **2** b): *How many calculations do you need to carry out to solve this problem?*
- Question **3** a): *How can you use the clues to help you complete the table?*

IN FOCUS In this part of the lesson, children are provided with further opportunity to develop their skills at answering more complex problems, using data presented in bar charts, tables and pictograms. Most questions require multiple steps, using different operations to solve problems.

STRENGTHEN Help children identify the different operations needed to solve a multi-step problem. Ask: *What data do you need to read from the graph/pictogram/table? What do you need to do next to this information in order to solve the problem?*

DEEPEN Encourage children to create their own two-step problem using a table or graph to set for their partner. This will help them consider how two parts of a question are related.

ASSESSMENT CHECKPOINT Use question **1** to assess whether children are able to accurately answer total and comparison questions based on a bar chart.

ANSWERS

Question **1**: Maple and Ash classes raised £60 more than Oak and Willow classes.

Question **1** a): The classes raised £420 altogether.

Question **1** b): There are 23 children in Oak class.

Question **2** a): Lions and owls.

Question **2** b): Lions and dogs made £100 for Year 3.

Question **3**:

Maple	£24
Ash	£36
Oak	£42
Willow	£30

In total Year 5 raised £132.

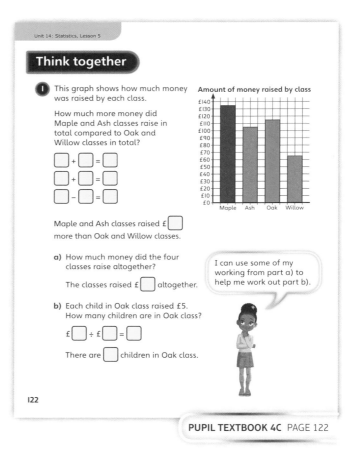

PUPIL TEXTBOOK 4C PAGE 122

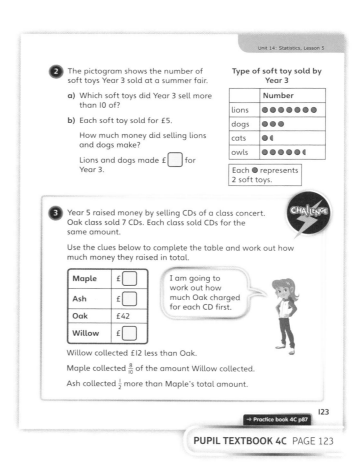

PUPIL TEXTBOOK 4C PAGE 123

Practice

WAYS OF WORKING Independent thinking

IN FOCUS Children are expected to solve problems based on all the ways of presenting data they have met so far: tables, pictograms, bar charts and line graphs. Question **3** allows children to identify and carry out all the steps needed to solve a complex problem. These questions continue to represent the style seen in summative assessments.

STRENGTHEN Provide scaffolding for children to complete which shows the operation needed for the different stages of a calculation, such as those provided in in the earlier stages of this section. Children could then gradually create their own frames, based on the operations that are needed to solve a problem.

DEEPEN Children should be able to make increasingly complex statements based on a chart or graph, and the charts provided in question **4** provide children with an opportunity to do this. Ask: *What other information can you tell from these charts?* Children could then be asked to create their own questions based on the information they have found.

ASSESSMENT CHECKPOINT Use question **3** d) to assess whether children can independently identify the multiple steps needed to solve a more complex problem. If children have not been successful with this question, ensure that you distinguish between calculation errors (but with a complete method) and an incomplete method.

ANSWERS Answers for the **Practice** part of the lesson appear in the separate **Practice and Reflect answer guide**.

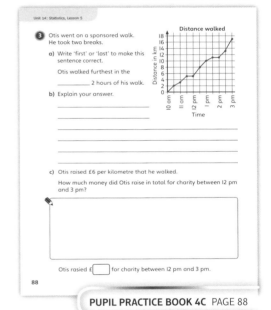

PUPIL PRACTICE BOOK 4C PAGE 87

PUPIL PRACTICE BOOK 4C PAGE 88

Reflect

WAYS OF WORKING Independent thinking

IN FOCUS In this activity, children must interpret the information given on a pictogram and a bar chart in order to devise two questions for a partner, based on the data provided.

ASSESSMENT CHECKPOINT Do children refer to both the bar chart and the pictogram in their questions?

ANSWERS Answers for the **Reflect** part of the lesson appear in the separate **Practice and Reflect answer guide**.

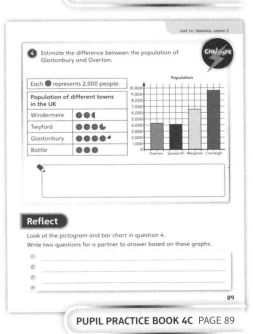

PUPIL PRACTICE BOOK 4C PAGE 89

After the lesson ⏸

- Are children secure at interpreting information and answering more complex questions based on various different types of data presentation?
- Are children stronger or weaker at analysing a particular way of presenting data?

End of unit check

> Don't forget the *Power Maths* unit assessment grid on p26.

WAYS OF WORKING Group work adult led

IN FOCUS The questions in the end of unit check focus on data presented in pictograms, bar charts, line graphs and tables. Through this, children's ability to interpret data is also assessed: care needs to be taken to distinguish between a data interpretation error and a calculation error.

ANSWERS AND COMMENTARY

Children who have mastered this unit can interpret data that is presented in a range of ways, including pictograms, bar charts, line graphs and tables. Children can use this data to answer a range of questions, including comparison, ordering and total questions. They can also make their own statements based on the data presented to them and are beginning to compare linked data which is presented across multiple sources, for example using linked data presented in a bar chart and table to answer and formulate their own questions. Children can answer more complex multi-step problems, which use information presented in a chart, graph or table.

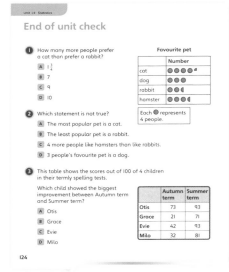

PUPIL TEXTBOOK 4C PAGE 124

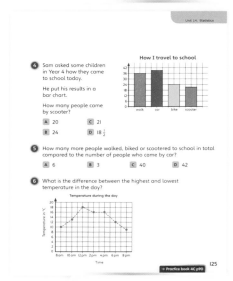

PUPIL TEXTBOOK 4C PAGE 125

Q	A	WRONG ANSWERS AND MISCONCEPTIONS	STRENGTHENING UNDERSTANDING
1	B	Choosing A suggests that the child is interpreting each symbol as representing 1 person.	Encourage children to use the key in the pictogram.
2	D	Choosing A and B indicates that the child is unfamiliar with the basic structure of a pictogram.	To help children with accurately reading from the vertical axis, link the vertical axis to a number line.
3	C	An incorrect answer suggests the child has carried out the wrong calculation.	Draw children's attention to the structure of the question and ask: • *What is the question asking you to do?* • *What operation could this involve?*
4	C	Choosing A, B or D indicates that the child is unsure of how to read a half value on the scale.	
5	D	A and B both suggest that children have not interpreted the steps needed to solve the problem.	For multi-step problems, encourage children to consider the different steps they need to take to solve the problem before they start to solve it.
6	**The difference between the highest and lowest temperature was 9 °C.**	Children must understood that a subtraction is required once the data has been read.	

My journal

WAYS OF WORKING Independent thinking

ANSWERS AND COMMENTARY

Support children to create their own statements by providing them with sentence structures to use; for example, you could provide them with the structures:

• Between _____ and _____ the value of the car increased by _____.
• The value of the car doubled between _____ and ___.
• The car increased in value by _____ between _____ and ___.

Power check

WAYS OF WORKING Independent thinking

ASK

• *What do you know now that you didn't know at the start of this unit?*
• *How confident do you feel about interpreting data in bar charts, pictograms, line graphs and tables?*

Power puzzle

WAYS OF WORKING Pair work

IN FOCUS Use this Power puzzle to identify whether children can use logic clues in order to complete a bar chart. Encourage children to work through the clues step by step, identifying which bar could refer to which child.

This Power puzzle also helps you identify if children understand the structure of a bar chart and how the different parts are related to each other.

ANSWERS AND COMMENTARY If children can complete the first part of the Power puzzle, it suggests they can logically follow clues to aid their interpretation of a chart. If they are not able to complete this, support them by asking specific questions about each clue; for example, ask:

• *We know Masie was 130 cm tall in January. Which bar is Masie?*
• *We know that Raj was 10 cm shorter than Finlay in December? What does that mean Raj's height was in December? Can you draw the bar for Raj in December to show this?*

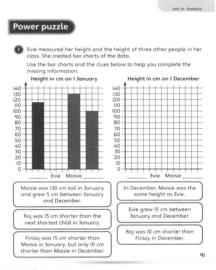

PUPIL PRACTICE BOOK 4C PAGE 90

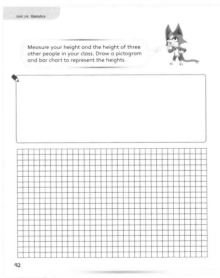

PUPIL PRACTICE BOOK 4C PAGE 91

PUPIL PRACTICE BOOK 4C PAGE 92

After the unit ⏸

• How can you continue to expose children to a range of statistical representations through your day-to-day classroom activities?
• What cross-curricular links can you make?

Strengthen and **Deepen** activities for this unit can be found in the *Power Maths* online subscription.

Unit 15
Geometry – angles and 2D shapes

Mastery Expert tip! "When I taught this unit, I made sure children were able to have as much experience with hands on manipulatives as possible. It made their ability to visualise shapes far stronger!"

Don't forget to watch the Unit 15 video!

WHY THIS UNIT IS IMPORTANT

This unit develops children's understanding of types of 2D shapes and their properties. Children begin by learning about three types of angles: acute, obtuse and right angles. They will use right angles as a way of recognising when angles are acute or obtuse. Children will then compare and order angles in ascending and descending order. Children will then learn about how shapes can be regular or irregular and will discover what this means and how it relates to the angles they have been learning about.

Children then learn about different types of triangles and different types of quadrilaterals. Children will be encouraged to apply all they have learnt to deduce facts about shapes and solve shape based problems and puzzles.

Finally, children will develop their understanding of symmetry, both inside and outside of shapes, and will complete symmetrical shapes and patterns.

WHERE THIS UNIT FITS

→ Unit 14: Statistics
→ **Unit 15: Geometry – angles and 2D shapes**
→ Unit 16: Geometry – position and direction

This unit builds upon the previous work children have done on recognising and identifying the basic properties of 2D shapes from Year 3. Children learnt to recognise angles as a turn and learnt about right angles. This unit also builds upon previous work children did on types of line in Year 3, where they learnt about horizontal and vertical lines including symmetry, and parallel and perpendicular lines.

Before they start this unit, it is expected that children:
• recognise and identify the basic properties of 2D shapes
• use basic vocabulary of shapes to describe 2D shapes
• recognise angles as a turn
• recognise horizontal and vertical lines of symmetry.

ASSESSING MASTERY

Children will demonstrate mastery by being able to confidently recognise and order acute, obtuse and right angles, explaining how right angles can help them to do so. They will be able to name and describe the different types of triangles and quadrilaterals, clearly explaining the similarities and differences. In the case of quadrilaterals, they will be able to point out where a shape may fit under more than one heading. Children will be able to confidently complete shapes and patterns across lines of symmetry in different orientations and will be able to apply their knowledge and understanding to solve problems.

COMMON MISCONCEPTIONS	STRENGTHENING UNDERSTANDING	GOING DEEPER
Children may incorrectly identify irregular polygons as regular, most commonly an oblong rectangle. They may fail to correctly identify the names of irregular polygons.	Provide children with opportunities to explore and sort a variety of triangles and polygons, discussing their similarities and differences.	Children could explore ways of creating different triangles and quadrilaterals by cutting them up or combining them.
Identifying all lines of symmetry can be challenging and some children may only identify those that bisect angles or bisect sides.	Allow children to draw and cut out different types of triangles and quadrilaterals and fold them in order to find the lines of symmetry. Also, provide mirrors so children can see the reflections of complex designs.	

WAYS OF WORKING

Talk through the key learning points, which the characters mention, and the key vocabulary. Do children have any misconceptions? Do they understand what the vocabulary means? A classroom display showing all of the key information will support children throughout this unit.

STRUCTURES AND REPRESENTATIONS

2D shapes: In this unit, children will learn more about the properties of 2D shapes, including whether they are regular or irregular and about the internal angles of shapes.

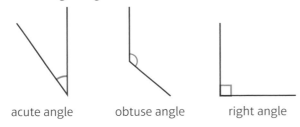

Angles: In this unit, children will be introduced to acute, obtuse and right angles.

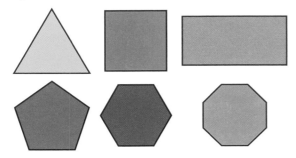

acute angle   obtuse angle   right angle

KEY LANGUAGE

There is some key language that children will need to know as part of the learning in this unit.

→ angle, acute, obtuse, right angle, quarter turn, half turn, interior angles, exterior angles

→ quadrilateral, square, oblong, rectangle, rhombus, parallelogram, trapezium, pentagon, hexagon, octagon, hexadecagon, kite arrowhead, polygon, circle

→ triangle, isosceles, equilateral, scalene

→ regular, irregular, side length, length, perimeter

→ symmetrical, symmetry, line of symmetry, horizontal, vertical, diagonal, reflective, sequence, pattern

→ sort, group, compare, order, properties

→ shape, vertices, parallel

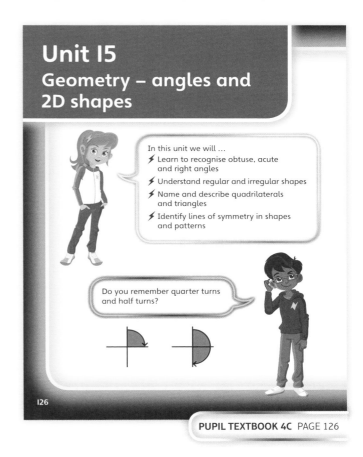

PUPIL TEXTBOOK 4C PAGE 126

PUPIL TEXTBOOK 4C PAGE 127

159

Identifying angles

Learning focus

In this lesson, children will compare angles and identify acute, obtuse and right angles.

Small steps

→ Previous step: Problem solving – graphs
→ **This step: Identifying angles**
→ Next step: Comparing and ordering angles

NATIONAL CURRICULUM LINKS

Year 4 Geometry – Properties of Shapes

Identify acute and obtuse angles and compare and order angles up to two right angles by size.

ASSESSING MASTERY

Children can identify right angles as a quarter turn and understand that angles less than a quarter turn are acute and that angles greater than a quarter turn but smaller than a half turn are obtuse. They can begin to apply this knowledge to describing the angles within 2D shapes.

COMMON MISCONCEPTIONS

Children may need support to identify the type of angle when the orientation means that neither line is vertical or horizontal. Ask:

• *What if you rotated the angle so that one line was horizontal (straight across) or vertical (straight up)? Would that make it easier to see what type of angle it is?*

STRENGTHENING UNDERSTANDING

Strengthen children's understanding by providing them with a square or a quarter circle so that they have a right angle that they can physically compare to other angles.

GOING DEEPER

Challenge children by giving them a paper square and ask them to draw two lines that join the opposite corners of the square. Ask: *Can you identify each angle? Are they acute, obtuse or right angles?*

KEY LANGUAGE

In lesson: angle, corner, size, larger, smaller, quarter turn, right angle, half turn, **obtuse**, **acute**, clock hand, point, shape, vertices, facing

Other language to be used by the teacher: 2D

STRUCTURES AND REPRESENTATIONS

angles, clock face

RESOURCES

Optional: a range of 2D shapes, paper squares, clock face

 In the eTextbook of this lesson, you will find interactive links to a selection of teaching tools.

Before you teach

• Are children aware that angles are a measure of a turn around a point?
• How secure are children in describing turns?
• What practical opportunities can you provide for children to explore turns in relation to acute, obtuse and right angles?

Discover

WAYS OF WORKING Pair work

WAYS OF WORKING Pair work

ASK

• Question **1** a): *Can you see any angles that are the same?*
• Question **1** a): *Do the angles of the bench match any angles in the garden?*
• Question **1** b): *How would you describe the different angles?*

IN FOCUS Question **1** b) encourages children to compare the different angles. Children may not be aware of the terms acute and obtuse, so encourage children to describe them in relation to the right angles.

PRACTICAL TIPS Get children to stand and make quarter turns in both directions so that they get a 'feel' of what a right angle is. Ask them to make a turn less than a right angle and a turn between a quarter turn and a half turn.

ANSWERS

Question **1** a): The bench can fit in corners **a** and **b**.

Question **1** b): Accept any features that are the same/different including:
Same: All of the angles measure the turn between two walls of the garden.
Different:
Angle **a** is a quarter turn or a right angle.
Angle **b** is larger than a right angle.
Angle **c** is smaller than a right angle.

Share

WAYS OF WORKING Whole class teacher led

ASK

• Question **1** a): *Why can the bench fit in corner **b** but not corner **c**?*
• Question **1** a) and b): *What can you say about the angles of the bench?*
• Question **1** a) and b): *Are there any other shapes that have the same angles as the bench?*

IN FOCUS Sparks's comment introduces children to the vocabulary of obtuse and acute and defines them by comparison to a quarter turn. It is important that children understand this definition. Therefore, provide children with the opportunity to compare angles practically with a right angle, using the corner of a square as a right angle. Ask: *Can you find any acute or obtuse angles around the classroom?*

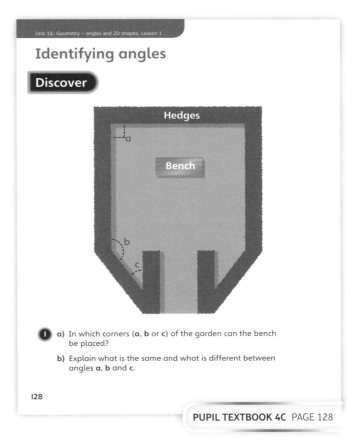

Identifying angles

Discover

a) In which corners (**a**, **b** or **c**) of the garden can the bench be placed?

b) Explain what is the same and what is different between angles **a**, **b** and **c**.

128

PUPIL TEXTBOOK 4C PAGE 128

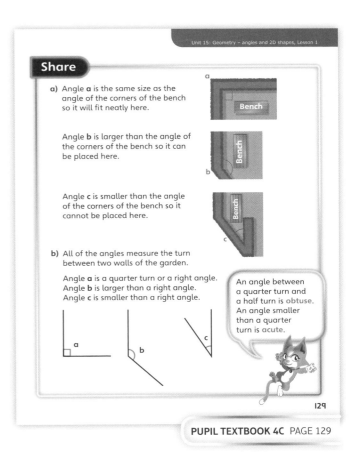

Share

a) Angle **a** is the same size as the angle of the corners of the bench so it will fit neatly here.

Angle **b** is larger than the angle of the corners of the bench so it can be placed here.

Angle **c** is smaller than the angle of the corners of the bench so it cannot be placed here.

b) All of the angles measure the turn between two walls of the garden.

Angle **a** is a quarter turn or a right angle.
Angle **b** is larger than a right angle.
Angle **c** is smaller than a right angle.

An angle between a quarter turn and a half turn is obtuse. An angle smaller than a quarter turn is acute.

129

PUPIL TEXTBOOK 4C PAGE 129

Think together

WAYS OF WORKING Whole class teacher led (I do, We do, You do)

ASK

- Question **2**: *Can you describe the angles on the bench?*
- Question **2**: *Can you think of any other shapes that would fit in the corner?*
- Question **3**: *Have you found all the possibilities?*

IN FOCUS Question **3** relates angles to the size of a turn around a point. Children could use clocks to explore this question in order to reinforce their understanding. Children will discover that there is only one answer for a right angle yet more than one for obtuse and acute. Some children may give possibilities for obtuse that go beyond half a turn. It is important to refer back to the definitions in the **Share** section so children understand that obtuse is between a quarter and half turn.

STRENGTHEN For question **1**, provide children with 2D shapes to represent the benches. This enables children to physically compare the angles between the hedges with the angles of the bench.

DEEPEN For question **3**, ask children: *A turn between which two numbers would create a right angle? Can you find all the possibilities?*

ASSESSMENT CHECKPOINT Questions **1** and **2** will demonstrate whether children can compare angles with a right angle. Question **3** will demonstrate whether children are able to identify acute, obtuse and right angles.

ANSWERS

Question **1**: The bench will fit in corners b, c and d.

Question **2**: The acute angle of the bench will fit in the corner if the bench is turned round.

Question **3** a): i) Numbers 1 and 2 will create an acute turn.
ii) Number 3 will create a right angle.
iii) Numbers 4 and 5 will create an obtuse turn.

Question **3** b): The hand started at number 2.

PUPIL TEXTBOOK 4C PAGE 130

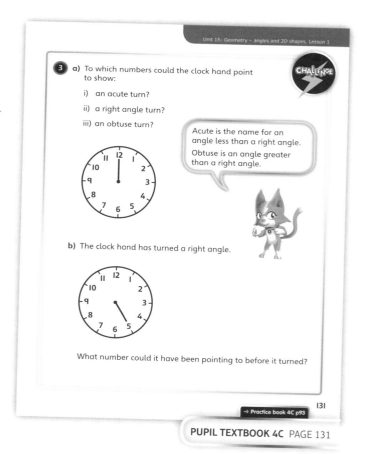

PUPIL TEXTBOOK 4C PAGE 131

Practice

WAYS OF WORKING Independent thinking

IN FOCUS Question **3** looks at sorting shapes by their types of angles. Children not only need to identify the types of angles in the shapes but also sort the shapes based on two criteria.

STRENGTHEN Using squared paper, ask children to draw a shape with only right angles, only obtuse angles or only acute angles. They can use a 2D square to check their angles.

DEEPEN Challenge children by providing them with a range of 2D shapes and asking them to sort them based on their angles. Ask: *Can you sort the shapes in different ways?*

ASSESSMENT CHECKPOINT Children should now be confident identifying and drawing acute, obtuse and right angles. Questions **3** and **4** will demonstrate whether children can identify angles within different 2D shapes.

ANSWERS Answers for the **Practice** part of the lesson appear in the separate **Practice and Reflect answer guide**.

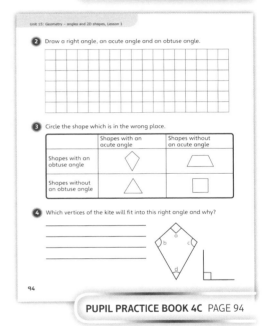

PUPIL PRACTICE BOOK 4C PAGE 93

PUPIL PRACTICE BOOK 4C PAGE 94

Reflect

WAYS OF WORKING Independent thinking

IN FOCUS This section asks children to give a definition for each of the three types of angles, in their own words. This will help to secure their understanding of acute, obtuse and right angles.

ASSESSMENT CHECKPOINT This section will demonstrate if children understand the definitions of acute, obtuse and right angles.

ANSWERS Answers for the **Reflect** part of the lesson appear in the separate **Practice and Reflect answer guide**.

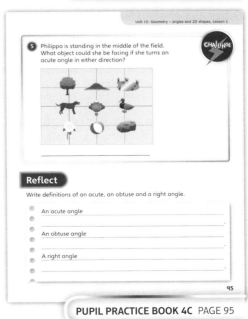

PUPIL PRACTICE BOOK 4C PAGE 95

After the lesson

- Were children able to relate angles to turns around a point?
- Are children secure in identifying the three types of angle?

Comparing and ordering angles

Learning focus

In this lesson, children will identify acute and obtuse angles, using what they already know about angles. They will compare the size of angles and use their comparisons to order them.

Small steps

→ Previous step: Identifying angles
→ **This step: Comparing and ordering angles**
→ Next step: Identifying regular and irregular shapes

NATIONAL CURRICULUM LINKS

Year 4 Geometry – Properties of Shapes

Identify acute and obtuse angles and compare and order angles up to two right angles by size.

ASSESSING MASTERY

Children can use what they know about angles to accurately identify acute, obtuse and right angles. They will be able to recognise which angles are larger or smaller than others and use their understanding to put them in ascending or descending order of size.

COMMON MISCONCEPTIONS

Children may think that a right angle is obtuse as it is not smaller than 90°. Ask:
• *What did you call this angle in the previous lesson? Is the angle you are looking at larger or smaller than a right angle?*

STRENGTHENING UNDERSTANDING

Take photos of children holding their arms wide, above their head, at different angles. Ask: *Can you order the pictures from the person who has their arms the widest to the person who has their arms held the least wide?*

GOING DEEPER

Challenge children by giving them a sequence of angles, ordered in ascending or descending order. Take one of the angles out, leaving a missing angle space in the sequence. Ask: *Was the angle I took away acute, obtuse or a right angle?* Ask children to draw missing angle. Ask: *Is this the only angle it could have been?*

KEY LANGUAGE

In lesson: acute, greater, smaller, right angle, larger, obtuse, sort, groups, compare, order, smallest, largest, fewest, most, four-sided, shape, size, interior, pattern, ascending

Other language to be used by the teacher: descending, triangle, equilateral triangle, pentagon, hexagon, octagon, rectangle, polygon

STRUCTURES AND REPRESENTATIONS

angles, 2D shapes

RESOURCES

Optional: 2D shapes, rulers, set squares

 In the eTextbook of this lesson, you will find interactive links to a selection of teaching tools.

Before you teach

• Are children confident at recognising angles inside and outside of a shape?
• Can children reliably identify right angles?

Discover

Unit 15: Geometry – angles and 2D shapes, Lesson 2

Comparing and ordering angles

Discover

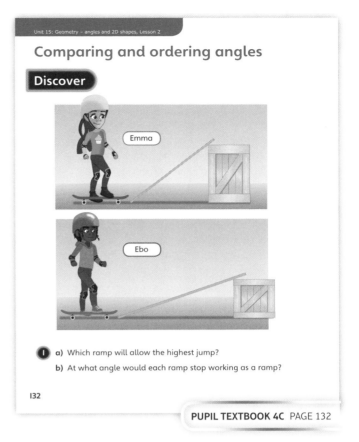

1 **a)** Which ramp will allow the highest jump?

b) At what angle would each ramp stop working as a ramp?

132

PUPIL TEXTBOOK 4C PAGE 132

WAYS OF WORKING Pair work

ASK

- Question **1** a): *How can you tell which ramp will allow for the highest jump?*
- Question **1** a): *What is the same and what is different about the two ramps?*
- Question **1** a): *Can you see any other angles in the picture?*

IN FOCUS Use this opportunity to remind children of right angles and discuss how the ramps they can see in the picture are similar and different to the angles they have met before. Encourage children to recognise how the ramps are set to smaller angles than a right angle.

PRACTICAL TIPS Give children the opportunity to create ramps as shown in the picture. This could also be linked to a science or PE lesson.

ANSWERS

Question **1** a): Emma's ramp will allow for the highest jump.

Question **1** b): A ramp set at a right angle would not work.

Share

WAYS OF WORKING Whole class teacher led

ASK

- Question **1** a): *What part of the ramp did you look at to find the angle?*
- Question **1** a): *How did you know which angle was bigger?*
- Question **1** a): *Could you use what you know about a right angle to help compare the two angles?*
- Question **1** a): *What is the same and what is different about acute and obtuse angles?*
- Question **1** b): *Why would a right angle not function as a ramp?*

IN FOCUS It will be important in this part of the lesson to make sure children are able to explain the properties of each of the three types of angle they are studying: acute, obtuse and right angles. Ensure that children understand that an obtuse angle is greater than a right angle but less than a straight line.

Unit 15: Geometry – angles and 2D shapes, Lesson 2

Share

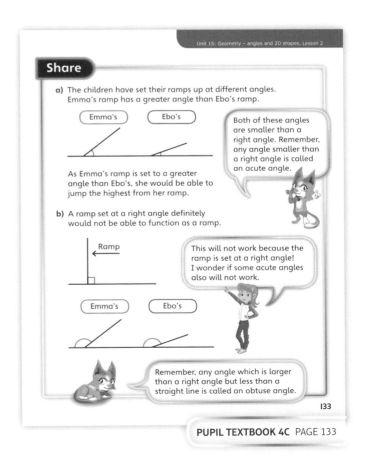

a) The children have set their ramps up at different angles. Emma's ramp has a greater angle than Ebo's ramp.

Emma's   Ebo's

As Emma's ramp is set to a greater angle than Ebo's, she would be able to jump the highest from her ramp.

Both of these angles are smaller than a right angle. Remember, any angle smaller than a right angle is called an acute angle.

b) A ramp set at a right angle definitely would not be able to function as a ramp.

Ramp

This will not work because the ramp is set at a right angle! I wonder if some acute angles also will not work.

Emma's   Ebo's

Remember, any angle which is larger than a right angle but less than a straight line is called an obtuse angle.

133

PUPIL TEXTBOOK 4C PAGE 133

Think together

Whole class teacher led (I do, We do, You do)

ASK

- Question **1**: *What types of angles can you see?*
- Question **1**: *How will you know which are acute angles, which are obtuse angles and which are right angles?*
- Question **2**: *Which angles will be easiest to sort first?*
- Question **3**: *Which angles will you look at in each shape?*

IN FOCUS At this point in the lesson, children begin to order angles based on size. Use questions **1** and **2** to discuss how the task of ordering angles can be broken down into two smaller steps, first sorting into type, then ordering them accurately.

STRENGTHEN To help children find which angles are larger or smaller than a right angle, offer them set squares to use. Ask: *How can you use the right angle on the set square to help you find acute and obtuse angles?*

DEEPEN Question **3** deepens children's understanding of angles within shapes. Children should recognise how angles found in shapes can be acute, obtuse or right angles. Challenge children by asking questions such as: *Are all the obtuse angles in each of the shapes the same? What would happen to the shape you drew if you used larger acute angles? What about smaller?*

ASSESSMENT CHECKPOINT Children should be able to use their understanding of right angles to identify whether they are looking at an acute or obtuse angle. Through observation, they should be able to more confidently order angles in ascending and descending order.

ANSWERS

Question **1**: Acute angles: a, e, f
Right angles: b
Obtuse angles: c, d

Question **2**: f, a, e, b, d, c

Question **3** a): Fewest to most acute angles: C, A, B
Fewest to most right angles: C, B, A
Fewest to most obtuse angles: B, A, C

Question **3** b): It is not possible to draw the shape described. For a four-sided shape with only one right angle, at least one of the other three angles must be bigger than a right angle.

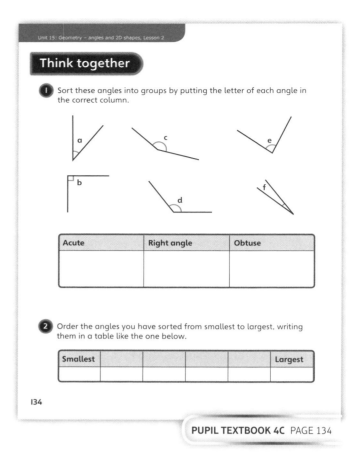

Think together

1 Sort these angles into groups by putting the letter of each angle in the correct column.

Acute	Right angle	Obtuse

2 Order the angles you have sorted from smallest to largest, writing them in a table like the one below.

Smallest					Largest

134

PUPIL TEXTBOOK 4C PAGE 134

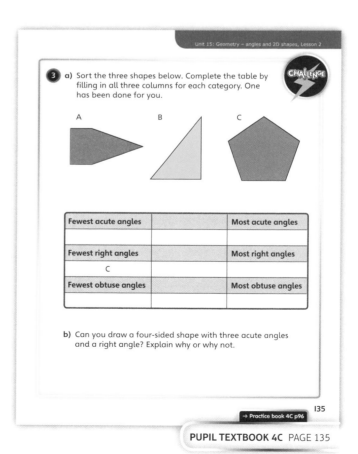

3 a) Sort the three shapes below. Complete the table by filling in all three columns for each category. One has been done for you.

A   B   C

Fewest acute angles		Most acute angles	
Fewest right angles		**Most right angles**	
C			
Fewest obtuse angles		**Most obtuse angles**	

b) Can you draw a four-sided shape with three acute angles and a right angle? Explain why or why not.

→ Practice book 4C p96

135

PUPIL TEXTBOOK 4C PAGE 135

Practice

WAYS OF WORKING Independent thinking

IN FOCUS Question **1** will give children the opportunity to compare and order angles. It will be important for children to recognise the varying ways in which angles can be ordered and recorded as it is not always in ascending order.

STRENGTHEN If children are finding it difficult to compare the angles by sight, ask: *Are there any angles you can recognise easily? How can you use those angles to help you begin to order the rest?* Children will need to use a set square or something that they know to be a right angle, such as the corner of a piece of paper, to help them judge angles that are close to a right angle.

DEEPEN Use question **4** to deepen children's reasoning. Ask questions such as: *Which two shapes make the smallest/largest obtuse angle? Are there two shapes which can't be used to make an obtuse angle? Is it possible to use any of the shapes to create an acute angle?* Encourage children to explain their ideas. Some children will find it easier if they have actual cut-out 2D shapes with which to work. Other children will quickly see that two acute angles do not always make an obtuse angle; they can also make a larger acute angle or a right angle.

ASSESSMENT CHECKPOINT Children should be able to confidently identify and order acute, obtuse and right angles. They should be able to fluently arrange angles in both ascending and descending order and be able to clearly explain how their understanding of right angles can help them.

ANSWERS Answers for the **Practice** part of the lesson appear in the separate **Practice and Reflect answer guide**.

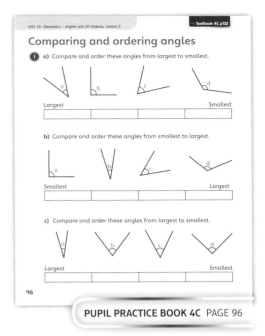

Comparing and ordering angles

1 a) Compare and order these angles from largest to smallest.

Largest · · · Smallest

b) Compare and order these angles from smallest to largest.

Smallest · · · Largest

c) Compare and order these angles from largest to smallest.

Largest · · · Smallest

96

PUPIL PRACTICE BOOK 4C PAGE 96

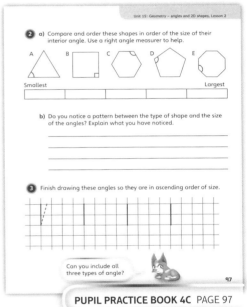

2 a) Compare and order these shapes in order of the size of their interior angle. Use a right angle measurer to help.

A   B   C   D   E

Smallest · · · Largest

b) Do you notice a pattern between the type of shape and the size of the angles? Explain what you have noticed.

3 Finish drawing these angles so they are in ascending order of size.

Can you include all three types of angle?

97

PUPIL PRACTICE BOOK 4C PAGE 97

Reflect

WAYS OF WORKING Independent thinking

IN FOCUS Give children time to consider what they have learnt in this lesson and then discuss this with a partner. Once they have done so, children should write their thoughts and share their ideas with the class.

ASSESSMENT CHECKPOINT Children should be demonstrating their understanding that the right angle can be used a reference point to easily spot acute and obtuse angles.

ANSWERS Answers for the **Reflect** part of the lesson appear in the separate **Practice and Reflect answer guide**.

After the lesson ⏸

- Are children confident at identifying all three types of angle?
- Have children recognised the importance of working systematically when ordering angles?

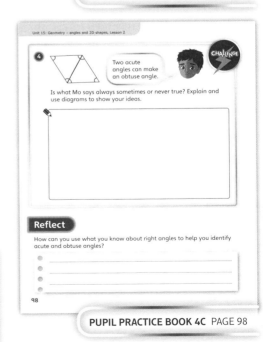

4 Two acute angles can make an obtuse angle.

Is what Mo says always sometimes or never true? Explain and use diagrams to show your ideas.

Reflect

How can you use what you know about right angles to help you identify acute and obtuse angles?

98

PUPIL PRACTICE BOOK 4C PAGE 98

Identifying regular and irregular shapes

Learning focus

In this lesson, children will recognise the similarities and differences between regular and irregular polygons. They will use this vocabulary to help their reasoning about 2D shapes.

Small steps

→ Previous step: Comparing and ordering angles
→ **This step: Identifying regular and irregular shapes**
→ Next step: Classifying triangles

NATIONAL CURRICULUM LINKS

Year 4 Geometry – Properties of Shapes

Compare and classify geometric shapes, including quadrilaterals and triangles, based on their properties and sizes.

ASSESSING MASTERY

Children can reliably identify regular and irregular shapes. They can fluently explain how the angles and side lengths can make a shape regular or irregular and can explain how only one property needs to be different for a shape to be classed as irregular.

COMMON MISCONCEPTIONS

Children may muddle interior and exterior angles when deciding if a shape is regular or not. Ask:
• *Which angles in a 2D shape have you been looking at? The ones on the inside or outside?*

When studying a shape with an interior reflex angle (larger than 180° but less than 360°), children may use the exterior angle instead as it will be smaller and more recognisable to them. Again, ask:
• *Where in the shape do the angles you have been comparing appear? On the inside or outside?*

STRENGTHENING UNDERSTANDING

Before learning the mathematical vocabulary introduced in this lesson, support children by asking them to organise shapes into different categories. For example, ask: *Can you find all the six-sided shapes? What other name do you know for six-sided shapes? What is the same and what is different about these shapes?*

GOING DEEPER

Children should use their learning from the previous lesson to deepen their understanding in this lesson. Challenge them to draw an irregular hexagon with four acute angles, one obtuse angle and one right angle.

KEY LANGUAGE

In lesson: regular, irregular, hexagonal, hexagon, side length, **interior angles**, equal, different, 2D

Other language to be used by the teacher: isometric dots, exterior angles, polygon

STRUCTURES AND REPRESENTATIONS

2D shapes

RESOURCES

Optional: 2D shapes, ruler

 In the eTextbook of this lesson, you will find interactive links to a selection of teaching tools.

Before you teach ⏸

• How will you ensure children recognise that they are studying the interior angles of shapes?
• What practical opportunities to find and compare regular and irregular shapes will you provide?

Discover

WAYS OF WORKING Pair work

WAYS OF WORKING Pair work

ASK

- Question ❶ a): *What shape tents are on the campsite?*
- Question ❶ a): *How do you know there is more than one hexagon?*

IN FOCUS Encourage children to notice that there are two hexagonal tents. Ask children to convince each other that there are definitely two hexagons. Discuss with children how they can be sure.

PRACTICAL TIPS Encourage children to find as many different types of one shape around the room as they can. Ask: *Can you find all the pentagons? What do you notice is the same and what is different about these shapes?* Children could be encouraged to take photos of the shapes to sort later.

ANSWERS

Question ❶ a): Richard could have lost his toy car near tent 3 or tent 4.

Question ❶ b): The two hexagons are similar as they both have six sides and six angles. They are different because their side lengths and interior angles are different sizes.

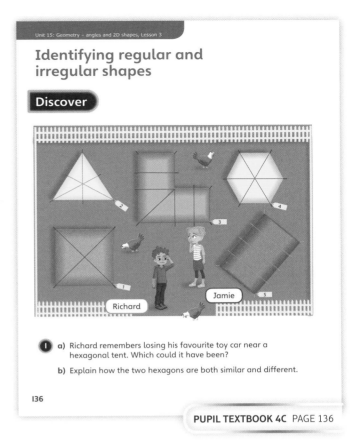

Identifying regular and irregular shapes

Discover

❶ a) Richard remembers losing his favourite toy car near a hexagonal tent. Which could it have been?

b) Explain how the two hexagons are both similar and different.

136

PUPIL TEXTBOOK 4C PAGE 136

Share

WAYS OF WORKING Whole class teacher led

ASK

- Question ❶ a): *How did you know which shapes were hexagonal?*
- Question ❶ b): *Which hexagonal shape was strange and why?*
- Question ❶ b): *Where would you look to find a shape's interior angles?*

IN FOCUS It will be important, during this part of the lesson, to make sure children are comfortable with what an 'interior angle' is and where it can be found. Remind children that 2D shapes are called polygons and that interior angles are found inside a shape. For example, the irregular hexagon (a compound L shape) has a three quarter turn interior angle, as well as smaller angles.

Share

a) All hexagons have six sides and six vertices. There are two hexagonal tent outlines on the campsite.

Richard's toy car could be near either tent 3 or 4.

b) This hexagon has six sides that are all equal. It also has six interior angles that are all equal. This means it is a regular shape.

This hexagon has six sides as well but they are different lengths. It also has six interior angles but they are also different sizes. This means it is an irregular shape.

I know that interior angles are the angles inside a polygon.

A shape is regular only if all sides are the same length **and** all angles are the same size.

The two hexagons are similar as they both have six sides and six angles. They are different because their side lengths and interior angles are different sizes.

137

PUPIL TEXTBOOK 4C PAGE 137

Think together

WAYS OF WORKING Whole class teacher led (I do, We do, You do)

ASK

- Questions **1** and **2**: *What properties will we need to look at when finding regular and irregular shapes?*
- Question **3**: *Can a shape be irregular if all the sides are the same?*

IN FOCUS Question **1** gives an opportunity to recap how only one of the properties needs to change for a shape to be irregular. Focus on the rectangle, where only the property of side length is different, to help scaffold this understanding.

STRENGTHEN For children who are still confusing the interior and exterior angles in each shape, it may be beneficial to encourage them to draw the shapes they are looking at. Ask: *What angles can you spot inside the shape? Can you compare all the interior angles you have found?*

DEEPEN Question **3** deepens children's reasoning by requiring them to interrogate each shape and work out where Alex has made a mistake. Encourage children's reasoning by asking: *What mistakes did Alex make? What advice would you give Alex to help her understand her mistake?*

ASSESSMENT CHECKPOINT At this point in the lesson, children should be able to discuss what makes a shape regular or irregular. Question **2** provides a good opportunity to check their understanding. They should be more confident at identifying regular and irregular shapes and should be able to explain their ideas using the correct vocabulary.

ANSWERS

Question **1**: The irregular shapes are the isosceles triangle and the rectangle.

Question **2**: The triangles (all equilateral) and the hexagon are regular. The rectangle and parallelograms are irregular.

Question **3**: Alex has mistakenly put the isosceles triangle (not regular) and the rectangle (not regular) in the wrong places in the table.
Other shapes that could go in each section:
A four-sided shape:
  Irregular: trapezoid
  Regular: square
Not a four-sided shape:
  Irregular: circle
  Regular: hexagon

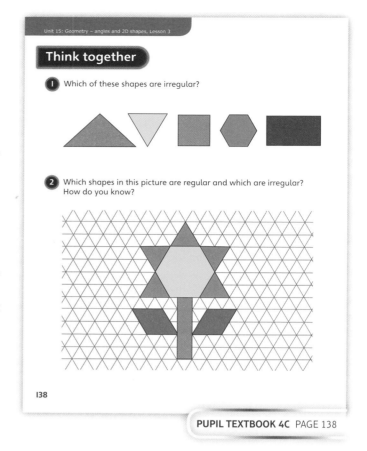

PUPIL TEXTBOOK 4C PAGE 138

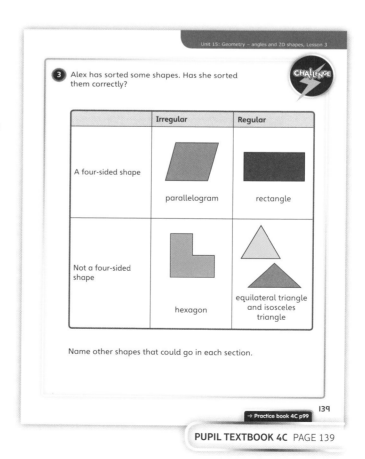

PUPIL TEXTBOOK 4C PAGE 139

Practice

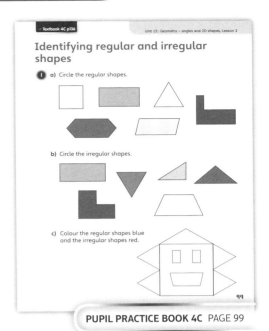

PUPIL PRACTICE BOOK 4C PAGE 99

WAYS OF WORKING Independent thinking

IN FOCUS For questions **2** and **3**, ensure that children are aware that the pattern of dotted paper is different in each question. This could be highlighted to children by asking: *What is the same and what is different about these two questions? How will the dotted paper help you? What do you need to be careful of when drawing your shapes?*

STRENGTHEN In questions **2** and **3**, it may be helpful to provide children with pictures of shapes or plastic 2D shapes for them to manipulate. Ask: *Which shape matches what you need to draw? Can you use the dots to help you draw that shape?*

DEEPEN When solving question **5**, deepen children's understanding and reasoning by asking them to provide proof of their findings. You could offer them pre-drawn, cut out versions of the shapes in the question. Alternatively, the children could be given isometric dotted paper to draw their own versions. Ask children how many solutions they can find and to prove that they have found all possibilities.

ASSESSMENT CHECKPOINT At this point in the lesson children should be able to confidently identify what makes a shape regular or irregular. Questions **2** and **3** are a good opportunity for children to demonstrate that they recognise that, for example, an irregular hexagon is still a hexagon. Question **1** provides children with an opportunity to demonstrate that they are able to confidently identify and sort shapes based on whether they are regular or irregular.

ANSWERS Answers for the **Practice** part of the lesson appear in the separate **Practice and Reflect answer guide**.

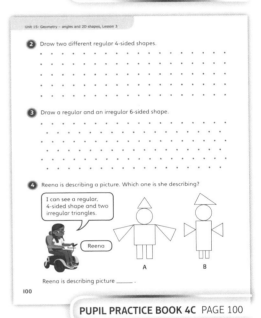

PUPIL PRACTICE BOOK 4C PAGE 100

Reflect

WAYS OF WORKING Independent thinking

IN FOCUS Children should formulate their ideas and summarise their learning about irregular shapes. Children should then be given the opportunity to share their ideas with a partner and in class discussion.

ASSESSMENT CHECKPOINT Children should be able to summarise clearly that it is important to remember that either the side lengths or angles should be different sizes if a shape is irregular. Look for children to point out that a shape is irregular if either both or only one of these things are not equal.

ANSWERS Answers for the **Reflect** part of the lesson appear in the separate **Practice and Reflect answer guide**.

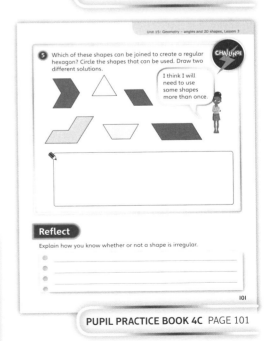

PUPIL PRACTICE BOOK 4C PAGE 101

After the lesson

- Are children confident at recognising what can vary in irregular shapes?
- Are children able to recognise and explain concisely how regular and irregular shapes are similar?

Classifying triangles

Learning focus

In this lesson, children will identify the three different types of triangles. They will understand the properties of scalene, isosceles and equilateral triangles in relation to their angles and the length of sides.

Small steps

→ Previous step: Identifying regular and irregular shapes
→ **This step: Classifying triangles**
→ Next step: Classifying and comparing quadrilaterals

NATIONAL CURRICULUM LINKS

Year 4 Geometry – Properties of Shapes

Compare and classify geometric shapes, including quadrilaterals and triangles, based on their properties and sizes.

ASSESSING MASTERY

Children can identify and classify scalene, isosceles and equilateral triangles. They can identify that equilateral triangles have three sides which are the same length and three angles the same size; that isosceles triangles have two sides which are the same length and two angles the same size; and that scalene triangles have three sides of different lengths and three angles of different sizes.

COMMON MISCONCEPTIONS

Children may need support to identify the different types of triangles when their orientation is unfamiliar. Ask:
• *Is it easier if you draw the shape and turn it around? Are the sides of the triangle all the same length? Are the interior angles of this triangle all the same?*

STRENGTHENING UNDERSTANDING

Provide children with a range of different triangles that they can sort, either drawn on paper, as 2D shapes, or photos of shapes. Discuss with children how they sort them and encourage them to look at the properties of the shapes. For example, hold up a scalene triangle and ask: *Which triangle is similar? Why?*

GOING DEEPER

Challenge children by giving them a large paper equilateral triangle and asking: *How many different triangles can you find by folding or cutting the paper?*

KEY LANGUAGE

In lesson: classify, triangle, similar, different, **isosceles**, **scalene**, **equilateral**, sides, angles, acute, quarter turn, geoboard, rotated, 90°, equal

Other language to be used by the teacher: longer, shorter, obtuse, half turn, right angle

STRUCTURES AND REPRESENTATIONS

2D shapes

RESOURCES

Optional: A range of different triangles, 2D shapes

 In the eTextbook of this lesson, you will find interactive links to a selection of teaching tools.

Before you teach

• What knowledge do children have of triangles?
• How secure are children in comparing angles?

Discover

WAYS OF WORKING Pair work

ASK

- Question **1** a): *Can you draw a scalene/isosceles triangle on a white board?*
- Question **1** b): *What can you tell me about the angles of the triangles?*
- Question **1** b): *What can you tell me about the sides of the triangles?*

IN FOCUS Question **1** b) encourages children to compare the triangles and think about their properties. Prompt children, if necessary, to look at the length of the sides and the size of the interior angles. This will lay the groundwork for identifying different types of triangles.

PRACTICAL TIPS Provide children with square and rectangular pieces of paper so that they can carry out the folding themselves. They will then be able to directly compare the two triangles.

ANSWERS

Question **1** a): Ambika and Lee have made triangles.

Question **1** b): Ways in which triangles are the same:
Both triangles have a right-angle.
Ways in which triangles are different:
When folded, the square makes a triangle that has two equal sides and two equal angles (an isosceles triangle) and the rectangle makes a triangle that has three unequal sides and three unequal angles (a scalene triangle).

Share

WAYS OF WORKING Whole class teacher led

ASK

- Question **1** a): *What type of triangle would it make if you folded the square piece of paper in half a second time?*
- Question **1** a): *Is it possible to make an equilateral triangle from either paper?*
- Question **1** b): *Could you draw a third triangle that is different to the two in the question?*

IN FOCUS Question **1** b) provides a definition of scalene and isosceles triangles. Ensure children understand these definitions. If necessary, get children to measure the sides of the triangles as proof. Give them two identical isosceles triangles so that they can directly compare the size of the angles.

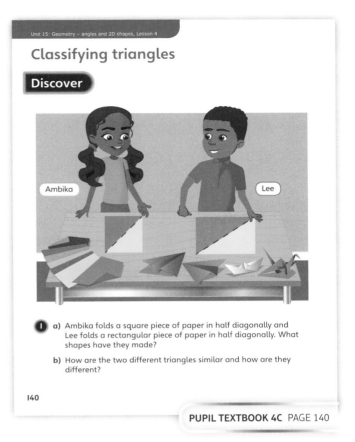

Classifying triangles

Discover

1 a) Ambika folds a square piece of paper in half diagonally and Lee folds a rectangular piece of paper in half diagonally. What shapes have they made?

b) How are the two different triangles similar and how are they different?

140

PUPIL TEXTBOOK 4C PAGE 140

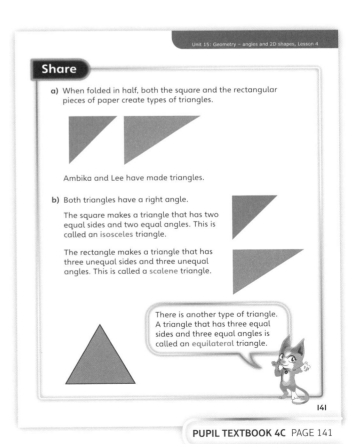

Share

a) When folded in half, both the square and the rectangular pieces of paper create types of triangles.

Ambika and Lee have made triangles.

b) Both triangles have a right angle.

The square makes a triangle that has two equal sides and two equal angles. This is called an isosceles triangle.

The rectangle makes a triangle that has three unequal sides and three unequal angles. This is called a scalene triangle.

There is another type of triangle. A triangle that has three equal sides and three equal angles is called an equilateral triangle.

141

PUPIL TEXTBOOK 4C PAGE 141

Think together

Whole class teacher led (I do, We do, You do)

ASK

- Question ❶: *Do all isosceles/scalene triangles look the same?*
- Question ❸: *How do you know which type of triangle you have created?*
- Question ❸: *How can you be sure that all of your triangles are different?*

IN FOCUS Question ❷ presents children with different isosceles triangles that look different both in orientation and size of angles. It is important to highlight that an isosceles triangle is only defined by two equal sides and two equal angles and that therefore isosceles triangles can look quite different from each other.

STRENGTHEN Provide children with a range of triangles that they can explore and sort. In order to compare angles within a triangle, children can draw around one triangle and then see if any of the angles match by comparing directly. For question ❶ children could measure the lengths of the sides using a ruler to help determine what type of triangle they are.

DEEPEN Challenge children to explore questions about triangles by providing them with triangles to draw around. Ask: *Can you join triangles together to make a new triangle? How many equilateral triangles are needed to make a larger equilateral triangle?*

ASSESSMENT CHECKPOINT Question ❸ will demonstrate whether children understand the properties of scalene, isosceles and equilateral triangles.

ANSWERS

Question ❶: C is a scalene triangle

Question ❷: A, C and E have 3 acute angles.

Question ❸ a): There are a number of triangles that can be made. Each triangle should be different in size or angles and/or length of sides, not just in orientation. There are 8 different triangles that can be made.

Question ❸ b): Ask children for suggestions as to how they know they have found them all. Discuss these suggestions as a class. The easiest way would be to draw a number of 3×3 grids or geoboards on squared paper and draw one triangle on each, until you cannot find any more.

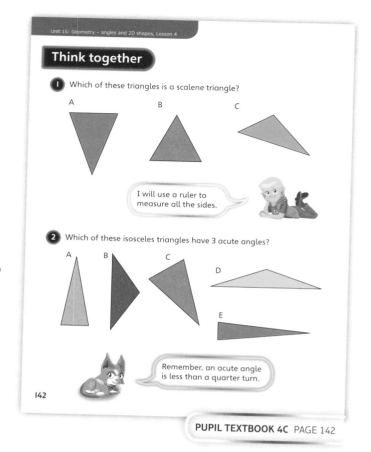

PUPIL TEXTBOOK 4C PAGE 142

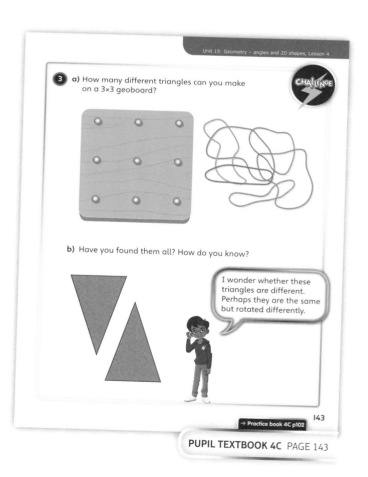

PUPIL TEXTBOOK 4C PAGE 143

Practice

WAYS OF WORKING Independent thinking

IN FOCUS Question **4** asks children to sort the triangles based on the properties that determine the type of triangle. Children need to look carefully at the length of sides and the size of the angles of each triangle in order to place them correctly in the table. The comment made by Ash should help children come to the realisation that if a triangle has two sides of equal length, then it will have two angles of equal size also.

STRENGTHEN Provide children with examples of each type of triangle with labels and definitions to refer to. They could look around their environment to try to find examples of each type of triangle.

DEEPEN To extend question **5**, give children a range of 2D shapes to draw around. Ask: *Which shapes can be divided like the pentagon in the question to create scalene/isosceles/equilateral triangles?*

THINK DIFFERENTLY Question **3** requires children to visualise the types of triangles required. They need to reason that in order to create an isosceles triangle, they will need to draw lines from the midpoint of one side to the two opposite corners. The children need to have a secure understanding of what makes a triangle an isosceles triangle in order to solve this problem.

ASSESSMENT CHECKPOINT Question **1** will demonstrate whether the children can identify equilateral, isosceles and scalene triangles. Questions **2** and **4** will demonstrate whether children are able to define the types of triangle, give them the correct properties and identify triangles with different dimensions and in different orientations.

ANSWERS Answers for the **Practice** part of the lesson appear in the separate **Practice and Reflect answer guide**.

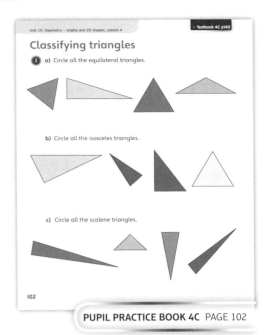

PUPIL PRACTICE BOOK 4C PAGE 102

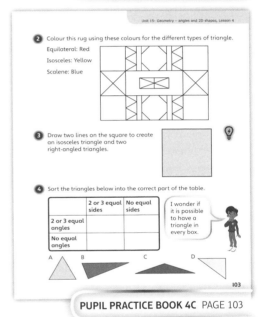

PUPIL PRACTICE BOOK 4C PAGE 103

Reflect

WAYS OF WORKING Independent thinking

IN FOCUS This section prompts children to discuss the properties of the different types of triangles. This will consolidate their learning from this lesson or help to identify any misconceptions about the properties of scalene, isosceles and equilateral triangles.

ASSESSMENT CHECKPOINT This section will determine whether children are secure in their understanding of the definitions of each type of triangle.

ANSWERS Answers for the **Reflect** part of the lesson appear in the separate **Practice and Reflect answer guide**.

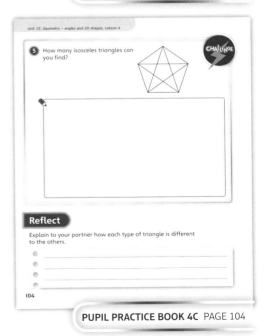

PUPIL PRACTICE BOOK 4C PAGE 104

After the lesson ⏸

- Do children have a secure understanding of the differences between the three types of triangle?
- How can you link the learning from this lesson to the next lesson on classifying and comparing quadrilaterals?

Classifying and comparing quadrilaterals

Learning focus

In this lesson, children will name, describe and identify quadrilaterals, recognising their similarities and differences. They will use their knowledge to classify and compare quadrilaterals.

Small steps

→ Previous step: Classifying triangles
→ **This step: Classifying and comparing quadrilaterals**
→ Next step: Deducing facts about shapes

NATIONAL CURRICULUM LINKS

Year 4 Geometry – Properties of Shapes

Compare and classify geometric shapes, including quadrilaterals and triangles, based on their properties and sizes.

ASSESSING MASTERY

Children can confidently identify quadrilaterals, giving each their specific name and describing their properties. They can explain how different quadrilaterals are similar and how they are different and can use this understanding to solve mathematical problems.

COMMON MISCONCEPTIONS

Children may assume that the word 'quadrilateral' is the name of only one shape. Create a visual reminder, such as a wall display, showing the quadrilaterals children will be studying. Ask:
• *What is similar about all these shapes? What is different?*

STRENGTHENING UNDERSTANDING

Give children a large loop of string. In groups of 4 to 6, ask children to create different four-sided shapes with the loop of string, holding it taut between them. Ask: *Can you draw each shape you make? What do you notice is similar and what is different about your shapes?*

GOING DEEPER

Encourage children to investigate different kinds of quadrilaterals. For example, ask children: *Can you find a quadrilateral that only has acute interior angles? Can you find a quadrilateral that only has obtuse interior angles? If you draw two lines through a quadrilateral, what types of triangles can you find?*

KEY LANGUAGE

In lesson: classify, compare, quadrilateral, regular, properties, different, sides, angles, 2D, rhombus, interior angles, square, irregular, equal, unequal, parallelogram, parallel, distance, trapezium, sorting circle, rectangle

Other language to be used by the teacher: same, kite, polygon

STRUCTURES AND REPRESENTATIONS

2D shapes

RESOURCES

Optional: 2D shapes, geo boards with elastic bands, geo strip kit

 In the eTextbook of this lesson, you will find interactive links to a selection of teaching tools.

Before you teach

• What manipulatives could you provide beyond plastic 2D shapes to help children visualise quadrilaterals?
• How will you link this lesson to children's learning about angles?

Discover

WAYS OF WORKING Pair work

ASK

- Question ❶ a): *What is the same about the shapes Olivia has made? What is different about them?*
- Question ❶ b): *Could she have made any different four-sided shapes?*
- Question ❶ b): *Are there any four-sided shapes you already know? Are there any you don't recognise in the picture?*

IN FOCUS During this part of the lesson it will be important, through discussion, to give children the opportunity to generalise about quadrilaterals. Using the practical tips below will help scaffold these generalisations.

PRACTICAL TIPS Provide children with geostrips or geoboards to create different four-sided shapes. Once they have made two or three shapes, ask: *Can you describe what is similar and what is different about these shapes? Can you compare them with your partner's shapes and describe the similarities and differences?*

ANSWERS

Question ❶ a): Properties which are the same: All have four sides and four angles so all of these shapes are quadrilaterals.
Differences: The shapes have different side lengths and angle sizes.

Question ❶ b): A regular quadrilateral with four sides and four angles is a square.

Share

WAYS OF WORKING Whole class teacher led

ASK

- Question ❶ a): *What is the same about all the sides in every quadrilateral? What is different?*
- Question ❶ a): *What is the same about all the angles in a quadrilateral? What is different?*
- Question ❶ b): *How is a rhombus different to a square? How is it similar?*
- Question ❶ b): *Which quadrilaterals are regular and which are irregular? How do you know?*

IN FOCUS Use this part of the lesson to discuss further the features of the quadrilaterals children have seen or made. Discuss how they each fit with the generalisations children made in the **Discover** section of the lesson. It will be interesting for children to discuss which quadrilaterals are regular and irregular, and discover that a square is the only regular quadrilateral.

Classifying and comparing quadrilaterals

Discover

❶ a) Olivia is making shapes with geostrips. What is the same and what is different about the shapes she has made?

b) What shape is a regular quadrilateral?

144

PUPIL TEXTBOOK 4C PAGE 144

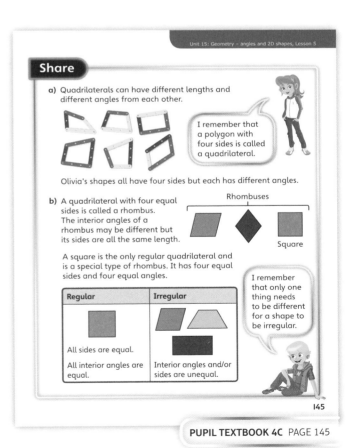

PUPIL TEXTBOOK 4C PAGE 145

Think together

WAYS OF WORKING Whole class teacher led (I do, We do, You do)

ASK

- Question **1** : *What is important about parallel lines?*
- Question **1** : *How can you identify parallel sides?*
- Question **2** : *How many different trapeziums can you draw?*
- Question **3** : *What quadrilaterals have a right angle? Can you find them all?*

IN FOCUS Throughout the activities in this section of the lesson, it would be beneficial to give children the opportunity to explore and create the shapes they are studying using geo boards and/or geo strips.

STRENGTHEN For question **2** , it may help to offer children pictures of different quadrilaterals. Ask: *Which of these quadrilaterals are trapeziums? Can you use the pictures to help you draw your own trapezium?*

DEEPEN When working on question **3** b), children who have successfully completed the sorting circle could be encouraged to come up with another criterion for a third circle or alternatively, three new criteria. Having done so, they could give their new sorting circle to a partner to sort their quadrilaterals into.

ASSESSMENT CHECKPOINT At this point in the lesson children should recognise quadrilaterals as shapes with four sides and four angles. They should recognise that there are many different types of quadrilateral and should be able to name some of them with more confidence.

ANSWERS

Question **1** : A, C and D are parallelograms.

Question **2** : Children should draw another, different, trapezium.

Question **3** a): Children should be able to create all the quadrilaterals they have studied so far.

Question **3** b): The quadrilaterals the children have created in part a) should be sorted correctly into the sorting circle.

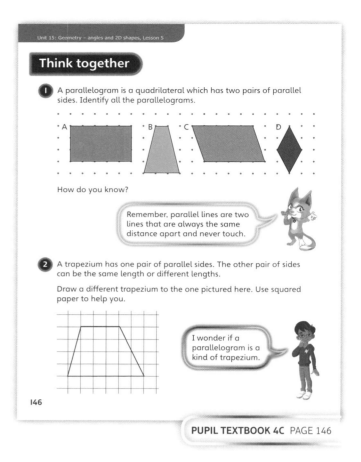

PUPIL TEXTBOOK 4C PAGE 146

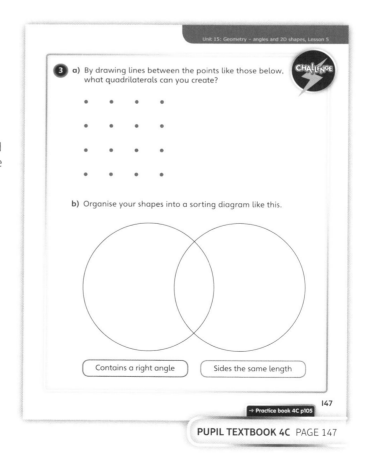

PUPIL TEXTBOOK 4C PAGE 147

Practice

WAYS OF WORKING Independent thinking

IN FOCUS While solving all the problems in this section of the lesson, ask children to name the shapes they see in each question or are drawing themselves. Discuss the properties of each shape and encourage children to link them to the mathematical shape name.

STRENGTHEN If children have difficulty drawing the quadrilaterals in questions **2** and **4** using isometric paper, offer them square dotted paper to help them draw the shapes more easily. Ensure children's understanding by continuing to encourage them to describe and name each quadrilateral they draw.

DEEPEN If children solve question **4**, their learning could be deepened by asking them to create similar challenges for a partner. Ask: *What is the fewest number of clues you can give to someone for them to be able to successfully guess and draw a rhombus?*

ASSESSMENT CHECKPOINT Children should be able to name and describe the different types of quadrilateral more confidently. They should be able to point out and explain why some quadrilaterals can be categorised under more than one name, for example a square could also be classed as a rhombus, a rectangle or a parallelogram.

ANSWERS Answers for the **Practice** part of the lesson appear in the separate **Practice and Reflect answer guide**.

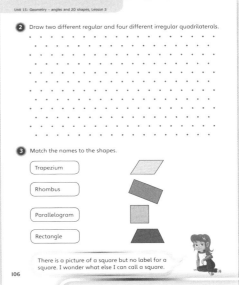

PUPIL PRACTICE BOOK 4C PAGE 105

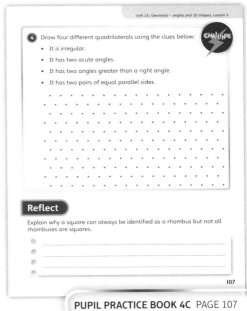

PUPIL PRACTICE BOOK 4C PAGE 106

Reflect

WAYS OF WORKING Pair work

IN FOCUS Give children time to discuss this question. Ask: *Are there any other instances of this kind of scenario that can happen with different quadrilaterals?* If children come up with other examples, encourage them to offer proof to support their ideas.

ASSESSMENT CHECKPOINT Children should be able to explain how the properties of one type of quadrilateral may encompass that of another type of quadrilateral.

ANSWERS Answers for the **Reflect** part of the lesson appear in the separate **Practice and Reflect answer guide**.

After the lesson

- How confident are children at naming all the types of quadrilateral?
- What support will you offer for those children who are still developing their understanding of quadrilateral names and properties?

PUPIL PRACTICE BOOK 4C PAGE 107

Deducing facts about shapes

Learning focus

In this lesson, children will consolidate their learning about 2D shapes and use it to help them solve shape problems and puzzles.

Small steps

→ Previous step: Classifying and comparing quadrilaterals
→ **This step: Deducing facts about shapes**
→ Next step: Lines of symmetry inside a shape

NATIONAL CURRICULUM LINKS

Year 4 Geometry – Properties of Shapes

Compare and classify geometric shapes, including quadrilaterals and triangles, based on their properties and sizes.

ASSESSING MASTERY

Children can confidently use the vocabulary and properties of 2D shapes and angles to understand and solve problems and puzzles. They can fluently explain their ideas and reasoning.

COMMON MISCONCEPTIONS

In this lesson, questions will focus on what shapes are created when pieces of paper are overlapped. Some questions will focus on the complete shape made by the two pieces of paper, other questions will focus on the smaller shape made by the overlap. Children may confuse these two ideas. Ask:
• *Have you read the question carefully? What does it ask you to do?*

STRENGTHENING UNDERSTANDING

Before the lesson, play some games with children that recap their learning about shapes. For example, hold a shape behind your back and describe it. Ask: *Can you guess the shape?* Alternately, children could play pairs – each child should have either a card with a picture of a shape or a card with the name of the shape written on it. The children have to find their pair (the person with the card that matches theirs).

GOING DEEPER

Encourage children to create puzzles, similar to those in the lesson, for their partners. Ask: *Can you create an overlapping puzzle for your partner?*

KEY LANGUAGE

In lesson: deducing, facts, overlapping, regular, hexagon, largest, corners, sides, equal, angles, hexadecagon, quadrilateral, equilateral, triangle, edge, different, square, rectangle, rhombus, trapezium, kite, arrowhead, pentagon, isosceles, perimeter, length, polygon

Other language to be used by the teacher: irregular, scalene, heptagon, octagon, acute, obtuse, right angle, polygon

STRUCTURES AND REPRESENTATIONS

2D shapes

RESOURCES

Optional: 2D shapes, paper squares, cards for pairs game – set of cards, half with a picture of a shape, the other half with the name of a shape

 In the eTextbook of this lesson, you will find interactive links to a selection of teaching tools.

Before you teach

• Are there any types of shapes that children are less confident with?

Discover

WAYS OF WORKING Pair work

ASK

- Question **1** a): *Why is Bella's shape irregular?*
- Question **1** b): *Can you make a regular hexagon?*
- Question **1** b): *What other shapes can you make?*
- Question **1** b): *Is it possible to make a shape with an acute angle using the two squares?*

IN FOCUS Ensure children understand how the questions in this lesson work. Be sure to point out how the hexagon has been created by the total area of the two overlapping shapes. Children will engage best with this part of the lesson if it is made as practical as possible; be sure to follow the advice below in **Practical Tips**.

PRACTICAL TIPS Make sure you give children an opportunity to copy the activity shown in the **Discover** picture. Children could investigate what other hexagons they can make or how many different shapes it is possible to make. It will be beneficial to give children square pieces of paper to use to recreate the shapes in this lesson. They could also use plain paper to draw the shapes they create as a way of recording them.

ANSWERS

Question **1** a): Bella's shape cannot be a regular hexagon as the angles and sides are unequal. Bella could make shapes such as a rectangle, an irregular heptagon and an irregular octagon.

Question **1** b): Bella could make a hexadecagon which has 16 corners.

Share

WAYS OF WORKING Whole class teacher led

ASK

- Question **1** b): *What shapes did you find?*
- Question **1** b): *Did you and your partner find similar shapes?*
- Question **1** b): *What was the shape with the fewest possible angles/sides?*
- Question **1** b): *What regular shapes were you able to create?*
- Question **1** b): *Was it easier to create regular or irregular shapes?*

IN FOCUS Encourage children to consider why some shapes are impossible to create with the given squares of paper. For example, they could be encouraged to reason why it will be impossible to make a shape that has an interior acute angle.

Deducing facts about shapes

Discover

I can make an irregular hexagon!

Bella

1 a) Bella has made a shape by overlapping two pieces of square paper. Explain why Bella's shape cannot be a regular hexagon.

What other shapes could Bella make?

b) What shape could Bella make with the largest number of corners?

148

PUPIL TEXTBOOK 4C PAGE 148

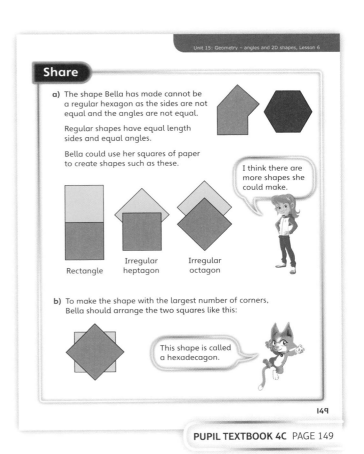

Share

a) The shape Bella has made cannot be a regular hexagon as the sides are not equal and the angles are not equal.

Regular shapes have equal length sides and equal angles.

Bella could use her squares of paper to create shapes such as these.

I think there are more shapes she could make.

Rectangle   Irregular heptagon   Irregular octagon

b) To make the shape with the largest number of corners, Bella should arrange the two squares like this:

This shape is called a hexadecagon.

149

PUPIL TEXTBOOK 4C PAGE 149

Think together

Whole class teacher led (I do, We do, You do)

ASK

- Question ❶: *What quadrilaterals have you learnt about? What are their properties?*
- Question ❷: *Is it possible to make a square using equilateral triangles?*
- Question ❷: *How can you prove your ideas?*
- Question ❷: *How will you know you have found all the possibilities?*
- Question ❸: *What type of angles can you see in this shape?*

IN FOCUS For all the questions in this part of the lesson, offer children practical opportunities to investigate the solutions. Have cut out shapes ready for children to manipulate. Question ❸ focuses on the shape made within the overlap of two squares of paper. It will be important for children to be aware of this to solve the problem successfully.

STRENGTHEN Have resources available for children to manipulate to visualise the shapes. These could include plastic 2D shapes or pictures of the shapes they have been studying. Ask: *Which shapes look like those in the textbook? Can you combine the shapes to make the ones pictured?*

DEEPEN Question ❸ will deepen children's understanding that a single shape can be classed as multiple types of quadrilateral. If children are insisting that a rhombus or a kite cannot be made, ask them about the rhombuses they made before: *Did they all look the same? Did some look like other shapes they know?*

ASSESSMENT CHECKPOINT Children should be showing confidence at using their knowledge and understanding to solve shape puzzles. They should be using the vocabulary they have learnt fluently to explain their reasoning.

ANSWERS

Question ❶: Different answers are possible, for example:
He used a trapezium and a parallelogram;
He used two parallelograms.

Question ❷: She could make:
A rhombus
An equilateral triangle
A trapezium
An irregular heptagon
An irregular hexagon
A parallelogram
An irregular pentagon

Question ❸:

Quadrilateral	Can it be made?
Square	Yes
Rectangle	Yes
Rhombus	Yes (as a square)
Trapezium	No
Kite	Yes (as a square)
Arrowhead	No

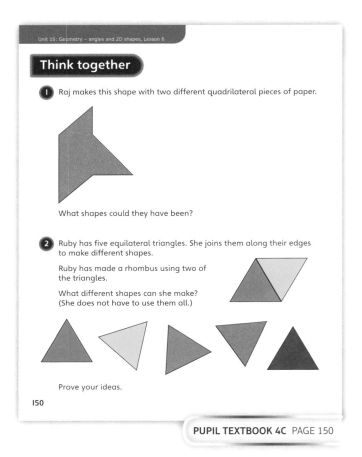

Think together

❶ Raj makes this shape with two different quadrilateral pieces of paper.

What shapes could they have been?

❷ Ruby has five equilateral triangles. She joins them along their edges to make different shapes.

Ruby has made a rhombus using two of the triangles.

What different shapes can she make? (She does not have to use them all.)

Prove your ideas.

150

PUPIL TEXTBOOK 4C PAGE 150

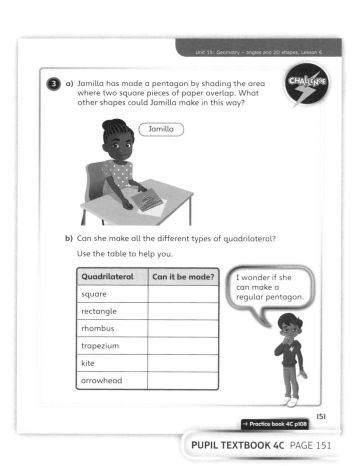

❸ a) Jamilla has made a pentagon by shading the area where two square pieces of paper overlap. What other shapes could Jamilla make in this way?

Jamilla

CHALLENGE

b) Can she make all the different types of quadrilateral?
Use the table to help you.

Quadrilateral	Can it be made?
square	
rectangle	
rhombus	
trapezium	
kite	
arrowhead	

I wonder if she can make a regular pentagon.

151

→ Practice book 4C p108

PUPIL TEXTBOOK 4C PAGE 151

Practice

WAYS OF WORKING Independent thinking

IN FOCUS Provide children with practical manipulatives to help them solve the puzzles in this part of the lesson.

STRENGTHEN To help children visualise triangles and quadrilaterals while solving questions ❸ and ❹, ask them about the triangles and quadrilaterals they have learnt about. Ask: *Can you draw what they look like?* Get children to compare their drawings to the shapes on the page. Ask: *Can you explain how they are similar?*

DEEPEN Extend question ❺ by asking children to find another way of completing the headings for the table. Ask: *How many solutions are there? How do they know?*

THINK DIFFERENTLY When solving question ❷, encourage children to investigate how the possible shapes that can be made change, depending on whether they are looking at the whole shape, or just the smaller shape within the overlap. Ask: *Are some shapes possible when looking at the whole shape but not when looking at the overlap of the shapes?*

ASSESSMENT CHECKPOINT Children should be confidently and fluently applying their knowledge and understanding, using appropriate vocabulary to describe the shapes and their properties, and sharing their reasoning concisely and clearly.

ANSWERS Answers for the **Practice** part of the lesson appear in the separate **Practice and Reflect answer guide**.

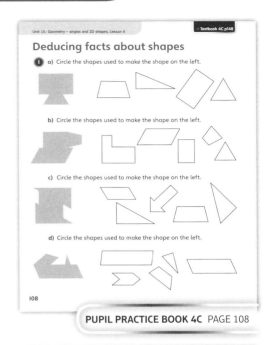

PUPIL PRACTICE BOOK 4C PAGE 108

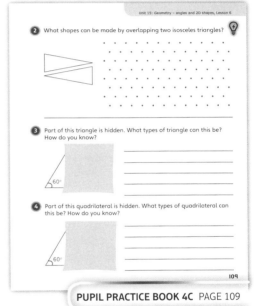

PUPIL PRACTICE BOOK 4C PAGE 109

Reflect

WAYS OF WORKING Independent thinking

IN FOCUS Give children time to formulate their own reasoning to finish the given sentence starter. Once they have written their ideas, share in partners and with the class.

ASSESSMENT CHECKPOINT Children should be able to list all the properties they need to consider to identify a polygon.

ANSWERS Answers for the **Reflect** part of the lesson appear in the separate **Practice and Reflect answer guide**.

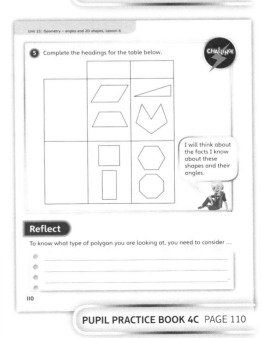

PUPIL PRACTICE BOOK 4C PAGE 110

After the lesson ⏸

- Were children more confident with certain shapes than with others?
- How confident were children at applying their problem-solving skills in this lesson?

Lines of symmetry inside a shape

Learning focus

In this lesson, children will explore reflective symmetry. They will identify lines of symmetry within regular and irregular polygons.

Small steps

- Previous step: Deducing facts about shapes
- **This step: Lines of symmetry inside a shape**
- Next step: Lines of symmetry outside a shape

NATIONAL CURRICULUM LINKS

Year 4 Geometry – Properties of Shapes

Identify lines of symmetry in 2D shapes presented in different orientations.

ASSESSING MASTERY

Children can identify lines of symmetry in a range of 2D shapes. They can identify when a shape does not have reflective symmetry and explain why. They can identify when a shape has multiple lines of symmetry and explain what symmetry means.

COMMON MISCONCEPTIONS

Children may think that if a shape can be folded in half, then it has symmetry. For example, an oblong rectangle can be folded along the diagonal, producing two similar triangles. However, they are not mirror images of each other. Ask:
- *Would the whole shape be shown if you put a mirror against the line of symmetry? If not, then is it symmetrical?*

STRENGTHENING UNDERSTANDING

Encourage children to explore symmetry by folding shapes. Explain that the two halves need to match exactly when they are folded. You could also provide children with mirrors to identify lines of symmetry. This helps children understand that opposite sides of the line of symmetry are mirror images of each other.

GOING DEEPER

Ask children to work in pairs. Give children squared paper and ask them to draw a vertical line of symmetry down the centre. Ask one child to draw half a polygon on the right side of the line. The other child then has to complete the left side so that it is symmetrical. Children can make the shape as complex as they like. This challenge can be further extended by drawing both a vertical and horizontal line of symmetry and then one child draws a quarter of a shape in the first quadrant.

KEY LANGUAGE

In lesson: reflective symmetry, symmetrical, lines of symmetry, square, equilateral, triangle, rectangle, hexagon, isosceles, regular, octagon, irregular, circle

Other language to be used by the teacher: isosceles, scalene, 2D, polygon

STRUCTURES AND REPRESENTATIONS

2D shapes

RESOURCES

Optional: range of 2D shapes, mirrors

 In the eTextbook of this lesson, you will find interactive links to a selection of teaching tools.

Before you teach

- Do children have experience with symmetry?
- Are children secure identifying and describing a range of 2D shapes?

Discover

ASK

- Question **1** b): *What do you think symmetry means?*
- Question **1** b): *What shapes do you know that are symmetrical?*
- Question **1** b): *How do you know if you have found a line of symmetry?*

IN FOCUS Question **1** b) requires children to visualise the triangle in order to identify the lines of symmetry. Children will have to draw on their knowledge of equilateral triangles from previous lessons in order to solve this problem.

PRACTICAL TIPS Provide children with paper squares and triangles for them to investigate the lines of symmetry. They could use mirrors to check if the lines they have found are lines of reflective symmetry.

ANSWERS

Question **1** a): Max is incorrect. The square has four lines of symmetry.

Question **1** b): There are three lines of symmetry of symmetry in an equilateral triangle.

Lines of symmetry inside a shape

Discover

I can find two ways to fold this square in half.

Max

1 a) Is Max correct? Has he found all the ways of folding the square in half?

b) How many lines of symmetry are there in an equilateral triangle?

152

PUPIL TEXTBOOK 4C PAGE 152

Share

ASK

- Question **1** a): *How can you prove that each line is a line of symmetry?*
- Question **1** a): *What do you notice about the number of lines of symmetry and the properties of the shape?*
- Question **1** b): *Does every triangle have a line of symmetry?*

IN FOCUS Ash's comment asks children to think about symmetry in other types of triangle. This could lead to a discussion about symmetry in regular and irregular polygons. Ask children to think about symmetry in other types of quadrilaterals. Ensure children understand the term 'reflective symmetry'. Explain that the shape on one side of a line of symmetry should be a mirror image of the shape on the other side.

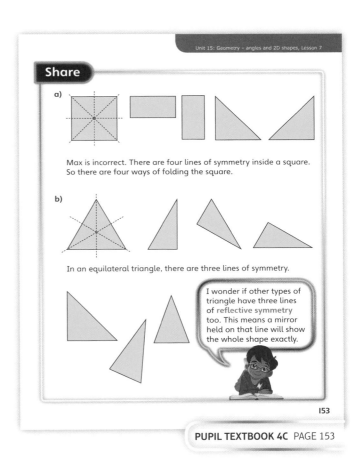

Share

a)

Max is incorrect. There are four lines of symmetry inside a square. So there are four ways of folding the square.

b)

In an equilateral triangle, there are three lines of symmetry.

I wonder if other types of triangle have three lines of reflective symmetry too. This means a mirror held on that line will show the whole shape exactly.

153

PUPIL TEXTBOOK 4C PAGE 153

Think together

WAYS OF WORKING Whole class teacher led (I do, We do, You do)

ASK

- Question **3**: *How can you tell if a shape has symmetry?*
- Question **3**: *Can you think of 2D shapes that do not have symmetry?*
- Question **3**: *What shape do you think will have the most lines of symmetry?*

IN FOCUS Question **3** looks at symmetry within different types of quadrilaterals. The first parallelogram may raise the misconception that it has a line of symmetry between opposite corners as it produces two identical scalene triangles. Children need to understand that reflective symmetry means that one half is the mirror image of the other and not just the same shape rotated.

STRENGTHEN Give children the 2D shapes in the questions so that they can fold or explore them with mirrors. This will help children to identify any lines of symmetry.

DEEPEN Challenge children to find shapes with different numbers of lines of symmetry. Ask: *Can you find a shape that has one line of symmetry? Two lines? Three lines? Four lines? Five lines?*

ASSESSMENT CHECKPOINT Question **1** will demonstrate whether children have an understanding of what symmetry means and question **3** will show whether children can identify symmetry in a range of quadrilaterals.

ANSWERS

Question **1**: Dominic is not correct as the two halves are not mirror images of each other.

Question **2**: The first hexagon has no lines of symmetry. The second hexagon has six lines of symmetry (because it is regular).

Question **3**: The kite has one line of symmetry. The parallelogram has no lines of symmetry. The reflex kite has one line of symmetry. The isosceles trapezium has one line of symmetry. The oblong has two lines of symmetry. The rhombus has two lines of symmetry. The square has four lines of symmetry. The right-angled trapezium has no lines of symmetry.

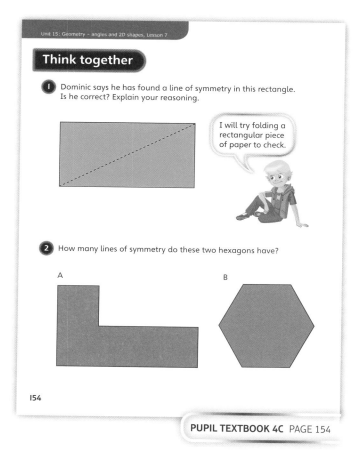

PUPIL TEXTBOOK 4C PAGE 154

PUPIL TEXTBOOK 4C PAGE 155

Practice

WAYS OF WORKING Independent thinking

IN FOCUS Question ④ asks children to create a hexagon with two lines of symmetry. Children have to take care that there are **only** two lines of symmetry. Some children may start by drawing a random shape with six sides, while others may start with a regular hexagon. Children need to think about how to adapt a regular hexagon so that it becomes a shape with only two lines of symmetry.

STRENGTHEN Provide children with mirrors in order to investigate the symmetry of the shapes. For question ④, children could use a geoboard and an elastic band to try to solve the problem.

DEEPEN Challenge children to investigate the relationship between the number of lines of symmetry and the number of sides of regular 2D shapes. Ask: *What do you notice? Can you explain why?*

ASSESSMENT CHECKPOINT Question ③ will demonstrate whether children can sort shapes based on lines of symmetry and whether the shapes are regular or irregular, while question ⑤ will show whether children can create a shape with a given number of lines of symmetry.

ANSWERS Answers for the **Practice** part of the lesson appear in the separate **Practice and Reflect answer guide**.

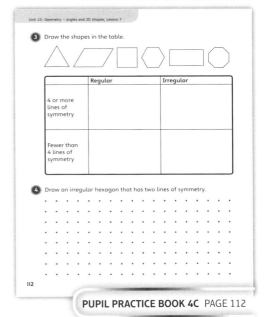

PUPIL PRACTICE BOOK 4C PAGE 111

PUPIL PRACTICE BOOK 4C PAGE 112

Reflect

WAYS OF WORKING Pair work

IN FOCUS This section requires children to think deeper about symmetry in shapes. The closer a regular 2D shape gets to a circle, the more lines of symmetry it has.

ASSESSMENT CHECKPOINT This section will determine whether children understand symmetry and how to find symmetry in 2D shapes.

ANSWERS Answers for the **Reflect** part of the lesson appear in the separate **Practice and Reflect answer guide**.

After the lesson ⏸

- Did children identify all the lines of symmetry?
- Were children able to apply their knowledge from previous lessons on 2D shapes?
- Do children still need practical activities to support their understanding of symmetry?

PUPIL PRACTICE BOOK 4C PAGE 113

Lines of symmetry outside a shape

Learning focus

In this lesson, children will identify symmetry within and outside shapes. They will learn to find symmetry within a range of patterns and designs.

Small steps

→ Previous step: Lines of symmetry inside a shape
→ **This step: Lines of symmetry outside a shape**
→ Next step: Completing a symmetric figure

NATIONAL CURRICULUM LINKS

Year 4 Geometry – Properties of Shapes

Identify lines of symmetry in 2D shapes presented in different orientations.

ASSESSING MASTERY

Children can identify lines of symmetry inside and outside of shapes and across a range of patterns and designs. They can identify when a shape has more than one line of symmetry and describe why a pattern is or is not symmetrical.

COMMON MISCONCEPTIONS

Children may mistake a repeating pattern as symmetrical or may think that there is symmetry when the order of shapes are reversed but the shapes themselves are not reflected. Ask:
• *Is one side the mirror image of the other?*

STRENGTHENING UNDERSTANDING

Provide children with mirrors to help them identify if or where a shape or design is symmetrical. Children may also benefit from a second copy of the pattern so they can make direct comparisons between the actual image and the image in the mirror.

GOING DEEPER

Challenge children by providing them with a pattern that does not have symmetry and ask: *What would need to change in order for the pattern to have a vertical/diagonal/horizontal line of symmetry?*

KEY LANGUAGE

In lesson: symmetry, vertical, diagonal, horizontal, continuous, reflective, sequence, symmetrical

Other language to be used by the teacher: polygon

STRUCTURES AND REPRESENTATIONS

2D shapes

RESOURCES

Optional: range of 2D shapes, mirrors

 In the eTextbook of this lesson, you will find interactive links to a selection of teaching tools.

Before you teach ⏸

• Are children confident finding lines of symmetry within a shape?
• Could you provide opportunities to find symmetry within the classroom?

Discover

Pair work

ASK

- Question ❶ a): *What do you look for when finding lines of symmetry?*
- Question ❶ a): *What is the direction of the line of symmetry?*
- Question ❶ b): *How do you know it is symmetrical?*

IN FOCUS Question ❶ b) requires children to look closely at the shapes in the monster face. They may see the symmetry of the monster face as a whole but miss the symmetry of the individual shapes within the face.

PRACTICAL TIPS The use of mirrors will help children to explore the symmetry in the pictures. You could ask children to go on a symmetry hunt around the school to find items that have been arranged symmetrically.

ANSWERS

Question ❶ a): A – The castle has a vertical line of symmetry.
B – The first pair of triangles have a diagonal line of symmetry.
C – The second pair of triangles have a vertical line of symmetry.
D – The title and pattern have a vertical line of symmetry. The individual shapes also have lines of symmetry.

Question ❶ b): E – The monster's eyes have vertical and horizontal lines of symmetry; the mouth and nose have vertical lines of symmetry; the face as a whole has a vertical line of symmetry.

Share

Whole class teacher led

ASK

- Question ❶ a): *What lines of symmetry did you miss?*
- Question ❶ a): *Does the pattern have a horizontal line of symmetry?*
- Question ❶ a): *How could you change the border so that it had a horizontal line of symmetry?*

IN FOCUS In question ❶ a), the symmetry of the title and the pattern D is the children's first introduction to symmetrical patterns. It is important to talk about how it is not only that the order of the shapes is reversed, but the shapes are also reflected, just as the title 'Symmetry' is reflected. The symmetry of the shapes is most evident from looking at the rhombus and triangle.

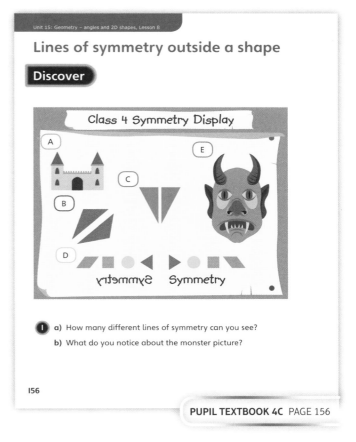

PUPIL TEXTBOOK 4C PAGE 156

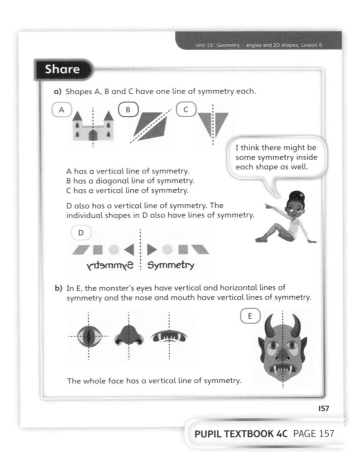

PUPIL TEXTBOOK 4C PAGE 157

Think together

WAYS OF WORKING Whole class teacher led (I do, We do, You do)

ASK

- Question **1**: *Describe how each monster is symmetrical.*
- Question **2**: *Can you draw your own symmetrical monster?*
- Question **3**: *What shapes would you include in a pattern to ensure that it had a horizontal line of symmetry?*

IN FOCUS Question **4** a) shows a pattern that has a number of possibilities for lines of symmetry. Children may find one vertical line of symmetry and stop there. However, the vertical line of symmetry could be drawn between any pair of rhombuses or down the centre of any hexagon as the pattern is continuous (repeating). The pattern also has a horizontal line of symmetry as the triangles are reflected along the central line and the other shapes have a horizontal line of symmetry.

STRENGTHEN Provide children with a mirror so they can explore the symmetry of each shape or pattern. You could provide the children with a simpler version of the patterns by presenting them with fewer shapes.

DEEPEN Challenge children to create a monster that has two lines of symmetry.

ASSESSMENT CHECKPOINT Questions **1**, **2** and **3** will demonstrate whether children can identify symmetry in complex shapes and simple patterns while question **3** will demonstrate whether children are able to find all lines of symmetry in a repeating pattern.

ANSWERS

Question **1**: A – the first monster has a vertical line of symmetry; B – the second monster has a horizontal line of symmetry; C – the third monster has vertical and horizontal lines of symmetry.

Question **2**: The monster has a diagonal line of symmetry.

Question **3** a) Pattern A has a vertical line of symmetry between the two triangles and a horizontal line of symmetry.

Pattern B can have a vertical line of symmetry between any pair of rhombuses or down the centre of any hexagon. It also has a horizontal line of symmetry.

Question **3** b): Children should draw symmetrical border patterns.

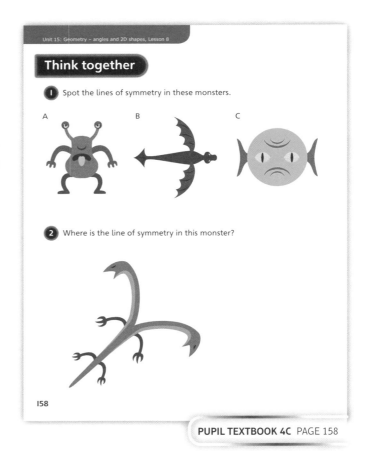

PUPIL TEXTBOOK 4C PAGE 158

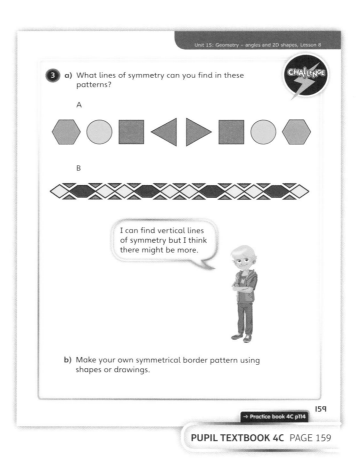

PUPIL TEXTBOOK 4C PAGE 159

Practice

WAYS OF WORKING Independent thinking

IN FOCUS Question **4** asks children to identify errors in a pattern that initially appears symmetrical. This addresses the misconception that if the shapes are repeated in reverse order, then the pattern is symmetrical. However, the shape itself also has to be reflected in the line of symmetry.

STRENGTHEN Create some simple symmetrical patterns using 2D shapes and ask children to identify the lines of symmetry. Provide the children with mirrors to help them explore the symmetry in the patterns.

DEEPEN Challenge children to think how they could adapt the pattern in question 4 so that it also had two diagonal lines of symmetry.

ASSESSMENT CHECKPOINT Questions **2** and **3** will demonstrate whether children can identify symmetry in a pattern with vertical, horizontal and diagonal lines of symmetry. Question **4** will demonstrate whether children can apply their knowledge of symmetry outside a shape to identify why a pattern is not symmetrical. It will also help to demonstrate if children have a secure understanding of what is required for a pattern to be symmetrical.

ANSWERS Answers for the **Practice** part of the lesson appear in the separate **Practice and Reflect answer book**.

PUPIL PRACTICE BOOK 4C PAGE 114

PUPIL PRACTICE BOOK 4C PAGE 115

Reflect

WAYS OF WORKING Independent thinking

IN FOCUS This section encourages children to consider the relationship between lines of symmetry and number of shapes. Children may reason that the number of times a shape appears will depend on whether or not the line of symmetry runs through a shape. This reasoning lays the foundations for reflection in the x- and y-axis in Year 5.

ASSESSMENT CHECKPOINT This part of the lesson will demonstrate whether children have a secure understanding of symmetry outside of a shape and symmetry in patterns.

ANSWERS Answers for the **Reflect** part of the lesson appear in the separate **Practice and Reflect answer book**.

After the lesson ⏸

- Were you able to provide practical opportunities to support children's learning, such as finding symmetry in their environment?
- How will you link the learning from this lesson to the next lesson on completing symmetrical patterns?

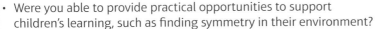

PUPIL PRACTICE BOOK 4C PAGE 116

Completing a symmetric figure

Learning focus

In this lesson, children will complete symmetric patterns when the lines of symmetry are given. They will reason about how shapes are affected by different lines of symmetry.

Small steps

→ Previous step: Lines of symmetry outside a shape
→ **This step: Completing a symmetric figure**
→ Next step: Completing a symmetric shape

NATIONAL CURRICULUM LINKS

Year 4 Geometry – Properties of shapes

Complete a simple symmetric figure with respect to a specific line of symmetry.

ASSESSING MASTERY

Children can complete and add to symmetric patterns with two or more lines of symmetry. They can create their own symmetric patterns with increasing complexity. Children can describe how shapes will be affected by vertical, horizontal and diagonal lines of symmetry.

COMMON MISCONCEPTIONS

When children try to complete a pattern they may forget to change the orientation of the shape according to the line of symmetry or they may make errors in the position of the reflected shape. Ask:
• *How will the shape look if it is reflected vertically/horizontally/diagonally?*

STRENGTHENING UNDERSTANDING

Ask children to make their own symmetric patterns using a range of 2D shapes. In this way they can physically flip or rotate the shapes in order to create the mirror image.

GOING DEEPER

Challenge children to come up with their own versions of the problems in the lesson for their partner to complete. They can make the challenge more difficult by adding more shapes, more lines of symmetry or by using more complex shapes.

KEY LANGUAGE

In lesson: symmetric, symmetrical, vertical, symmetry, horizontal, diagonal, oblong

Other language to be used by the teacher: polygon

STRUCTURES AND REPRESENTATIONS

2D shapes

RESOURCES

Optional: A range of 2D shapes, mirrors, geoboards and elastic bands

 In the eTextbook of this lesson, you will find interactive links to a selection of teaching tools.

Before you teach

• What practical opportunities can you provide to strengthen children's understanding?
• How will you address misconceptions about how a shape's orientation changes when reflected?

Discover

WAYS OF WORKING Pair work

ASK

- Question **1** a): *Can you identify the lines of symmetry? How do you know?*
- Question **1** a): *How do you know you have chosen the correct tile?*
- Question **1** b): *How is each design the same or different?*

IN FOCUS Question **1** a) requires children to first identify the line of symmetry from an incomplete pattern. They have to reason about what information they have in order to do this. This question should promote a high level of discussion. Ensure that children are prompted to justify their choices throughout.

PRACTICAL TIPS Provide children with coloured squares so that they can replicate the designs. By having 'tiles' that they can move, they can try out their ideas, review and adapt if necessary.

ANSWERS

Question **1** a): Tiles needed in order from top to bottom, left to right are: yellow, yellow, red, yellow.

Question **1** b): Tiles needed in order from top to bottom, left to right are: red, red, purple, orange.

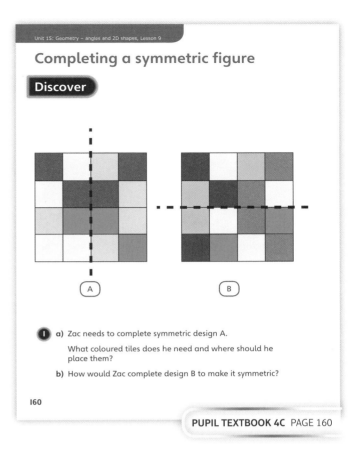

Completing a symmetric figure

Discover

1 a) Zac needs to complete symmetric design A.
What coloured tiles does he need and where should he place them?

b) How would Zac complete design B to make it symmetric?

160

PUPIL TEXTBOOK 4C PAGE 160

Share

WAYS OF WORKING Whole class teacher led

ASK

- Question **1** a): *How do you know there is only one line of symmetry?*
- Questions **1** a) and b): *Could the tiles have been other colours?*
- Questions **1** a) and b): *What would have to change for the patterns to have three lines of symmetry?*

IN FOCUS Question **1** b) has a different line of symmetry than the pattern in question **1** a). This means that children have to adjust their thinking and how they visualise the pattern in order to complete it. Due to how the patterns are organised, it would be easy to make the error of thinking that they have diagonal lines of symmetry. Ask: *Identify why the patterns do not have diagonal symmetry?*

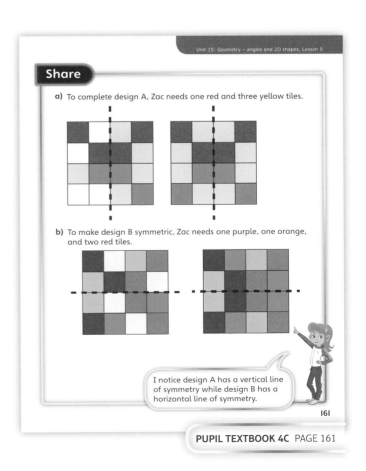

Share

a) To complete design A, Zac needs one red and three yellow tiles.

b) To make design B symmetric, Zac needs one purple, one orange, and two red tiles.

I notice design A has a vertical line of symmetry while design B has a horizontal line of symmetry.

161

PUPIL TEXTBOOK 4C PAGE 161

Think together

WAYS OF WORKING Whole class (I do, We do, You do)

ASK

- Questions ❶ and ❷: *How are the patterns here different from the patterns in the **Discover** section?*
- Question ❶: *Is there more than one possibility?*
- Question ❸: *Why doesn't it have diagonal lines of symmetry?*

IN FOCUS Question ❹ asks children to come up with their own symmetric design. Due to the fact that there is an odd number of tables, children will have to place one in the centre. Children need to reason that the number of desks they have in one quadrant will have to be repeated in each of the quadrants. This question would be straightforward if the number of desks were divisible by four.

STRENGTHEN Provide children with mirrors so that they can test their ideas. Giving children coloured squares to manipulate allows them to test and adapt their ideas in a concrete way.

DEEPEN Challenge children to extend question ❹. Ask: *How would your design change if you added one more table? How about if you had 13 tables? Is there a number of tables where it is impossible to have two lines of symmetry?*

ASSESSMENT CHECKPOINT Question ❸ will demonstrate whether children are able to correctly identify the design and orientation of a tile to complete a symmetric design. In question ❹, children demonstrate whether they are able to create their own symmetric designs.

ANSWERS

Question ❶: Tiles needed in order from top to bottom, left to right are: yellow, orange, yellow, orange.

Question ❷: The design has vertical and horizontal lines of symmetry.

Question ❸: Tile B is missing from the left side of the design.
Tile A is missing from the right side.

Question ❹: Children should have a design using 11 rectangles with horizontal and vertical lines of symmetry.

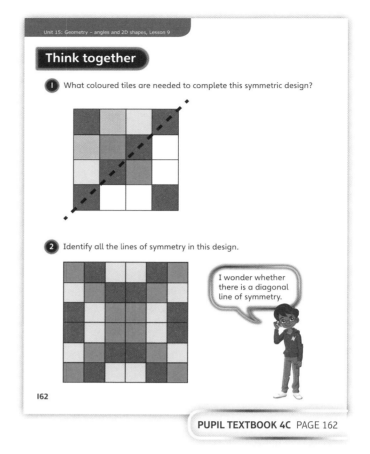

PUPIL TEXTBOOK 4C PAGE 162

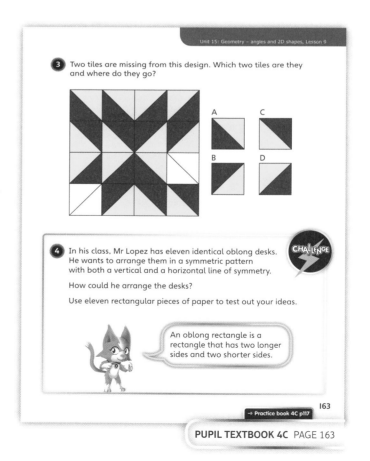

PUPIL TEXTBOOK 4C PAGE 163

Practice

WAYS OF WORKING Independent thinking

IN FOCUS Question **7** requires children to reason about how the orientation of the shape changes with vertical, horizontal and diagonal lines of symmetry. Children need to visualise how the shape changes and describe the transformation. This question may expose misconceptions about how the orientations of shapes are changed by reflection.

STRENGTHEN For questions **1** and **2**, provide children with mirrors so that they can see how the completed design should look. For questions **4** and **5**, allow children to explore using real geoboards so that they can easily review and adapt their designs.

DEEPEN Challenge children to work in pairs to create a symmetric design. Each child has a blank grid with a vertical and horizontal line of symmetry. The first child draws a shape on the right side of their design. The second child then draws the reflected image on the left side of their design. Then the second child then adds another shape on the left side and the first child draws the reflected shape on the right side of their design. Repeat for as long as required. The children then join their designs and check that they have created between them a design that has horizontal and vertical symmetry.

THINK DIFFERENTLY In question **6**, the lines drawn suggest that it is part of a square. However, by drawing two lines to make it a square, the end shape would have four lines of symmetry. Children need to create a convex (familiar kite shape) or concave ('arrowhead' kite shape) kite. It has a diagonal line of symmetry. That the shape has a diagonal line of symmetry may not be immediately obvious to children, so they have to apply what they know about the properties of quadrilaterals in order to solve this problem. You could prompt children by asking them to draw the line of symmetry first and then complete the shape.

ASSESSMENT CHECKPOINT Question **7** will demonstrate whether children have secure understanding of how shapes are transformed when reflected along vertical, horizontal and diagonal lines.

ANSWERS Answers for the **Practice** part of the lesson appear in the separate **Practice and Reflect answer book**.

Reflect

WAYS OF WORKING Pair work

IN FOCUS To create their own symmetry problems for each other, children need to have a good understanding of symmetry and how symmetric patterns work. They can challenge themselves appropriately by making the design as complex as they can.

ASSESSMENT CHECKPOINT This section will demonstrate whether children understand symmetry and how symmetric patterns work.

ANSWERS Answers for the **Reflect** part of the lesson appear in the separate **Practice and Reflect answer book**.

After the lesson ⏸

- Do children understand what happens to a shape when it is reflected along vertical, horizontal and diagonal lines?
- Could children contribute to a class or school display that allows them to apply the skills learnt in this lesson?

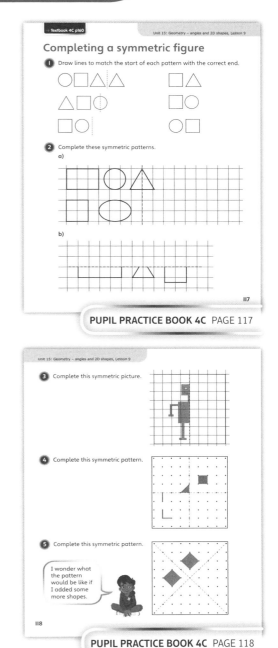

PUPIL PRACTICE BOOK 4C PAGE 117

PUPIL PRACTICE BOOK 4C PAGE 118

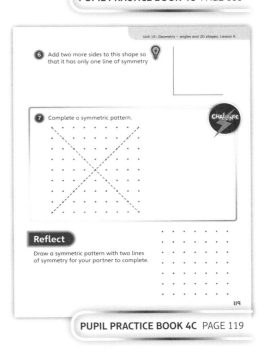

PUPIL PRACTICE BOOK 4C PAGE 119

Completing a symmetric shape

Learning focus

In this lesson, children will continue to develop their understanding of symmetry by completing symmetric shapes using a given line of symmetry.

Small steps

→ Previous step: Completing a symmetric figure
→ **This step: Completing a symmetric shape**
→ Next step: Describing position (1)

NATIONAL CURRICULUM LINKS

Year 4 Geometry – Properties of Shapes

Complete a simple symmetric figure with respect to a specific line of symmetry.

ASSESSING MASTERY

Children can reliably complete a symmetric shape. They can confidently use a line symmetry, regardless of its orientation, to complete a shape.

COMMON MISCONCEPTIONS

Children may need support to recognise how symmetry works when a line of symmetry is orientated at an angle other than vertical or horizontal (for example, at 45°). Ask:
• *What could you use to check what the shape should look like? What is different about this line symmetry to those you have seen before?*

STRENGTHENING UNDERSTANDING

Children may benefit from having the opportunity to spot lines of symmetry inside shapes. This could be done by showing them shapes or pictures and asking them to identify where the lines of symmetry are inside the shape. Recapping this skill will help them in readiness for this lesson.

GOING DEEPER

Encourage children to complete a pattern or shape where multiple lines of symmetry have been placed more haphazardly. Children should investigate how this affects the final shape or pattern. Ask: *Was this easier or trickier to complete? How did it affect the final shape or pattern?*

KEY LANGUAGE

In lesson: symmetric, octagonal, symmetry, lines of symmetry, irregular, octagon, vertical, horizontal, pattern, obtuse

Other language to be used by the teacher: acute, right angle, symmetrical, polygon

STRUCTURES AND REPRESENTATIONS

a range of 2D shapes and angles

RESOURCES

Mandatory: lolly sticks

Optional: mirrors, 2D shapes

 In the eTextbook of this lesson, you will find interactive links to a selection of teaching tools.

Before you teach

• How confident are children in their learning from the previous lesson on symmetry?
• Are there any misconceptions you will need to tackle before moving forward in this lesson?

Discover

Completing a symmetric shape

Discover

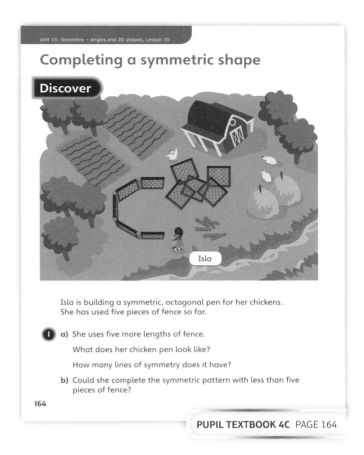

Isla is building a symmetric, octagonal pen for her chickens. She has used five pieces of fence so far.

1 **a)** She uses five more lengths of fence.

What does her chicken pen look like?

How many lines of symmetry does it have?

b) Could she complete the symmetric pattern with less than five pieces of fence?

164

PUPIL TEXTBOOK 4C PAGE 164

WAYS OF WORKING Pair work

ASK

- Question **1** a): *What shape do you predict her chicken pen will be?*
- Question **1** b): *Is there a minimum amount of fence panels she needs to use?*
- Question **1** b): *Is there a maximum number she could use?*

IN FOCUS It will be important to use this opportunity to recap symmetry and the children's learning from the previous lesson to ensure speedy progress through this lesson.

PRACTICAL TIPS This activity could be carried out in class practically with lolly sticks. The activity could be extended by giving similar questions about different shaped pens.

ANSWERS

Question **1** a):

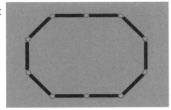

The pen will have two lines of symmetry.

Question **1** b): The pen can be finished symmetrically using only three pieces of fence.

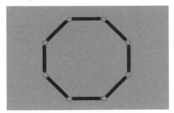

Share

Share

a) Isla's chicken pen would look like this once it has been completed with five more pieces of fence.

This shape has two lines of symmetry.

This irregular octagon has one vertical and one horizontal line of symmetry.

b) Isla could complete a symmetric, octagonal pen by using only three more pieces of fence. This is what the pen would look like.

This regular octagon has 8 lines of symmetry.

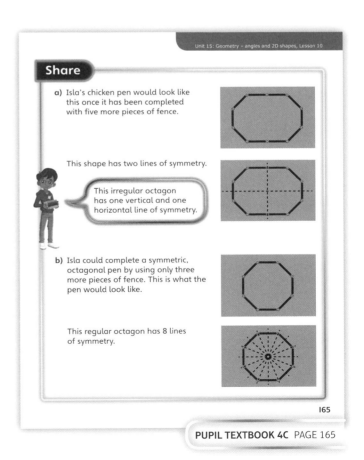

165

PUPIL TEXTBOOK 4C PAGE 165

WAYS OF WORKING Whole class teacher led

ASK

- Question **1** a): *Did your octagon look like the one in the picture?*
- Question **1** a): *How was your shape the same as your partner's and how was it different?*
- Question **1** b): *Did you find another way of completing the shape?*
- Question **1** b): *What does the line of symmetry represent?*

IN FOCUS Discuss with children what tools they can use to help them predict what a symmetric shape will look like after it has been completed and to help check their work once they have completed it. Children should recognise that a mirror can help them predict and check their work.

Think together

WAYS OF WORKING Whole class teacher led (I do, We do, You do)

ASK

- Questions **1** and **2**: *What is similar and what is different about the lines of symmetry?*
- Questions **1** and **2**: *How will you complete the shapes?*
- Questions **1** and **2**: *How can you check the symmetric shapes?*
- Question **3**: *How can you prove or disprove the conjectures?*

IN FOCUS For question **2** in particular, it will be important to focus on the lines of symmetry that are not horizontal or vertical. Encourage children to investigate what happens when a shape is mirrored across a line of symmetry that is set to a 45° angle. Ask: *How is this line of symmetry similar and how is it different to those you have seen before? How can you predict and check what the shape should look like?*

STRENGTHEN To help children prove or disprove the conjectures made in question **3**, ask: *What could you do to test your ideas?* You could also ask: *Are there any resources you could use to help you investigate?*

DEEPEN Challenge children to come up with their own conjectures, as in question **3**. Ask: *Can you come up with a conjecture about how angles change across a line of symmetry? What do you think might happen if you mirror a shape across two lines of symmetry?*

ASSESSMENT CHECKPOINT At this point children should be able to complete a symmetric shape across lines of symmetry of different orientations.

ANSWERS

Question **1** a): Children should have completed the shape correctly using 5 sticks.

Question **1** b): Children should have completed the shape correctly using 5 sticks.

Question **2** a): Children should have completed the shape correctly using 6 sticks.

Question **2** b): Children should have completed the shape correctly using 6 sticks.

Question **3**: 1. True – you can draw a right angled trapezium, for example.
2. False – it will depend where the line of symmetry is.
3. False – it will depend where the line of symmetry is.

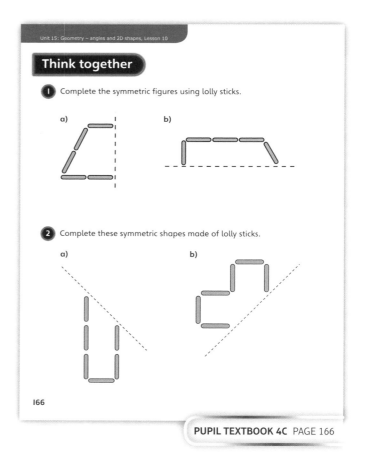

PUPIL TEXTBOOK 4C PAGE 166

PUPIL TEXTBOOK 4C PAGE 167

Practice

WAYS OF WORKING Independent thinking

IN FOCUS The questions in this part of the lesson help children to become more fluent and flexible in their use of lines of symmetry. Be sure to help children realise that the lines of symmetry appear at different angles, both on and between the gridded dots, and in differing numbers.

For question **5**, encourage children to consider what shapes they know of that would fit the properties given in the question. They may neglect to consider irregular shapes and only investigate regular ones. Ask: *Is that the only type of pentagon (or other shape with an odd number of sides) you can draw?*

STRENGTHEN It may help children to have visual reminders around the classroom or at their workspaces to help scaffold their work. Ask: *Now that you have completed the symmetric shape, can you find a similar one on the in the classroom?*

DEEPEN Challenge children to create their own symmetry challenges for their partner. Ask: *Can you create a symmetric shape or pattern for your partner to finish? Remember to consider: where the lines of symmetry will go; how many lines of symmetry; what type of gridded paper to use.* Children could also be encouraged to investigate how a line of symmetry would work if it was placed through a shape.

ASSESSMENT CHECKPOINT Children should be able to confidently mirror any shape across a line of symmetry of any orientation.

ANSWERS Answers for the **Practice** part of the lesson appear in the separate **Practice and Reflect answer book**.

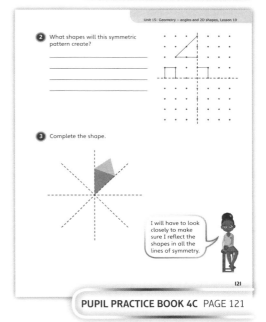

PUPIL PRACTICE BOOK 4C PAGE 120

PUPIL PRACTICE BOOK 4C PAGE 121

Reflect

WAYS OF WORKING Independent thinking

IN FOCUS Give children time to formulate their own reasoning to finish the given sentence starter. Once they have written their ideas, share in partners and with the class. Children should compare their ideas. Do they agree on what is important? Can they convince their partner of their ideas?

ASSESSMENT CHECKPOINT Look for children's ability to explain the process of finishing symmetric shapes and patterns. They may mention how mirrors can be used to predict and check a symmetric shape.

ANSWERS Answers for the **Reflect** part of the lesson appear in the separate **Practice and Reflect answer book**.

After the lesson ⏸

- Are children confident with lines of symmetry at all orientations?
- How were children's reasoning skills supported and developed in this lesson?

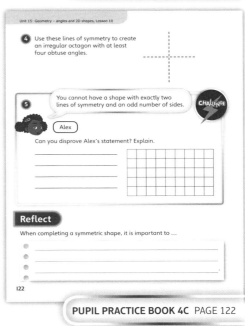

PUPIL PRACTICE BOOK 4C PAGE 122

End of unit check

> Don't forget the *Power Maths* unit assessment grid on p26.

WAYS OF WORKING Independent work

IN FOCUS

- This end of unit check will allow you to focus on children's understanding of angles and 2D shapes including symmetry, and whether they can apply their knowledge to solve problems.
- Questions **1** and **3** ask children to identify particular types of irregular and regular shapes.
- Question **2** and **5** assess children's ability to recognise and complete a symmetrical pattern and identify lines of symmetry.
- Question **4** assesses children's understanding of different types of angles.
- Question **6** is a SAT-style question and assesses children's recognition of angles and types of triangles.

ANSWERS AND COMMENTARY

Children who have mastered the concepts in this unit will be able to confidently recognise and order acute, obtuse and right angles, and explain how right angles can help them to do so. They will be able to name and describe the different types of triangles and quadrilaterals, and explain the similarities and differences. They will be able to point out where a quadrilateral may fit under more than one heading. Children will be able to confidently complete shapes and patterns across lines of symmetry in different orientations and will be able to apply their knowledge and understanding to solve problems.

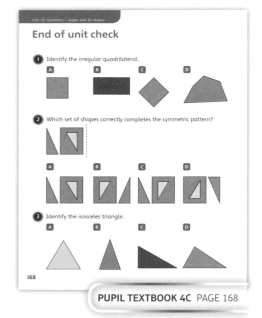

PUPIL TEXTBOOK 4C PAGE 168

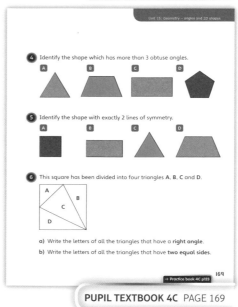

PUPIL TEXTBOOK 4C PAGE 169

Q	A	WRONG ANSWERS AND MISCONCEPTIONS	STRENGTHENING UNDERSTANDING
1	B	A indicates a lack of understanding about what irregular means.	**Symmetry:** Give children a mirror to help them check the lines of symmetry inside and outside of the shapes. **Angles:** Remind children about how they can use a right angle to help them judge whether an angle is acute or obtuse.
2	B	A indicates children have just repeated the first shape, not mirrored it. C and D indicate that children have not fully understood how symmetrical patterns and lines of symmetry alter shapes.	
3	B	A, C or D indicate children are unsure about types of triangle.	
4	D	A, B, or C indicate children are unsure about types of angle.	
5	B	A indicates children have neglected diagonal lines of symmetry. C or D indicates that children are unsure about lines of symmetry in 2D shapes.	
6 a)	A, B, D	Not identifying them all may suggest that children fail to identify right angles in unfamiliar orientations.	
6 b)	A, C	B and/or D suggests that children have compared lengths of sides incorrectly.	

My journal

WAYS OF WORKING Independent thinking

ANSWERS AND COMMENTARY Question **1** : For this question, look for children's ability to visualise the types of triangles and quadrilaterals that may be possible to create using the interior of a regular hexagon. Ask:
- *What types of quadrilaterals and triangles are there?*
- *Can you see how any of those shapes might fit into the hexagon? Can you make any of those shapes by drawing two lines across the hexagon?*

Answer: There are two correct answers. (6 vertices numbered from 1st to 6th clockwise around a hexagon.)
1. Draw a line from the 1st vertex to the 4th vertex and a second line from the 2nd vertex to the 5th vertex.
2. Draw a line from the 1st vertex to the 4th vertex and a second line from the 3rd vertex to the 5th vertex.

Children may represent these ways of dividing the hexagon but in a different orientation.

Question **2** : When solving this question, look for children to be experimenting and finding evidence. When solving the question and providing their ideas, encourage children's reasoning by asking:
- *How have you proven your ideas?*
- *What is it about obtuse angles that means Greg cannot be correct?*
- *How many obtuse angles could he have? Why?*

Answer: Greg cannot be correct because if you draw two lines that meet to create an obtuse angle, in order to join them with a third line to create a triangle, the other two angles have to be acute so two angles in a triangle cannot be obtuse. Children may support their argument with a picture.

Power check

WAYS OF WORKING Independent thinking

ASK
- *How confident are you at recognising acute and obtuse angles?*
- *Could you name and identify all types of triangle?*
- *Can you identify different quadrilaterals and their properties?*
- *Do you think you can complete any symmetrical shape or pattern now?*

Power play

WAYS OF WORKING Pair work

IN FOCUS This activity will help you see if children are able to identify different quadrilaterals and triangles. Discuss with children the properties of the shapes they are making and ask them to justify how they know what shape they have made.

ANSWERS AND COMMENTARY If children are able to create the different shapes and justify what they have done, then this shows they have a good understanding of the properties of quadrilaterals and triangles. If they are unsuccessful, then this suggests that the children need support in comparing angles and sides of 2D shapes.

After the unit ⏸

- Can children find quadrilaterals and triangles in the environment in the classroom? How could you link the learning from this unit with the next?

PUPIL PRACTICE BOOK 4C PAGE 123

PUPIL PRACTICE BOOK 4C PAGE 124

PUPIL PRACTICE BOOK 4C PAGE 125

Strengthen and **Deepen** activities for this unit can be found in the *Power Maths* online subscription.

Unit 16
Geometry – position and direction

Don't forget to watch the Unit 16 video!

WHY THIS UNIT IS IMPORTANT

Coordinate geometry is one of the most powerful ideas in basic mathematics. Coordinates use numbers to describe positions on a grid and connect the worlds of arithmetic and geometry. In later work, coordinates will be used with algebra to allow children to visualise the behaviour of mathematical rules, connections and conditions. This unit focuses on the use of coordinates to describe positions and movements, and provides a solid foundation in some key ideas that will be used in a wide variety of more advanced concepts.

WHERE THIS UNIT FITS

→ Unit 15: Geometry – angles and 2D shapes

→ **Unit 16: Geometry – position and direction**

This unit introduces children to coordinate grids, using them to describe positions of points and translations from one point to another. It builds on the knowledge developed in Unit 15 of properties and symmetry of 2D shapes to identify and represent such shapes using coordinates.

Before they start this unit, it is expected that children:
• know how to read positions on a number line (to the nearest half unit)
• understand how maps and plans can be used to represent a 'real-life' scene
• understand a range of simple ideas and vocabulary related to position and direction: for example left/right and horizontal/vertical.

ASSESSING MASTERY

Children can read and write coordinates for positions in the first quadrant, i.e. points to the right of and above the origin (0,0). They can plot points given a pair of coordinates and understand the convention that the first coordinate represents the horizontal distance to the right of the origin and the second coordinate represents the vertical distance above the origin. They understand translations as movements on the coordinate grid; they can describe the result of making a translation described in words and they can find the translation required for the movement between given positions. They can use simple geometrical reasoning on a coordinate grid to draw patterns and complete shapes.

COMMON MISCONCEPTIONS	STRENGTHENING UNDERSTANDING	GOING DEEPER
Children may confuse the order of coordinates.	Explain that the order of coordinates is *conventional*, in the sense that it is a convention that everyone has agreed to follow.	Provide children with a variety of coordinates, including half units, and ask them to plot them on a grid.
Children may confuse the ideas of coordinates and translations.	Be clear that coordinates tell us where things are, and have a simple notation in the form (6,5); translations tell us how to move, and are written out in words.	At a deeper level, coordinates *are* translations – from the origin to the point we are interested in. Ask children to describe the translation to go from the origin to a point and to explain the pattern that they find.

WAYS OF WORKING

Use these pages to introduce the unit focus to children. Use the characters to discuss concepts and phrases that children have not heard before.

STRUCTURES AND REPRESENTATIONS

Coordinate grid: Children use coordinate grids throughout the unit to describe positions of points and translations from one point to another.

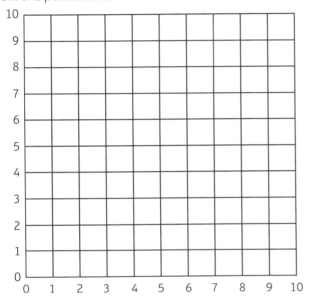

KEY LANGUAGE

There is some key language that children will need to know as part of the learning in this unit.

→ coordinates
→ position
→ horizontal, vertical
→ up, down
→ left, right
→ square, rectangle
→ vertex, vertices

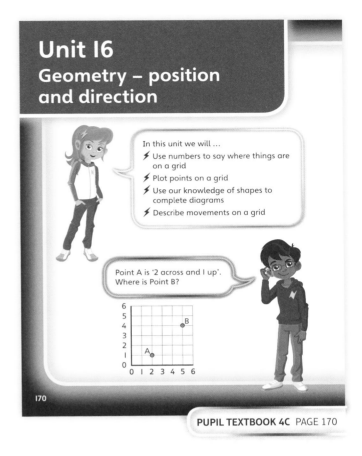

Unit 16
Geometry – position and direction

In this unit we will …
⚡ Use numbers to say where things are on a grid
⚡ Plot points on a grid
⚡ Use our knowledge of shapes to complete diagrams
⚡ Describe movements on a grid

Point A is '2 across and 1 up'. Where is Point B?

170

PUPIL TEXTBOOK 4C PAGE 170

We will need some maths words. Which ones go together?

position	horizontal	vertical
up	down	left	right
coordinate	square	rectangle
plot	vertex	vertices
point	grid

You will need to know how to find numbers on a number line. What are the numbers marked with letters?

171

PUPIL TEXTBOOK 4C PAGE 171

Describing position ❶

Learning focus

In this lesson, children will describe relative positions on a map, initially without a grid and then with a grid. They will develop understanding and skills that will be needed when numbered axes and coordinates are introduced in the next lesson.

Small steps

→ Previous step: Completing a symmetric shape
→ **This step: Describing position (1)**
→ Next step: Describing position (2)

NATIONAL CURRICULUM LINKS

Year 4 Geometry – Position and Direction

Describe positions on a 2D grid as coordinates in the first quadrant.

ASSESSING MASTERY

Children can describe the relative positions of objects using terms such as near, closest, centre, between, and half-way between. They can use a grid to describe the positions of objects in relation to others, counting squares as necessary.

COMMON MISCONCEPTIONS

Children may need support to identify when places are half-way between other places. Ask:
• *Describe the position of A relative to B and C. What can you tell me about the distance from A to B and from A to C? Are they the same? Complete this sentence: A is _____ between B and C.*

STRENGTHENING UNDERSTANDING

To strengthen understanding of how to describe relative position, position children around the classroom or the playground and ask them to describe their position relative to other children. Encourage them to describe their position in different ways.

GOING DEEPER

Ask children to find a map on the internet and to make up questions about the locations of places. A partner can then try to find the places from the information.

KEY LANGUAGE

In lesson: map, next to, near, closest, centre, between, half-way between, **grid**, left, right, up, down

Other language to be used by the teacher: horizontal, vertical

RESOURCES

Optional: access to the internet, simple maps

 In the eTextbook of this lesson, you will find interactive links to a selection of teaching tools.

Before you teach ❚❚

• Can children describe their position relative to other children or objects?
• Have children met situations where they need to find places on maps?

Discover

WAYS OF WORKING Pair work

ASK

- Question **1** a): *Tell me some places you can see on the map.*
- Question **1** a): *Which places are close to each other? Which places are far apart?*
- Question **1** a): *How many playgrounds are there?*

IN FOCUS This activity develops the ability to describe one place relative to another, encouraging children to use different ways to describe position.

PRACTICAL TIPS Use a real map (perhaps of the local area around your school) as an alternative or addition to the map shown here.

ANSWERS

Question **1** a): Bella is looking for the roller coaster.

Question **1** b): The roller coaster is half-way between the log flume and the dropzone ride. (Other descriptions are possible.)

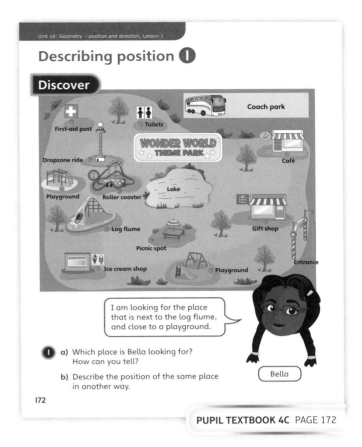

PUPIL TEXTBOOK 4C PAGE 172

Share

WAYS OF WORKING Whole class teacher led

ASK

- Question **1** a): *Why does Dexter say he needs to use both pieces of information?*
- Question **1** b): *Whose description gives a better idea of where the roller coaster is: Astrid's or Flo's?*
- Question **1** b): *Can you describe the position of the roller coaster in any other way?*

IN FOCUS This activity establishes that the location of one place can be described relative to other places in different ways. It introduces terms such as 'next to' and 'between'. Question **1** b) introduces the idea that descriptions can be made more precise by using words such as 'half-way'.

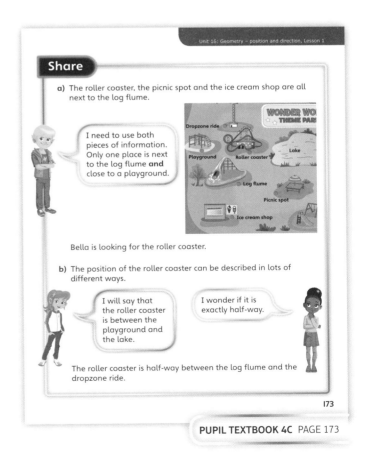

PUPIL TEXTBOOK 4C PAGE 173

Think together

Whole class teacher led (I do, We do, You do)

ASK

- Question ❷ a): *Which place is closest to the ice cream shop? Which place is furthest away?*
- Question ❷ a): *Does your description only apply to the café, or could it be describing another place? Do you need to add to your description?*
- Question ❸ a): *How many squares are there across the map? How many squares up and down?*
- Question ❸ a): *How can you use the squares to find somewhere half-way between two points?*

IN FOCUS Question ❸ introduces a grid of squares, which makes it easier to describe where places are. Emphasise that since the squares are all the same size, locations can be given accurately by counting the number of squares. The grid uses horizontal and vertical lines – introduce this terminology, making sure that children understand which is which.

STRENGTHEN Give children additional practice in identifying locations from your descriptions before asking them to describe locations for themselves. Put children in pairs to describe locations to each other to help them develop the idea that they need to be precise, so that only one location fits the description.

DEEPEN Challenge children to think about the most efficient way to describe locations. Before the grid is introduced, you could encourage them to use left/right and above/below as well as near/far and so on.

ASSESSMENT CHECKPOINT Use question ❶ to assess whether children can find places given a description of their location. Use question ❷ to assess whether they can describe locations unambiguously.

ANSWERS

Question ❶ a): The toilets.

Question ❶ b): The lake.

Question ❶ c): The gift shop.

Question ❶ d): The roller coaster.

Question ❷ a): Example: The ice cream shop is close to the bottom of the map, near the log flume.

Question ❷ b): Example: The café is between the gift shop and the coach park.

Question ❷ c): Example: The dropzone ride is next to the playground and the roller coaster.

Question ❷ d): Example: The first aid post is at the top left of the map.

Question ❸ a): The log flume.

Question ❸ b): The toilets.

Question ❸ c): The gift shop.

Think together

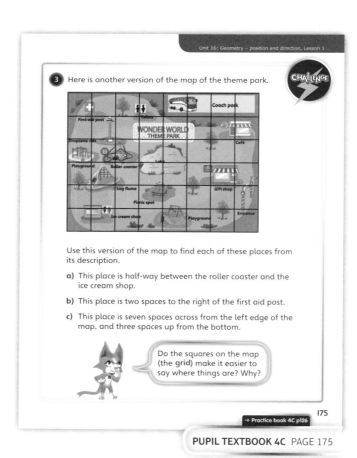

❶ Identify each of these places from its description.

a) The place near the top of the map, close to the coach park.

b) The feature in the centre of the map.

c) The closest place to the entrance.

d) The closest place to the lake.

❷ Describe the positions of these places. There may be more than one way to describe each one.

a) The ice cream shop c) The dropzone ride

b) The café d) The first aid post

174

PUPIL TEXTBOOK 4C PAGE 174

---

❸ Here is another version of the map of the theme park. **CHALLENGE**

Use this version of the map to find each of these places from its description.

a) This place is half-way between the roller coaster and the ice cream shop.

b) This place is two spaces to the right of the first aid post.

c) This place is seven spaces across from the left edge of the map, and three spaces up from the bottom.

> Do the squares on the map (the **grid**) make it easier to say where things are? Why?

→ Practice book 4C p126

175

PUPIL TEXTBOOK 4C PAGE 175

Practice

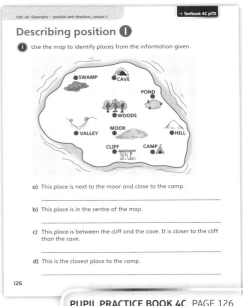

PUPIL PRACTICE BOOK 4C PAGE 126

WAYS OF WORKING Independent work

IN FOCUS Question ❷ involves describing locations relative to other places on a map. Encourage children to use a variety of ways of describing locations, rather using the same term (for example, 'next to') in all their descriptions. Question ❹ clarifies that all places between two points are not necessarily half-way between.

STRENGTHEN In question ❺, ask children questions about the grid (for example, 'How many squares across …' and 'How many squares up …'). Describe some locations for them to identify using the grid before they use it to describe locations to a partner.

DEEPEN Ask children to investigate how many places they need to reference to describe a location. For example, 'the moor is half-way between the valley and the hill' references two locations – the valley and the hill. Ask them to explain how many places they need to reference when using a grid: only one, as the other information is given by the number of squares in two directions.

ASSESSMENT CHECKPOINT Use question ❶ to assess whether children can find places given a description of their location. Use question ❷ to assess whether they can describe locations unambiguously. Use question ❸ to check that they are confident at identifying positions that lie on a given straight line.

ANSWERS Answers for the **Practice** part of the lesson appear in the separate **Practice and Reflect answer guide**.

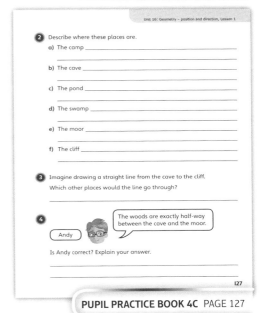

PUPIL PRACTICE BOOK 4C PAGE 127

Reflect

WAYS OF WORKING Independent thinking

IN FOCUS This activity provides an opportunity for children to reflect on the maps they have used, with and without grids, and the different ways in which they have specified locations.

ASSESSMENT CHECKPOINT Check that children understand the importance of providing descriptions that identify only one possible location. They may realise that this is easier to do with a grid.

ANSWERS Answers for the **Reflect** part of the lesson appear in the separate **Practice and Reflect answer guide**.

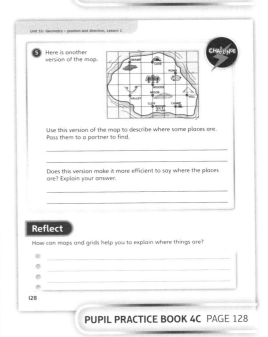

PUPIL PRACTICE BOOK 4C PAGE 128

After the lesson

- Can children describe positions relative to other locations?
- Were children confident in using directions left/right and up/down on a grid?
- Are children prepared for the introduction of a formal system of coordinates in the next lesson?

Describing position ❷

Learning focus

In this lesson, children will use coordinates in the first quadrant to describe positions on a grid, using the conventional order and notation.

Small steps

→ Previous step: Describing position (1)
→ **This step: Describing position (2)**
→ Next step: Drawing on a grid

NATIONAL CURRICULUM LINKS

Year 4 Geometry – Position and Direction

Describe positions on a 2D grid as coordinates in the first quadrant.

ASSESSING MASTERY

Children can use coordinates to describe the positions of objects on a grid. They understand the importance of being consistent in the order in which the coordinates are given (horizontal then vertical), and they recognise and use the conventional notation for coordinates.

COMMON MISCONCEPTIONS

Children may write coordinates in the wrong order. Indicate point (4,2) and ask:
• *How many squares along is this point? How many squares up? Which do you put first when writing coordinates?*

STRENGTHENING UNDERSTANDING

It may be useful for some children to think about the coordinate axes as number lines. For example, you could ask: *How far along this number line [the horizontal axis] do you need to go? And how far up this number line [the vertical axis]?*

GOING DEEPER

More confident learners can be challenged to answer questions 'without the pictures'. For example, ask them which is closer to (4,4): (9,4) or (4,0), and encourage them to explain their answer.

KEY LANGUAGE

In lesson: coordinates, position

Other language to be used by the teacher: parentheses, horizontal, vertical, origin, grid

STRUCTURES AND REPRESENTATIONS

coordinate grid

RESOURCES

Optional: computer geometry package

 In the eTextbook of this lesson, you will find interactive links to a selection of teaching tools.

Before you teach

• Are children confident in describing relative positions on an unnumbered grid?
• Do children appreciate the usefulness of measuring positions from a common reference point?

Discover

WAYS OF WORKING Pair work

ASK
- Question **1** a): *What is different about this map compared to the maps in the last lesson?*
- Question **1** a): *What do you think the numbers in (2,2) mean?*

IN FOCUS This activity introduces the coordinate grid and the concept that the location of objects on the map can be given by two numbers (the horizontal and vertical coordinates). Question **1** a) has been chosen so that the order of the coordinates does not matter and question **1** b) establishes that there needs to be an agreed order for the numbers.

PRACTICAL TIPS Do not explain the order of the coordinates at this stage. The most important idea to establish is that there needs to be *some* consistent order for the coordinates – the remainder of the lesson will be used to reinforce what the conventional order is.

ANSWERS

Question **1** a): The sword was found at position (2,2).

Question **1** b): The gold cup was found at position (2,1).

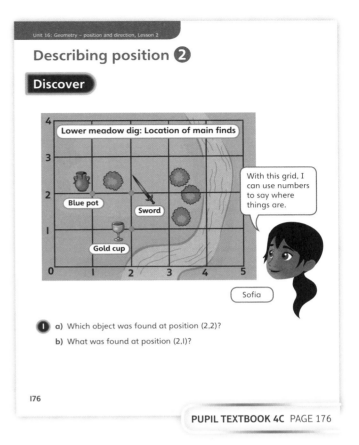

PUPIL TEXTBOOK 4C PAGE 176

Share

WAYS OF WORKING Whole class teacher led

ASK
- Question **1** a): *What do you notice about the two numbers? Does it matter whether you go across or up first?*
- Question **1** b): *Does it matter whether you use the first number to go across or up?*
- Question **1** b): *What is at (1,2)?*

IN FOCUS This introduces children to a number of important concepts: always give the 'across' number first, followed by the 'up' number; these numbers are called coordinates; and coordinates are written as two numbers, separated by a comma and surrounded by parentheses. Also draw attention to the fact that the grid numbering starts from the bottom left corner, so that the horizontal coordinate is measured to the right, and the vertical coordinate is measured upwards.

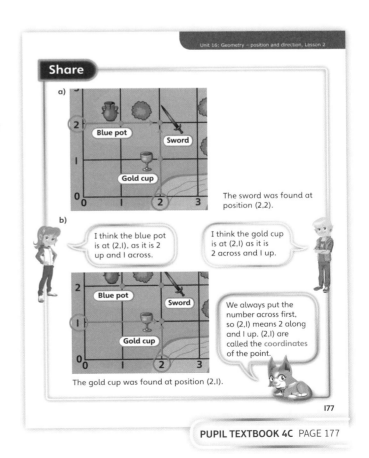

PUPIL TEXTBOOK 4C PAGE 177

Think together

Think together

WAYS OF WORKING Whole class teacher led (I do, We do, You do)

ASK

- Question **1**: *Can you see that some other things have been found and marked on the map?*
- Question **3**: *Do you think coordinates are a good way of recording where things were found? Would it be easier to just say something like 'The silver pin was found near the trees'?*

IN FOCUS Question **3** emphasises the advantage of coordinates over word descriptions to accurately describe positions.

STRENGTHEN Reinforce children's understanding of the correct order of coordinates by asking questions such as: *Which position would be in the river: (4,1) or (1,4)?* Draw a grid on the board clearly showing going across then up.

DEEPEN Ask further questions based on the map of the dig. For example: *Imagine that another gold cup was found, one grid space from the first one: what could its coordinates be? A shield was found half-way between the spear and the red pot: what were its coordinates?*

ASSESSMENT CHECKPOINT Use question **1** to assess whether children can find locations given by coordinates. Use question **2** to check that children can give coordinates of specified locations correctly.

ANSWERS

Question **1** a): The blue pot is located at (1,2).

Question **1** b): The statue is located at (5,3).

Question **1** c): The spear is located at (2,3).

Question **2** a): The coordinates of the silver tray are (1,1).

Question **2** b) i):   The red pot was found at (0,3).

Question **2** b) ii):   The coin was found at (4,0).

Question **2** b) iii):   The vase was found at (5,1).

Question **3**: The pin could not have been found at C (2,3).

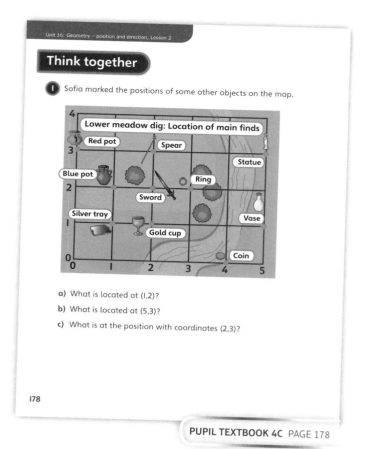

PUPIL TEXTBOOK 4C PAGE 178

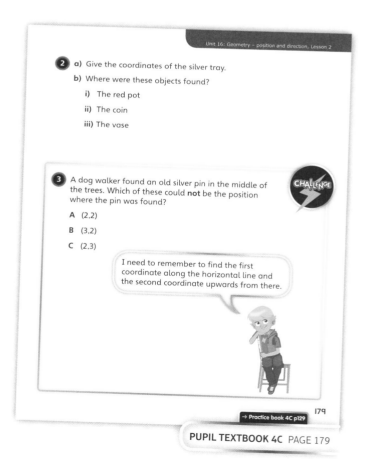

PUPIL TEXTBOOK 4C PAGE 179

Practice

WAYS OF WORKING Independent thinking

IN FOCUS Questions **4** and **7** require children to interpret the information given on the plan to decide where to plant. Question **5** introduces children to the origin of the grid – that is, the reference point from which all of the distances on the grid are measured. If necessary, discuss what makes this a sensible choice of origin: all measurements can be made to the right and up, and the location of any position in the diagram can be expressed by a pair of positive coordinates.

STRENGTHEN Children who are still finding it difficult to remember the correct order of coordinates may benefit from additional practice using a computer geometry package. This approach can take away some of the risk and uncertainty involved in trying to remember the order – instead, children can simply enter the coordinates and see where the computer plots a point.

DEEPEN Ask children to mark a tree on the map of Jamie's garden and then write out the coordinates of that tree. Their partner can describe the position of a new object using coordinates which they then have to plot.

THINK DIFFERENTLY Question **6** is more open-ended and allows an element of interpretation as the sides of the shed are parallel to the house, giving more than one possible answer. Children are likely to keep to integer coordinates, as used throughout this lesson. So the points furthest from the house could be (0,6) or (1,6).

ASSESSMENT CHECKPOINT Use questions **1** and **2** to assess whether children are writing coordinates correctly, giving the 'distance across' followed by 'distance up'.

ANSWERS Answers for the **Practice** part of the lesson appear in the separate **Practice and Reflect answer guide**.

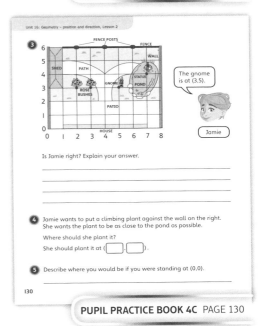

PUPIL PRACTICE BOOK 4C PAGE 129

PUPIL PRACTICE BOOK 4C PAGE 130

Reflect

WAYS OF WORKING Independent thinking

IN FOCUS This activity provides a final opportunity to revisit the key learning point for this lesson – the use of coordinates to specify positions in the first quadrant.

ASSESSMENT CHECKPOINT Check that children understand that the coordinates represent horizontal and vertical distances from the origin (in that order), and so the example given is incorrect.

ANSWERS Answers for the **Reflect** part of the lesson appear in the separate **Practice and Reflect answer guide**.

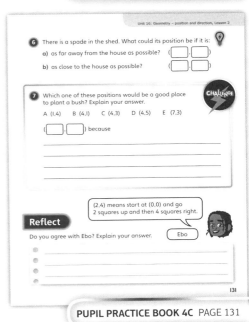

PUPIL PRACTICE BOOK 4C PAGE 131

After the lesson

- Are children using coordinates correctly?
- What opportunities can you provide for additional practice in plotting points?

Drawing on a grid

Learning focus

In this lesson, children will use coordinates to plot points in the first quadrant and to construct simple shapes by plotting their vertices. They will also plot points to complete shapes.

Small steps

→ Previous step: Describing position (2)
→ **This step: Drawing on a grid**
→ Next step: Reasoning on a grid

NATIONAL CURRICULUM LINKS

Year 4 Geometry – Position and Direction

Plot specified points and draw sides to complete a given polygon.

ASSESSING MASTERY

Children can plot points in the first quadrant. They can continue simple patterns, determining and plotting the coordinates that are required, and they can draw simple geometric shapes, given a list of coordinates for the vertices.

COMMON MISCONCEPTIONS

Children may still interpret coordinates in the wrong order. Children need to know that the order matters (and that we therefore need to agree on one order or the other) and they also need to know what the conventional order is. Indicate point (4,2) and ask:

• *Does it matter whether you give the across coordinate first, or the up coordinate first? How will I know which you are giving first?*

STRENGTHENING UNDERSTANDING

All of the plotting exercises in this lesson could usefully be carried out (or repeated) using a computer geometry package. Seeing the same coordinate system used in as many different contexts as possible should help to strengthen understanding of the system. In the previous lesson, children used coordinates used on maps – this lesson introduces floor robots and more abstract grids as additional contexts in which the same rules apply.

GOING DEEPER

Challenge more confident children to research how computer games designers use coordinates to specify positions on the screen of a device.

KEY LANGUAGE

In lesson: plot, coordinates, **point**, vertices, horizontal, vertical, predict

Other language to be used by the teacher: rule, vertex, pattern, rectangle, square, triangle, pentagon

STRUCTURES AND REPRESENTATIONS

coordinate grid

RESOURCES

Mandatory: squared paper

Optional: computer geometry package, squared paper, ruler

 In the eTextbook of this lesson, you will find interactive links to a selection of teaching tools.

Before you teach

• Do children understand the conventional order of coordinates?
• What support will you provide for children who need additional practice?

Discover

Pair work

ASK

- Question ❶ a): *The robot is plotting a new point. How many points has it plotted before this one?*
- Question ❶ a): *How do the numbers on the grid help you to see where the points will be plotted?*

IN FOCUS This activity provides further experience with coordinates, in a new context. The use of a 'robot' moves the emphasis from 'remembering what the correct order of coordinates is' to 'using the available clues to work out what the robot is doing'. Check that children understand the idea of 'plot a point' – it may be necessary to explain that this is simply the way that the robot is told where to draw the little circles on the grid.

PRACTICAL TIPS If available, use a simple computer geometry package to demonstrate plotting different points.

ANSWERS

Question ❶ a): The command Reena used to plot the third dot is: Plot a point at (3,5).

Question ❶ b): Reena should plot the points (4,4), (5,3), (6,2), and (7,1) to continue the dots in a straight line.

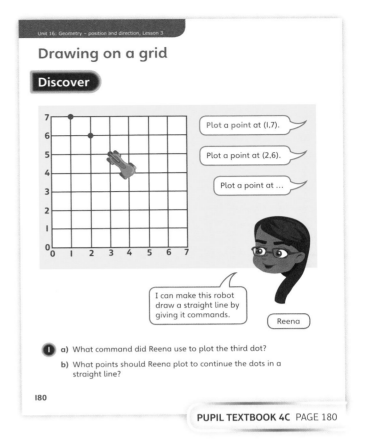

Drawing on a grid

Discover

I can make this robot draw a straight line by giving it commands.

Reena

❶ a) What command did Reena use to plot the third dot?

 b) What points should Reena plot to continue the dots in a straight line?

180

PUPIL TEXTBOOK 4C PAGE 180

Share

Whole class teacher led

ASK

- Question ❶ a): *Why did Dexter choose to count from zero? Why does he count across and then up? Do you know the meaning of 'horizontal' and 'vertical'?*
- Question ❶ b): *How does Flo find where the next points are? Could you find them without drawing the line?*
- Question ❶ b): *If you say the numbers in the wrong order, where will the robot will plot the points?*

IN FOCUS Remind children of the terms 'horizontal' and 'vertical' from their work in Unit 14 with graph axes. Make reference to the similarities to grids here and the order in which coordinates are written and carried out.

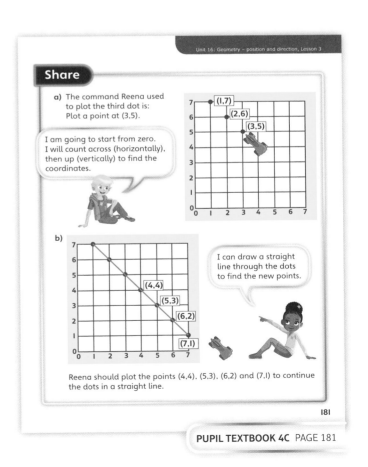

Share

a) The command Reena used to plot the third dot is: Plot a point at (3,5).

I am going to start from zero. I will count across (horizontally), then up (vertically) to find the coordinates.

b)

I can draw a straight line through the dots to find the new points.

Reena should plot the points (4,4), (5,3), (6,2) and (7,1) to continue the dots in a straight line.

181

PUPIL TEXTBOOK 4C PAGE 181

Think together

Whole class teacher led (I do, We do, You do)

ASK

- Question **1**: *How many squares do you need to go across for the point (0,2)? How will you plot that?*
- Question **2**: *Can you see a pattern in the coordinates? Can you predict the next point without drawing the line?*

IN FOCUS Question **1** provides an opportunity to focus on the role of 0 on the axes. Children need to plot a point on the vertical axis and so the grid needs to have a properly labelled origin.

STRENGTHEN Children may need extra support when reading coordinates with 0, remind them that the bottom left corner is at (0, 0). Ask them to give the coordinates of the top left corner and the bottom right corner.

DEEPEN Extend question **3** by giving children the coordinate (10,10) and ask them to predict what the coordinates of the points would be if they were to draw a straight diagonal line towards (0,0).

ASSESSMENT CHECKPOINT Use question **1** to assess whether children can plot given points. Use question **2** to assess whether they can work out the coordinates of points to complete shapes or continue lines. Use question **3** to assess whether children know how to work out coordinates between whole-number values.

ANSWERS

Question **1**: The points lie on a straight diagonal line from (0,2) to (5,7).

Question **2** a): (10,0), (9,1) and (8,2)

Question **2** b): (7,3), (6,4), (5,5), (4,6), (3,7), (2,8), (1,9), (0,10)

Question **3**: Plot (3,3). Plot (1,3). Plot (1,2·5). Plot (2,2·5). Plot (2,1·5). Plot (1,1·5). Plot (1,1). Plot (3,1). Plot (3,0). Plot (0,0).

(The decimals can be written as fractions – for example, $2\frac{1}{2}$ instead of 2·5, and so on.)

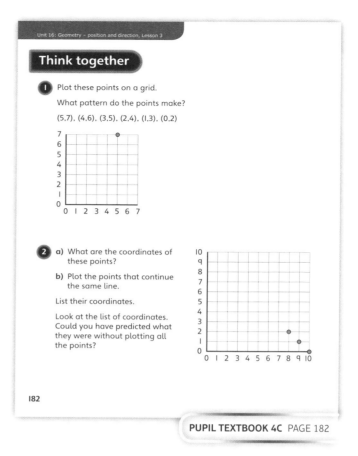

PUPIL TEXTBOOK 4C PAGE 182

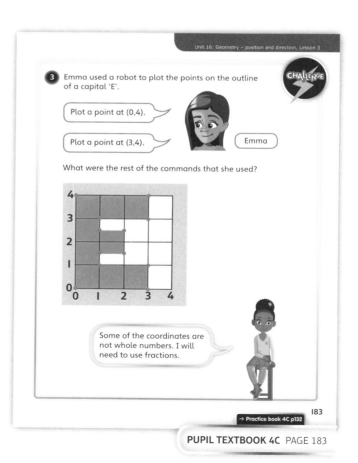

PUPIL TEXTBOOK 4C PAGE 183

Practice

WAYS OF WORKING Independent thinking

IN FOCUS Question ② links this lesson's work on coordinates with children's existing knowledge of shapes, as well as providing further practice in plotting coordinates. Make sure that children understand the term 'vertices', as well as 'triangle', 'rectangle' and 'pentagon'.

STRENGTHEN Question ① provides an opportunity to reinforce children's understanding of the coordinate system. All of the required points could fit on the grid, even if plotted in the wrong order. Where children find this difficult, refer back to the examples used earlier in the lesson.

DEEPEN Encourage more confident children to think more deeply about the properties of shapes and their relationships to coordinates. For example, you could use question ③ to ask: *Do three points always make a triangle, and five points a pentagon, and so on?* The answer is no – where three consecutive points are in a straight line, the 'middle' one would not be a vertex of a polygon.

ASSESSMENT CHECKPOINT Use questions ① and ② to assess whether children can plot given points. Use question ③ to check children's familiarity with the conventional order of coordinates. Children who understand that the first coordinate is measured horizontally should be able to spot that line 1 will be horizontal, because the distance 'across' changes but the distance 'up' is constant. Similarly, line 2 must be vertical because the points are all the same distance 'across' the grid.

ANSWERS Answers for the **Practice** part of the lesson appear in the separate **Practice and Reflect answer guide**.

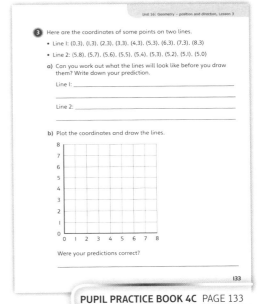

PUPIL PRACTICE BOOK 4C PAGE 132

PUPIL PRACTICE BOOK 4C PAGE 133

Reflect

WAYS OF WORKING Independent thinking

IN FOCUS This question provides a simple check on the main learning from this lesson, ensuring once again that children are using the order of coordinates properly, and that they can visualise vertical and horizontal straight lines, given a sequence of coordinates.

ASSESSMENT CHECKPOINT Assess whether children can explain why the line is vertical. Explanations should include the idea that both points are three units across from (0,0), but at different heights.

ANSWERS Answers for the **Reflect** part of the lesson appear in the separate **Practice and Reflect answer guide**.

After the lesson ⏸

- Children should now be familiar with the idea that coordinates can be used to draw a variety of shapes, as well as plotting simple points. Can you provide examples of how this is used – for example, in computer graphics?

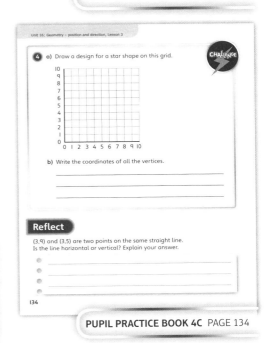

PUPIL PRACTICE BOOK 4C PAGE 134

Reasoning on a grid

Learning focus

In this lesson, children will use the properties of shapes and points to help them make constructions on the coordinate grid.

Small steps

→ Previous step: Drawing on a grid
→ **This step: Reasoning on a grid**
→ Next step: Moving on a grid

NATIONAL CURRICULUM LINKS

Year 4 Geometry – Position and Direction

Describe positions on a 2D grid as coordinates in the first quadrant.

ASSESSING MASTERY

Children can use simple properties of shapes to plot missing points and complete geometrical diagrams.

COMMON MISCONCEPTIONS

Children may need support to link their developing understanding of coordinates with their existing knowledge of the properties of shapes. Ask:

• *What do you know about the sides of a square? How can you use that to work out where the next vertex will be plotted?*

STRENGTHENING UNDERSTANDING

Use a computer geometry package to provide additional practice with the material covered in this lesson and to check solutions to the exercises. Also note that some of the exercises contain incomplete information, and some assumptions will be needed, for example assuming that some angles on sketched shapes are intended to be right angles. If this step proves difficult, ask questions such as: *Where do you think this line is supposed to go – will it be straight up, or at an angle?*

GOING DEEPER

Ask children to explore more complex problems, perhaps using a computer geometry package. For example, they could try to identify the remaining two vertices of squares where (5,4) and (9,4) are opposite vertices; or where (3,5) and (9,6) are adjacent vertices.

KEY LANGUAGE

In lesson: grid, coordinates, symmetry, vertices, vertex, line, square, rectangle, horizontal, vertical, plotted

STRUCTURES AND REPRESENTATIONS

coordinate grid

RESOURCES

Optional: computer geometry package, squared paper, chalk, tape

 In the eTextbook of this lesson, you will find interactive links to a selection of teaching tools.

Before you teach

• Are children confident in working with properties of simple shapes – for example, finding the area of a square, or understanding that the opposite sides of a rectangle have equal lengths?

Discover

WAYS OF WORKING Pair work

ASK

- Question ❶ a): *Where did the robot start drawing?*
- Question ❶ a): *How many lines will it have to draw in total? How long will they be?*

IN FOCUS This exercise provides a simple example of using geometrical knowledge (the fact that the sides of a square are of equal length) to complete a construction using coordinates. The robot is again used here to take the focus away from trying to remember the correct order of coordinates – instead, children can simply look at the robot and see how it responded to the commands that were already given. This means that it may not be necessary to remind children how the coordinate system works – children who are still unsure of the order of the coordinates should be encouraged to use the information in the question to check.

PRACTICAL TIPS Create a simple grid on the floor (using tape) or outside in the playground (using chalk). Children can alternate being the 'robot'. Ask children to plot specific coordinates so together they create different shapes.

ANSWERS

Question ❶ a): The next command Richard should give is: Draw a line to (4,4).

Question ❶ b): The final command that is needed to finish the square is: Draw a line to (1,4).

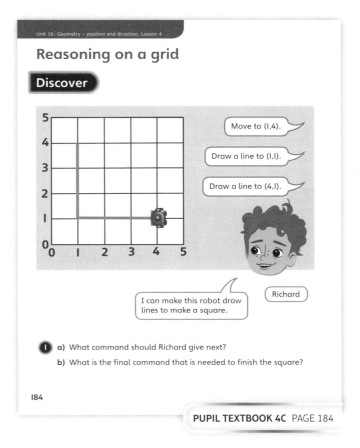

Reasoning on a grid

Discover

Move to (I,4).

Draw a line to (I,I).

Draw a line to (4,I).

I can make this robot draw lines to make a square.

Richard

❶ a) What command should Richard give next?

  b) What is the final command that is needed to finish the square?

184

PUPIL TEXTBOOK 4C PAGE 184

Share

WAYS OF WORKING Whole class teacher led

ASK

- Question ❶ a): *How has Dexter worked out where the square will be?*
- Question ❶ b): *It took five commands to draw the square – but a square has only got four sides! Why is there an extra command?*

IN FOCUS Ensure children understand that the idea of shading the square is simply to help locate the final corner. In this question, children need to focus on the lengths and directions of lines rather than the area of the square.

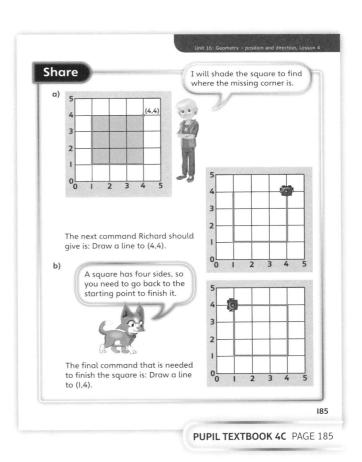

Share

I will shade the square to find where the missing corner is.

a) (4,4)

The next command Richard should give is: Draw a line to (4,4).

b) A square has four sides, so you need to go back to the starting point to finish it.

The final command that is needed to finish the square is: Draw a line to (I,4).

185

PUPIL TEXTBOOK 4C PAGE 185

Think together

Whole class teacher led

ASK

- Question **1**: *There are no angles marked on the diagram. What should the angles be? Have you got enough information to draw the shape accurately?*
- Question **2**: *What shape are you trying to draw? What do you know about the sides of that shape?*

IN FOCUS Question **2** is a 2-step problem: children need to work out the length of the side of the square from the given points and then use this knowledge to work out the other two coordinates. Question **3** has a number of possible answers, depending on whether the given points are taken as adjacent or opposite corners of the square.

STRENGTHEN Children who need additional practice could use a computer geometry package to reproduce the diagram from question **1**.

DEEPEN Encourage children to look for patterns in the coordinates for the original and reflected shapes in question **4**. They should notice that the horizontal coordinates do not change and they should be able to relate this to the fact that the reflected points move directly downwards.

ASSESSMENT CHECKPOINT Use questions **1**, **2** and **3** to assess whether children can use their knowledge of the properties of squares and rectangles to find missing coordinates. Use question **4** to assess whether they can apply reflecting a shape in a mirror line to a coordinate grid.

ANSWERS

Question **1**: The coordinates of the final corner are (7,5).

Question **2**: The other two corners are at (2,7) and (8,7).

Question **3**: If the two marked points are taken as adjacent vertices of the square, then the remaining vertices are at (4,1) and (8,1), or at (4,9) and (8,9). If the marked corners are taken as opposite vertices of the square, the remaining vertices are at (6,3) and (6,7).

Question **4**: The coordinates required to complete the shape are: (1,2), (2,1), (5,2), and (6,1).

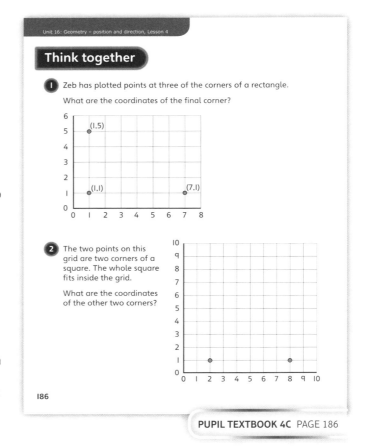

PUPIL TEXTBOOK 4C PAGE 186

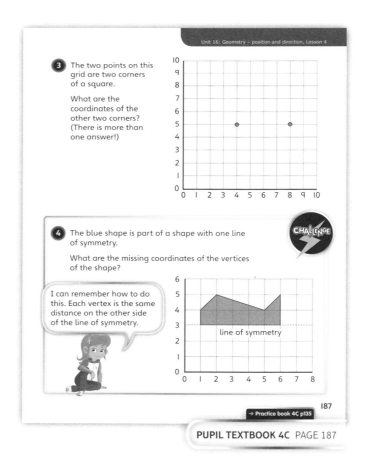

PUPIL TEXTBOOK 4C PAGE 187

Practice

WAYS OF WORKING Independent thinking

IN FOCUS Question **2** provides a further opportunity to combine the properties of shapes with the context of drawing on a coordinate grid. Use opportunities like this to explain that, although mathematics is taught as a series of separate topics, in reality there are many links and connections. Focusing on mathematical connections is a good means of changing the emphasis of learning – away from memorising, and towards understanding.

Question **4** requires some deeper thinking. Children will need to consider the possible orientations of the rectangle in part b). Since these are not specified in the question, the width could be taken as 5 units and the height as 7, or vice versa.

STRENGTHEN Ask children to visualise what the completed rectangle in question **1** will look like. If children find it difficult to picture the completed shape, cut out a small piece of paper that will fit in the required space.

DEEPEN Give children practice questions in which they are given, for example, three vertices of a parallelogram and need to find the fourth vertex. Ask them to explain how they found the fourth vertex.

THINK DIFFERENTLY Question **3** is a more open-ended task – there are four different possible orientations for the rectangle, depending on which of the vertices is taken to be at (4,4). Note that the question indicates the orientation of the rectangle; without this there would be further solutions.

ASSESSMENT CHECKPOINT Use question **2** to assess whether children can work accurately with coordinates and that they can make effective use of their understanding of the properties of shapes.

ANSWERS Answers for the **Practice** part of the lesson appear in the separate **Practice and Reflect answer guide**.

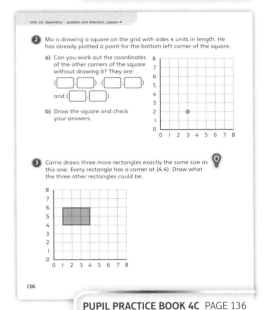

PUPIL PRACTICE BOOK 4C PAGE 135

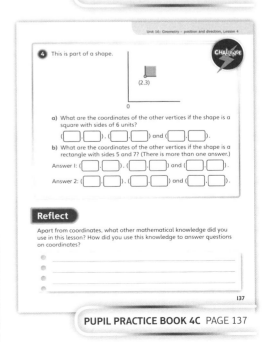

PUPIL PRACTICE BOOK 4C PAGE 136

Reflect

WAYS OF WORKING Independent thinking

IN FOCUS This activity asks children to think about the other mathematical ideas that were needed in this lesson and is a further opportunity to establish connections between topics.

ASSESSMENT CHECKPOINT Check that children appreciate that many of the geometrical ideas that they already know (such as symmetry and reflection, and the side and angle properties of squares and rectangles) can be usefully applied on a coordinate grid.

ANSWERS Answers for the **Reflect** part of the lesson appear in the separate **Practice and Reflect answer guide**.

PUPIL PRACTICE BOOK 4C PAGE 137

After the lesson ⏸

- Are children readily making connections between mathematical ideas?
- What further opportunities can you provide for making this kind of connection?

Moving on a grid

Learning focus

In this lesson, children will carry out simple translations on a coordinate grid, following instructions given in the form 'left/right and up/down'.

Small steps

→ Previous step: Reasoning on a grid
→ **This step: Moving on a grid**
→ Next step: Describing a movement on a grid

NATIONAL CURRICULUM LINKS

Year 4 Geometry – Position and Direction

Describe movements between positions as translations of a given unit to the left/right and up/down.

ASSESSING MASTERY

Children can carry out simple translations – they can explain the effect of moving an arbitrary distance to the left/right and up/down. (The terminology of translations will be fully introduced in Year 5.) They can find the coordinates of a destination point, given the coordinates of the starting point and the translation. They know the conventional order in which translations will be given (horizontal movement, vertical movement). They can combine a succession of translations to produce a 'journey' with multiple stages.

COMMON MISCONCEPTIONS

Children may confuse the horizontal and vertical components of a translation with the corresponding coordinates of a point: for example, they may confuse 'move 2 right and 3 up' with (2,3). Ask:
• *What is your starting point? How many squares are you moving to the right/left/up/down? What is your end point?*

Some children count grid lines instead of squares, incorrectly starting the count at 1 at the starting point rather than counting 1 at a distance of one unit from the starting point. Ask:
• *What is your starting point? What is 1 right/up from your starting point? How do you know?*

STRENGTHENING UNDERSTANDING

To strengthen understanding of translations, children could use a computer geometry package to give instructions to move right/left and up/down. Alternatively, use a grid on the ground and ask children to carry out the translation by moving on the grid.

GOING DEEPER

Encourage more confident children to see a translation as a single (diagonal) movement from the starting point to the end point. Ask why it is convenient to describe each journey using two components (horizontal and vertical), even though it might make more sense to carry out the journey as a single (diagonal) movement.

KEY LANGUAGE

In lesson: across, right, left, up, down

Other language to be used by the teacher: horizontal, vertical, coordinates

STRUCTURES AND REPRESENTATIONS

coordinate grid

RESOURCES

Optional: computer geometry package

 In the eTextbook of this lesson, you will find interactive links to a selection of teaching tools.

Before you teach

• Are children confident in using coordinates?
• Do you have a suitable space inside or outside the classroom where you could model translations using spoken instructions to move a child to a destination?

Discover

WAYS OF WORKING Pair work

ASK

- Question **1** a): *Can you see where the position of the drone is marked on the screen?*
- Question **1** a): *What are the coordinates of the drone? How does Sofia want it to move?*

IN FOCUS This activity provides a simple practical context in which the importance of being able to give instructions for movements should be clear. Notice that although this has returned to the context of a map, there is no scale given and the drone would need to be using the same set of coordinates as Sofia.

PRACTICAL TIPS You could use a practical activity to introduce the idea of translations: ask a child to move around the classroom (or other suitable space) following simple instructions such as 'Move 2 paces left, then 3 paces back'. This kind of activity helps to reinforce the idea that the points on the grid never move: the point (4,2) is always 4 across and 2 up from the origin, although a drone originally at that position can move to a new one.

ANSWERS

Question **1** a): Sofia wants to look at the jetty.

Question **1** b): Sofia sent the drone to the castle.

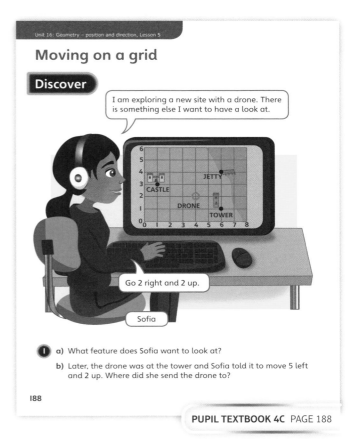

PUPIL TEXTBOOK 4C PAGE 188

Share

WAYS OF WORKING Whole class teacher led

ASK

- Question **1** a): *How did Astrid mark the starting point for the drone?*
- Question **1** b): *Can you see how you could work out where the drone went without drawing?*

IN FOCUS Working out the final position of the drone without drawing is an important step. State that in **1** b), the drone is at (6,1), and moves 5 left. Ask which number will change, the 6 or the 1. Ask children to explain how they know.

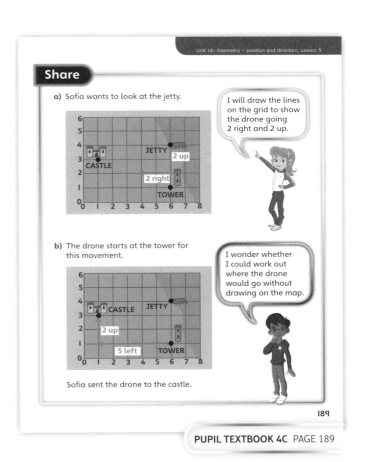

PUPIL TEXTBOOK 4C PAGE 189

Think together

WAYS OF WORKING Whole class teacher led (I do, We do, You do)

ASK

• Question **1**: *This drone is going to do all of these journeys, one after the other. What is the first place it will go to? Where will it go after that?*

IN FOCUS Question **2** can be tackled in a variety of ways. You could suggest trial and error – for each translation, try each of P, Q, and R as potential starting points until they find one that works. A better approach is to think about what each of the translations means; for example, if (3 right, 1 up) finishes on one of the marked locations it cannot start at R (which is already the rightmost point), and it cannot start at Q (which is already further 'up' than the other two points).

STRENGTHEN Provide further practice by asking other questions based on the diagram in question **1**. For example, ask: *I am at A and I go 6 right and 1 down. Where do I finish?*

DEEPEN In question **2**, ask children if they can see a link between, for example, the journey from P to Q and the journey from Q to P. Ask them to investigate whether this pattern is the same for the other journeys and to explain their findings.

ASSESSMENT CHECKPOINT Use questions **1** and **2** to assess whether children can carry out simple translations. Check that they understand translations with a single component, such as '4 down' in question **1**, and that this could be written as '0 right, 4 down'.

ANSWERS

Question **1**: B, D, C, E, A

Question **2** a): Q to P

Question **2** b): P to R

Question **2** c): R to P

Question **2** d): Q to R

Question **2** e): R to Q

Question **3**: B moves to (7,7), C to (11,7), and D to (11,4).

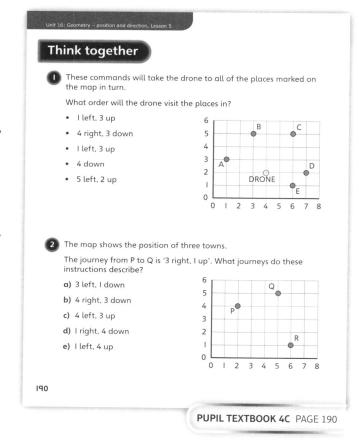

PUPIL TEXTBOOK 4C PAGE 190

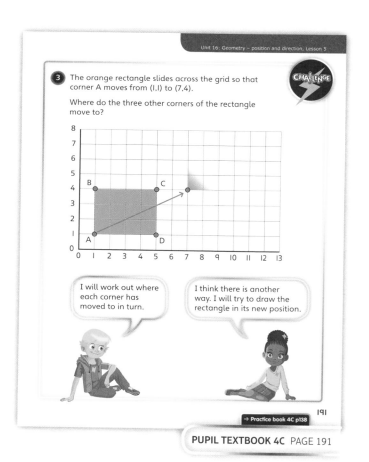

PUPIL TEXTBOOK 4C PAGE 191

Practice

WAYS OF WORKING Independent thinking

IN FOCUS Question ① provides further practice at working out the effects of translations on the coordinate grid. Make sure that children understand that these movements all start from the marked position of the boat – they are not intended to be carried out in succession.

STRENGTHEN Use question ② to check that children can follow a series of instructions to move to a succession of points on the coordinate grid. To give children additional practice, ask further questions based on this diagram, for example: *I am at (3,7), and I move 6 right and 3 down. Where am I now?*

DEEPEN Ask children questions similar to question ⑤, where the required translation will move the shape off the grid provided, for example move 10 right and 8 up. Children will need to use reasoning to work out the coordinates of the translated shape.

THINK DIFFERENTLY Question ④ requires children to use reasoning without the support of a grid showing the translation. In question ④ b) they need to 'think backwards' – they are given the end point and a displacement, and have to work out the start point.

ASSESSMENT CHECKPOINT Use questions ① and ③ to assess whether children can carry out simple translations. Use question ② to check whether they can follow a series of translations around the coordinate grid.

ANSWERS Answers for the **Practice** part of the lesson appear in the separate **Practice and Reflect answer guide**.

Reflect

WAYS OF WORKING Independent thinking

IN FOCUS This question provides an opportunity to reflect on the effect of a translation on the coordinates of a point.

ASSESSMENT CHECKPOINT Check that children understand that the first coordinate will increase after a translation to the right and decrease after a translation to the left; and that the second coordinate will increase after a translation upwards and decrease after a translation downwards.

ANSWERS Answers for the **Reflect** part of the lesson appear in the separate **Practice and Reflect answer guide**.

After the lesson ⏸

- Are children able to determine the coordinates of the image of a point following a translation?

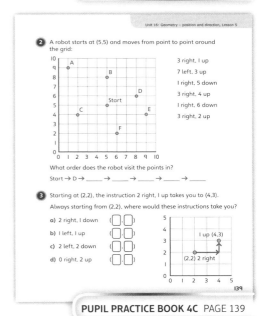

PUPIL PRACTICE BOOK 4C PAGE 138

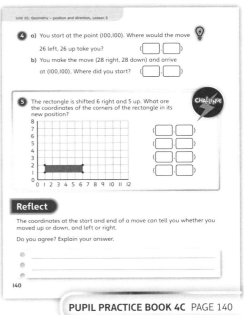

PUPIL PRACTICE BOOK 4C PAGE 139

PUPIL PRACTICE BOOK 4C PAGE 140

Describing a movement on a grid

Learning focus

In this lesson, children will work out the translations (expressed in the form 'right/left, up/down') that are needed to move from one position on the coordinate grid to another.

Small steps

→ Previous step: Moving on a grid
→ **This step: Describing a movement on a grid**

NATIONAL CURRICULUM LINKS

Year 4 Geometry – Position and Direction

Describe movements between positions as translations of a given unit to the left/right and up/down.

ASSESSING MASTERY

Children can state the translation that is required to move between any two points on a coordinate grid, giving their answer in the form '3 left, 2 up'. They can apply their understanding to a range of grid systems (including maps, scale diagrams and abstract coordinate grids).

COMMON MISCONCEPTIONS

Children may not immediately see that the type of translation that they have already met can be used in a range of practical situations. Ask:

• *Does this look like something you have done before? What does this remind you of? What do you think you could try?*

STRENGTHENING UNDERSTANDING

Make sure that children understand the change in emphasis here; in the previous lesson, they were working out the effect of a given translation, while in this lesson they find the translation that is needed to produce a certain movement. You may find it helpful to 'personalise' some of the questions in order to prompt children to think about the translations as an active and dynamic process of moving from one point to another: *If you were at this point A, and you wanted to move to this point B, what move would you need to make?*

GOING DEEPER

Challenge more confident children to investigate games where movements can be described using translations, for example chess, draughts or peg/Chinese solitaire. Ask them to find examples of cities laid out on a grid system, where translations might be a sensible way of describing journeys.

KEY LANGUAGE

In lesson: grid, move, journey, left, right, up, down

Other language to be used by the teacher: horizontal, vertical

STRUCTURES AND REPRESENTATIONS

coordinate grid

RESOURCES

Optional: computer geometry package, chess board

 In the eTextbook of this lesson, you will find interactive links to a selection of teaching tools.

Before you teach

• Are children able to use coordinates to describe positions on a coordinate grid?
• Can they describe movements on the grid using translations (in words)?

Discover

WAYS OF WORKING Pair work

ASK

- Question **1** a): *Have you ever seen a city with a grid of streets like this? Why would you design a city like this?*
- Question **1** a): *Luis is standing at the crossroads of Second Street and First Avenue. Where are the other children?*

IN FOCUS This question provides another example of a situation where a grid system might be used and where it would be important to be able to describe movements in a consistent way.

PRACTICAL TIPS It may be necessary to acknowledge that the system of crossroads used here will only provide approximate locations. For example, Sam's position at the crossroads of Second Street and First Avenue does not mean that he is standing in the middle of either of those thoroughfares. Despite this lack of complete precision, the grid system is useful and will enable the convenient location of places or (as in this example) people.

ANSWERS

Question **1** a): Jamilla could write her journey to Luis as '2 left, 1 up'.

Question **1** b): The journeys are the same so both are correct.

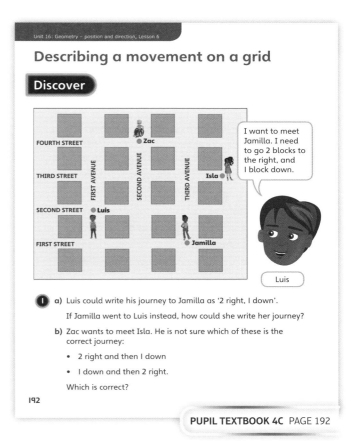

PUPIL TEXTBOOK 4C PAGE 192

Share

WAYS OF WORKING Whole class teacher led

ASK

- Question **1** a): *Why does Flo say that Jamilla's journey is the opposite of Luis's?*
- Question **1** b): *Can you explain why the two journeys are the same?*

IN FOCUS This activity encourages children to look at the journeys as translations – that is, a movement of a particular distance in a particular direction, rather than between two specific points.

PUPIL TEXTBOOK 4C PAGE 193

Think together

Whole class teacher led (I do, We do, You do)

ASK

- Question ❶ c): *How many squares up or down does Luis go? How can you describe this?*
- Question ❸: *Where does this corner of the rectangle move to? Do all the corners move by the same amount?*

IN FOCUS Question ❶ starts with translations that have both horizontal and vertical components, as in the **Share** activity. However, questions ❶ c) and ❶ d) are examples where one of the components is zero. Discuss whether children need to write 0 up/right, or whether they can omit this component. It is possible to leave the 'missing' component out completely (so, for example, a translation of 5 units right could simply be written as '5 right'), or include it with a zero value (for example, '5 right, 0 up'). Although the second option is slightly longer, it is more consistent and makes it clear than the missing component has not just been forgotten. In question ❷, opposite journeys have been arranged side by side to encourage children to spot the pattern. Tell children to lay the answers out like this in their exercise books when answering the question.

STRENGTHEN Use question ❷ to reinforce the idea that a translation should be described in the order **distance across**, **distance up** (or down). If children write the components in the 'wrong' order the translation will of course still work – '2 up then 1 right' is equivalent to '1 right then 2 up'. However, it is sensible to be consistent and give the components in the same order as is used with coordinates; this will reinforce the idea of 'horizontal first'.

DEEPEN Challenge children to generalise the process for finding the 'opposite' of a journey (i.e. finding the translation B to A, given the translation A to B).

ASSESSMENT CHECKPOINT Use questions ❶ and ❷ to assess whether children can find the horizontal and vertical components of any translation on a grid. Check that children know what to do if one component is zero.

ANSWERS

Question ❶ a): Zac's journey is 1 right, 2 down.

Question ❶ b): Both Isla and Zac are right, although Isla's description is the order that will be used in more advanced work.

Question ❶ c): Luis's journey is 2 right and 0 down or 0 up and 2 right.

Question ❶ d): Jamilla's journey is 1 up.

Question ❷: B to A: 5 right, 2 down
A to C: 3 left, 3 down   C to A: 3 right, 3 up
B to C: 2 right, 5 down   C to B: 2 left, 5 up

Question ❸: The journeys are:
a): 2 right, 3 up
b): 4 right
c): 1 left, 2 down

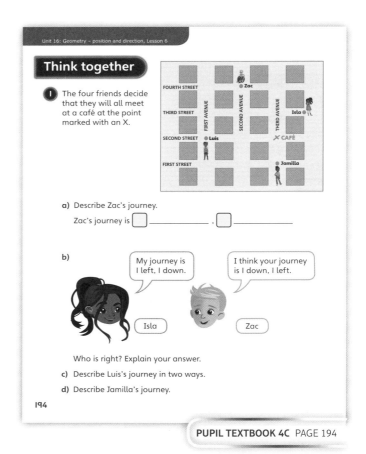

PUPIL TEXTBOOK 4C PAGE 194

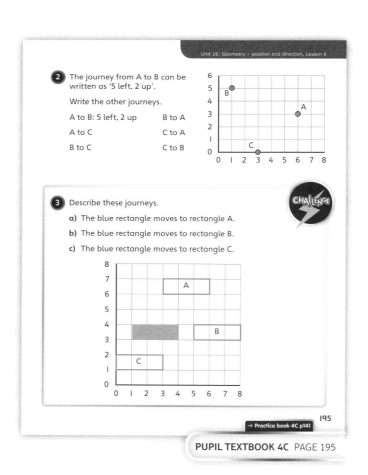

PUPIL TEXTBOOK 4C PAGE 195

Practice

WAYS OF WORKING Independent thinking

IN FOCUS Question ❶ uses the same grid scenario that was introduced in the **Discover** exercise, but this time applies it to a different context: counting shelving blocks in a library. This helps to emphasise the idea that the same mathematical techniques can be applied to a variety of practical situations. Question ❹ makes the point that a translation can be described using numbers, even without knowing the coordinates of any of the points.

STRENGTHEN Draw a grid on the board and mark two points. Ask a child to trace the distance across and then up/down, describing it as they do so. Repeat for different pairs of points until children can confidently state the journey.

DEEPEN In question ❷, tell children to write down the coordinates of A, B and C. Ask them to look for patterns connecting the journey and the coordinates. If necessary, suggest that they look at the horizontal coordinates and journey components together, and similarly the vertical coordinates and components.

ASSESSMENT CHECKPOINT Use question ❶ to assess whether children can describe translations on a grid system. Use question ❷ to check that they can apply this knowledge to a coordinate grid.

ANSWERS Answers for the **Practice** part of the lesson appear in the separate **Practice and Reflect answer guide**.

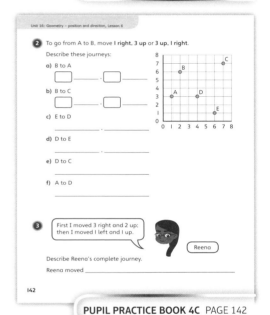

PUPIL PRACTICE BOOK 4C PAGE 141

PUPIL PRACTICE BOOK 4C PAGE 142

Reflect

WAYS OF WORKING Independent thinking

IN FOCUS This question looks at the idea of finding the opposite of a journey – that is, the translation that takes us back to the starting point. This provides an opportunity to think about translations in a more abstract way, finding the opposite of any journey, rather than a particular case.

ASSESSMENT CHECKPOINT Check that children can describe the process of finding the opposite of a particular journey (i.e. an example they choose). A more complete explanation should describe a more general process (for example: 'If it says "up", change it to "down"').

ANSWERS Answers for the **Reflect** part of the lesson appear in the separate **Practice and Reflect answer guide**.

PUPIL PRACTICE BOOK 4C PAGE 143

After the lesson ⏸

• Can children confidently find translations on a coordinate grid?

End of unit check

> **Don't forget the *Power Maths* unit assessment grid on p26.**

WAYS OF WORKING Group work adult led

IN FOCUS

- Question ❶ provides an opportunity to check that children understand the order of coordinates when identifying and plotting points.
- Question ❷ allows children to show their understanding of how shapes can be plotted on a coordinate grid.
- Questions ❸, ❹ and ❺ enable children to demonstrate that they understand translations and the convention of right/left and up/down on a coordinate grid.
- Question ❻ is a SATs style question that provides the children with an opportunity to give reasoning with their answer.

ANSWERS AND COMMENTARY

Children who have mastered the concepts in this unit can read, write and plot coordinates. They can use simple geometrical reasoning on a coordinate grid to draw patterns and complete shapes. They understand translations as movements on the coordinate grid; they can describe the result of making a translation described in words, and they can find the translation required for the movement between given positions.

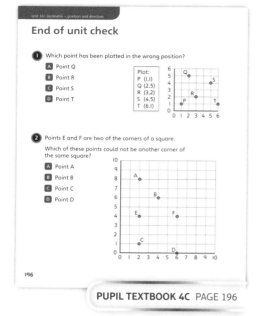

PUPIL TEXTBOOK 4C PAGE 196

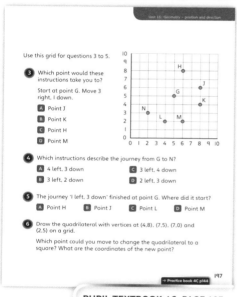

PUPIL TEXTBOOK 4C PAGE 197

Q	A	WRONG ANSWERS AND MISCONCEPTIONS	STRENGTHENING UNDERSTANDING
1	C	A, B or D suggests that the child has not fully grasped the correct order of coordinates.	Children who need further practice may benefit from using a computer graph plotting package. These packages are very easy to use and children could use them to check their answers.
2	C	B suggests that the child has not understood that E and F could be opposite corners. D suggests that they think the given coordinates form the base of the square.	
3	B	A suggests that the child does not understand the direction of the components of a translation.	
4	B	C suggests that they have applied the magnitudes in the wrong order. D suggests that they have identified the magnitude of the two movements, but not the correct order.	
5	A	C suggests that they have started at G instead of finishing there.	
6	(4,8) to (2,0)	Some children may plot the coordinates in the wrong order.	

My journal

WAYS OF WORKING Independent thinking

ANSWERS AND COMMENTARY

Cards A and D will combine to give a translation of 5 right, 5 up, which represents the movement from (5,5) to (10,10).

There are several stages involved in this solution – children will first need to identify the required translation, and then use their number sense and understanding of relative movement to identify the required pair of cards.

Question **2** uses a game which children have likely played before, where they must place four counters in a row without being intercepted. This could also be used in the classroom, where children must announce the position of each counter as they play.

Kim should place her counter in position (4,5) to win the game.

Power check

WAYS OF WORKING Independent thinking

ASK

- *Had you seen maps and plans used to show where things are before you started this unit?*
- *Do you think you are better able to describe positions and movements after doing the unit?*
- *Can you explain how to write a coordinate?*

Power play

WAYS OF WORKING Pair work

IN FOCUS Use the game of battleships to provide a further example of the use of coordinates in a practical context.

ANSWERS AND COMMENTARY In this game, children extend the idea of a set of coordinates to include naming positions on a game board using the conventions that have been developed in this chapter – first give the direction across to the right, then the distance up. Model placing the battleships on a grid to emphasise that ships must not occupy adjacent points, including diagonally.

After the unit ⏸

- How will the work in this unit prepare children for more advanced work, where directed numbers are used to describe translations, and coordinates in other quadrants?
- The order of coordinates is a good example of a mathematical convention – we could use any order, but we all need to agree on the same one. What other conventions will children need to know in mathematics?

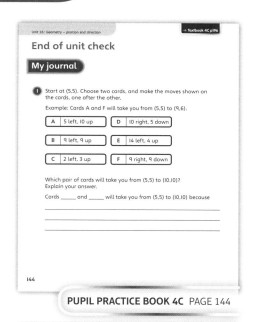

PUPIL PRACTICE BOOK 4C PAGE 144

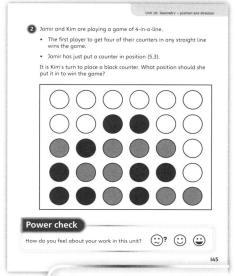

PUPIL PRACTICE BOOK 4C PAGE 145

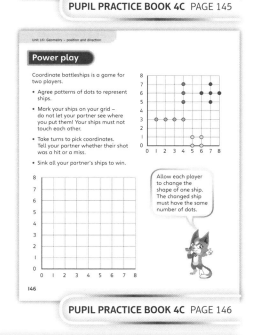

PUPIL PRACTICE BOOK 4C PAGE 146

Strengthen and **Deepen** activities for this unit can be found in the *Power Maths* online subscription.

Published by Pearson Education Limited, 80 Strand, London, WC2R 0RL.

www.pearsonschools.co.uk

Text © Pearson Education Limited 2018
Edited by Pearson, Little Grey Cells Publishing Services and Haremi Ltd
Designed and typeset by Kamae Design
Original illustrations © Pearson Education Limited 2018
Illustrated by Laura Arias, John Batten, Fran and David Brylewski, Diago Diaz, Nigel Dobbyn, Virginia Fontanabona, Adam Linley and Nadene Naude at Beehive Illustration; and Emily Skinner at Graham-Cameron Illustration.
Cover design by Pearson Education Ltd
Back cover illustration © Diago Diaz and Nadene Naude at Beehive Illustration.

Series Editor: Tony Staneff
Consultants: Professor Liu Jian and Professor Zhang Dan

The rights of Tony Staneff, David Board, Emily Fox, Tim Handley, Derek Huby, Jill Todd, Timothy Weal, Rachel Webster and Paul Wrangles to be identified as authors of this work have been asserted by them in accordance with the Copyright, Designs and Patents Act 1988.

First published 2018

21 20 19 18
10 9 8 7 6 5 4 3 2 1

British Library Cataloguing in Publication Data
A catalogue record for this book is available from the British Library

ISBN 978 0 435 19020 0

Printed in Slovakia by Neografia

www.activelearnprimary.co.uk

Note from the publisher
Pearson has robust editorial processes, including answer and fact checks, to ensure the accuracy of the content in this publication, and every effort is made to ensure this publication is free of errors. We are, however, only human, and occasionally errors do occur. Pearson is not liable for any misunderstandings that arise as a result of errors in this publication, but it is our priority to ensure that the content is accurate. If you spot an error, please do contact us at resourcescorrections@pearson.com so we can make sure it is corrected.